MW01634350

By moonlight or candlelight. . .
. . . discover the joy of
Christmas love.

An Old Fashioned Christmas

Four Inspirational
Love Stories from
Christmases Gone By

Sally Laity
Loree Lough
Tracie Peterson
Colleen L. Reece

ISBN 1-59789-139-8

This book is a work of fiction. Names, characters, places, and incidents are either products of the author's imagination or used fictitiously. Any similarity to actual people, organizations, and/or events is purely coincidental.

Published by Barbour Publishing, Inc., P.O. Box 719, Uhrichsville, Ohio 44683, www.barbourbooks.com

Our mission is to publish and distribute inspirational products offering exceptional value and biblical encouragement to the masses.

Printed in the United States of America.
5 4 3 2 1

An Old Fashioned Christmas

For the Love of a Child

Sally Laity

Chapter 1

Philadelphia, 1878

Angelina Matthews closed the back door of Mistress Haversham's Dress Shop behind her and stepped cautiously out onto Front Street. A frigid December wind, fraught with dampness from the Delaware River a stone's throw away, flung icy shards of falling snow mercilessly against her face. Switching her lantern to her other hand, she gave her scarf an extra wrap and buried her nose deeper into its confines. Then she set off through the growing darkness toward her rented house on Elfreth's Alley.

On either side, the shops and warehouses lay dark and silent. *No doubt the other businesses had closed early, at the very onset of the storm,* she surmised with irritation. If only Mistress Haversham afforded her employees the same consideration! But with the Christmas festivities fast approaching, there were endless orders for new party frocks. And unless Angelina and Ruby, the other hired seamstress, toiled until closing time every day, the gowns would never be finished on schedule.

Angelina sought the likeliest route through the gathering drifts, bolstering herself against the pain in her withered leg as she limped over the uneven cobbles.

Once she reached home, a grand fire in the hearth and a pot of hot tea would erase the misery of this blizzard from her mind for the night. Tomorrow, thankfully, was Saturday, and she wouldn't have to be at work until noon. If it weren't December, she would have had the entire day free.

The wind howled over the narrow street—an eerie, almost human whine that whistled around the brick and stone buildings, leaving snow in its wake. Angelina shivered and pressed on.

The wind wailed louder—but another sound mixed with the storm's ghostly moan, and she paused to listen. What was that? A cry?

Holding her breath, she raised her lantern high, peering beyond the scant circles of light cast by the gas lamps. Perhaps a kitten had gotten lost, she mused, straining to hear over the fury of the elements.

The sound came again, stronger. . .and almost sounded like a plaintive "Mama. . ." She shook her head. It had to be her imagination.

But as each step brought her closer to the source of the cries, they became all the more recognizable. All the more wrenching. Ahead, Angelina made out a small shape huddled between the bare branches of a shrub and a vacant warehouse. She moved toward it as quickly as her weakened leg would allow and held the light aloft.

Her breath caught in her throat. A child!

She bent to touch the little one's shoulder. "I'll help you, dear," she crooned.

The young girl of about three started and looked up, then let out an ear-shattering wail.

"Shh, shh," Angelina coaxed. The child's threadbare coat looked at least a size too small and did little to protect the spindly arms or legs. Setting down the lantern, Angelina bent down and gathered the shivering form close. "What on earth are you doing out in this storm?" she asked, as much to the heavens themselves as to the child.

"C–c–cold!" the little girl chattered, swallowing a sob.

Angelina removed her scarf and tied it about the short, damp curls, then unbuttoned her long wool coat and picked up the urchin. Tucking her against the warmth of her own body, she wrapped the thin little legs as best she could. She couldn't imagine from whence the youngster had come, or what circumstances might have cast her alone in this dark business district. But she had far more urgent matters to consider, like getting help. Now. But from where?

St. Joseph's Church was known around the city for providing refuge to the downtrodden and dispossessed . . .but even if Angelina left the lantern behind, she could not possibly carry the little girl all the way to Willing's Alley. And Christ Church was also much too far to get to in a blizzard.

Then she recalled a smaller house of worship Ruby had mentioned one day, where occasional homeless souls had been given shelter. On Second, wasn't it? Just the next street over and not really out of her way. Once the little girl had been deposited in the care of the person in charge, Angelina could continue up the street and enter Elfreth's Alley the back way.

Thus decided, she tightened her hold on the little one

and started toward the church, the wind whipping her own dark tresses in every direction as she went.

"What's your name, sweetheart?" she asked, trying to keep the child calm as she labored toward Second Street.

"N–Noely." The breathless voice was almost a whisper. "Noely?" Angelina repeated, and felt the small head nod against her shoulder. "My, that's a pretty name. I'm Angelina." She paused. "Does your mama know you're outside in the dark, Noely?"

A leftover sob racked the tiny frame.

"Well, I'll take you to some nice people who can help you find her, dear."

Noely sniffed.

For such a little thing, she was surprisingly heavy, and Angelina tired by the minute. Surely it couldn't be too much farther.

At last the brick structure loomed into view. With renewed strength she trudged across the intersection separating them. The church sat in darkness, but warm lamplight glowed from the appealing two-story house next door. She hoped it was the parsonage. Shifting Noely's weight to her right arm, Angelina lifted the brass knocker and rapped.

Astounded that anyone could be out on such a night, Gabe Winters laid aside his Bible and sermon notes and hurried to answer the summons, ill-prepared for the arctic blast that stole his breath. On the stoop stood a fragile, dark-haired young woman with the most exquisite features he had ever seen. Her luminous brown eyes peered up at him through a fringe of long lashes. In her arms she carried a young child. . .and both of them were flocked head to toe with snow. Realizing he was gawking, Gabe quickly yanked the door wide and stepped back. "Please come inside. Warm yourselves by the fire."

"Thank you," the woman breathed. She entered, setting the little one down.

As they gravitated to the hearth, Gabe closed the door, then went to the hall. "Aunt Clara," he called up the staircase. "Any of that hot cocoa still left?"

"Sure an' there is," came her reply, the *r*'s rolling smoothly from her Irish brogue. "I'll be fetchin' it right away."

When he returned to the parlor, he found the pair kneeling before the blazing warmth. The little one's wet outerwear had already been shed, and now she extended her hands toward the heat. He switched his attention to the woman. "What might I do for you and your little girl?"

"Oh!" she gasped. "She isn't mine. I only just found her shivering outside in the storm. I thought perhaps you might help her. You are a minister, are you not?"

He nodded. "Gabe Winters. I pastor the Baptist Church here. And you're—"

"Forgive me, Reverend," she murmured, rosy patches heightening those the fire had already called forth on her fine cheekbones. "Angelina Matthews. I'm a seamstress on Front Street. And this is Noely," she added, turning the little girl to face him. "But I'm afraid that's all I know."

Gabe had no reason to doubt her word, but even if he had, the uncertainty would have evaporated as he compared her and the child. Noely's complexion was fair, nowhere near the rich olive tones of Miss Matthews. Nor were her huge blue eyes in the slightest way similar to the expressive doe-like ones of her rescuer. The girl's features—far from being delicately feminine—were stark, almost too mature for her little face, yet Gabe had no doubt she would grow into them one day.

On the other hand, he couldn't help wondering why someone as fetching as Angelina Matthews would find necessity to be employed, rather than married and a mother herself.

Her voice cut across his contemplations. "The child hasn't told me about her parents. She cried when I inquired after them."

"Well, now, little Noely," he said, sinking to one knee beside her. "Once we've managed to get you all warm and dry, perhaps you'll tell us a few things about yourself."

She tucked her chin and inched shyly against Miss Matthews.

Aunt Clara bustled in just then, bearing a tray. She set it on a lamp table, then passed steaming mugs around. "This has got extra milk, darlin'," she said, giving one to the child, "so it'll not be burnin' your tongue. Are ye hungry?"

Noely gave a slow nod.

"Well, then, we'll be settin' that problem to rights. Come see what we can find, will ye now?" She held out a hand.

Huge wary eyes sought those of Miss Matthews for encouragement, then she hesitantly put her small fingers inside the older woman's plump ones. The two of them ambled toward the kitchen, with Noely intent upon not spilling the cocoa she clutched in her other hand.

Gabe caught the furtive glance the youngster cast over her shoulder before exiting the parlor with his motherly aunt. He switched his attention to the dark-haired woman a few feet away. Her long, loose waves, held back at each side in pearl combs, were already beginning to dry. "So the little thing hasn't told you how or why she happened to be caught out in the weather."

"Not a word." She drank the remainder of the warm drink, then rose stiffly to her feet. "And since she'll be in such good hands, there is no reason for me to stay longer. In fact, it might be best if she didn't see me leave. I shall trust her to your care and be on my way. Thank you for your hospitality—and your aunt's, of course."

"But the storm—"

The young woman leaned over to retrieve the short cape and the scarf from the braided rug, then she deftly put them on. "I'll be fine. I live not far from here." She hobbled across the room.

Gabe's heart caught at the sight of her ungainly walk. He easily beat her to the door. "I do thank you, Miss Matthews, for bringing the child to us. We'll do our best to discover the whereabouts of her parents. And until then, we'll take very good care of her, be assured of that."

"I have no doubt of it. Goodnight, Reverend."

"God be with you, miss."

Leaving the comfortably furnished brick home behind, Angelina realized her last comment had been made in all honesty. The warmth she had found at the parsonage had every bit as much to do with the loving atmosphere as it did the burning logs in the fireplace. The sandy-haired pastor—she smiled to herself recalling the giant he had seemed, towering over her and Noely—probably had to duck his head to go out the door! But his kindly face had a certain openness about it, a gentle appeal, especially with the merry twinkle radiating from his clear blue eyes.

And something about his aunt Clara reminded Angelina of her own mother. Not so much the woman's stature, but her manner and bearing, her soothing voice. They awakened memories Angelina only remembered in hazy snatches. Noely should be fine there until her parents could be contacted. Thus comforted, she picked her way carefully through the snowdrifts.

Finally turning onto Elfreth, where simple row houses appeared to nestle against one another for warmth, she used the glow from the windows to get her bearing as she made her way to her own residence, the second from the end. It was nowhere near as grand as the homey abode she had so recently left, she conceded, and it would be cold and dark after sitting empty all day, but at least the wind would be kept at bay while a fire took hold. She unlocked the door and entered, lit the lamps, then disposed quickly of her wet clothes. Once she had replaced them with a warm nightgown and flannel wrapper, she padded to the small, plain parlor to start the fire.

Heat from the crackling logs soon eradicated the chill. Angelina unwrapped the heavy blanket with which she had enshrouded herself and poured a cup of tea to have with her bread and cheese. No doubt little Noely had enjoyed a grand feast, but no one could begrudge her that. . .poor little thing. What could her parents have been thinking, to allow such a young child to wander about on her own? She only hoped the Reverend Winters would give them a sound talking-to when he found them.

Angelina's thoughts lingered for a time on the pastor as she contemplated his sensitive manner. *Curious*, she thought, *such a nice-looking man without a wife—or the woman surely would have been home on a night such as this!* But at least his aunt was there to take charge of a child's welfare. Angelina could almost picture the older woman fussing over Noely, tucking her into a feather bed piled with quilts, tending to her every need.

Yes, she surmised with a yawn, the little girl would probably have the time of her life at the parsonage, then be reunited with her own family. In time she wouldn't even remember getting lost in a blizzard. No reason Angelina shouldn't forget the whole affair herself, really.

But warm thoughts of a nice pastor—and even more disturbing ones of a heart-stealing little girl—weren't so easily turned away.

Chapter 2

A shaft of sunlight slanted across Angelina's bed, right into her eyes. Turning her head away, she yawned and stretched, flung the patchwork quilt aside and rose, slipping into her warm wrapper and knitted slippers. Then she padded to the window.

Beneath the clear blue sky, a two-foot blanket of downy snow glistened as if studded with millions of diamonds. It was hard to believe the elements had put on such a wild show last night—or that she had slept until ten. Now long icicles hung from the eaves of every building, dripping in the blazing sun. Most of the goodwives in the neighborhood had already swept their stoops, Angelina noticed, and bundled children frolicked in the snowdrifts. Undoubtedly their white wonderland would diminish with each hour, turning quickly into dreary slush and mud. But in the meanwhile, the little ones would take full advantage.

Angelina smiled. The sight was so like her own sweet childhood. . .until the carriage accident had turned her whole world upside down. Never would she forget waking up in the hospital that awful day, her whole body racked with unspeakable pain from her shattered left leg. But far worse an agony was learning that her mother had died instantly, and her father, who had lingered for several hours, had succumbed as well.

After being transported to the orphan asylum for the remainder of her childhood, Angelina was granted precious few carefree moments to cherish.

Sloughing off memories which could so easily swamp her in bitterness, she hurried downstairs to stoke up the fire in the stove and make porridge and tea. Then she ate slowly, mulling over the previous night's events in her mind.

How had little Noely fared? Angelina had tried in vain to banish the mental image of the sweet face turned fearfully toward her while being ushered to the kitchen. Angelina had hoped to prevent the pain of parting by taking her leave unnoticed. But whether that had been a wise move, she could only wonder.

Noely's parents must have been frantic when they discovered their little girl missing. Hopefully there would be a grand reunion before the day was spent.

Oh well, what was done was done. Perhaps sometime next week she would drop by the parsonage and ask after the little girl. That decided, she filled a pitcher with warm water and ascended the stairs to her bedroom. She had yet to freshen up and dress for the extra half-day's work required each week in December.

An hour later, she arrived at the dress shop. Tucked between that of a candlemaker and a leathercraft store, Mistress Haversham's tiny endeavor had but one big window facing Front Street. Each month it displayed a new and attractive ensemble in current vogue, complete with the latest accessories to show it off to perfection.

The charming main room with its counter, two fitting rooms, and a niche with a velvet settee and round lamp table had already been tidied for the day, she noted upon entering, but all seemed unusually quiet as she went on through to the cramped back room.

In stark contrast to the outer room's neatness, the work room fairly overflowed with dress patterns, fashion catalogs, colorful bolts of fabric, and assorted buttons and fancy trims. Works in progress draped every available spot.

Frail, auburn-haired Ruby Chambers looked up from the emerald velvet sleeve she was pinning to the bodice of a partially finished gown on the dress form. "Hi, Angie."

"Mistress Haversham isn't here?" Angelina asked, hanging her coat on the rack by the back door.

"Came in to open up," the girl mumbled around the straight pins clamped between her lips, "then went to deliver that burnished gold silk frock we finished yesterday to uppity Mrs. Worthingham. Personally."

"I see."

"That lady is nothin' short of a bother." Ruby jabbed the final dress pin into place, then nudged her spectacles higher with a free finger. "Always has Mistress in such a dither, comin' by every day without fail to check on her gown. You'd think hers was the only order to be done before Christmas!"

Angelina nodded. "Has the hem been marked yet?" she asked, indicating the emerald gown.

"Mm-hmm. All pinned and ready. That and the sleeves are all that's left."

"I'll help you, then, and we'll be able to cross one more off the list." Moving to the cluttered worktable, she retrieved a pin cushion and a spool of thread, then eased down onto a stool at the foot of the dress form. She threaded her needle and deftly knotted the end.

"My, that was some tempest blowed through last night," Ruby exclaimed. "Come near to bein' buried in a snowdrift 'fore I made it home. Percy got there five minutes sooner and was just about to come lookin' for me."

Angelina shot her an understanding smile. "I arrived home a little late myself. I had to take a detour."

"In that storm? Whatever for?"

"It's a long story."

"Well, we got half a day, you know, and Mistress won't be back for at least an hour. She'll be wantin' to fit that gown herself to make sure it suits her highness."

"You're right." Angelina took a deep breath, gathering her thoughts as she worked. "It was the most unexpected thing. Partway home, I thought I heard what sounded like a cry. When I went to investigate, I found a child—a little girl—stranded outside."

"No!" Ruby's mouth dropped open. She wrinkled her nose twice to nudge her spectacles higher as Angelina gave a solemn nod. "What'd you do? The orphanage is way across town."

"And that's the last place I'd take a child anyway," Angelina stated flatly. "I know firsthand what it's like. I took her to the Baptist Church you told me about, on Second."

"I declare." Pulling a basting thread to ease the fullness of the sleeve she was attaching, the painfully thin seamstress peered down at Angelina. "The pastor's decent enough, from what I hear around. He'll find a home for the orphan right quick."

"Actually, I'm not sure she is an orphan. She barely uttered a word. All I found out was her first name." Remembrances of last evening brought a smile. "Noely, she said it was. The little thing's so plain she's really quite endearing."

Ruby grimaced. "Odd way of puttin' it, if I do say so."

"Perhaps. Anyway, I thought I'd go by in a few days and see what became of her. She was on my mind all through the night." Concentrating on her task, Angelina added a few more stitches.

"Why wait so long?"

She met her coworker's green eyes straight on and considered the remark. "Why, indeed! I'll go home that way again tonight. Pastor Winters and his aunt shouldn't mind my concern. . .after all, I did find the child. Naturally I'd be interested in her welfare."

The thought of putting her mind to rest about Noely carried her through the remainder of the day as she and Ruby finished not only the emerald velvet but a cranberry taffeta as well, much to their employer's delight. And to their own delight, they were dismissed half an hour early.

This time the sky wasn't so dark when Angelina reached the red brick building with its pristine steeple. She admired the black shutters on the charming parsonage and the neat window boxes which, come spring, would surely overflow with flowers, if she were any judge of the minister's aunt. Angelina's pulse accelerated. She hoped her appearance wouldn't seem an intrusion. But no one could object to her merely asking about Noely. Bolstering her courage, she paused on the stoop to rest her leg momentarily before rapping with the brass knocker.

She'd forgotten how tall the minister was until the light from the parlor lamps outlined the sandy-haired giant's form in doorway. She swallowed.

"Yes?" Then as recognition dawned, Pastor Winters grinned. "Oh! Miss Matthews. Come in, come in."

"Thank you, Reverend." She stepped past him as he held the door. "I've just come to inquire after—"

A childish shriek sounded from the dining room. Noely, seated at the table with the Reverend's aunt, charged toward the entry and flung her arms about Angelina's waist. "Ang'lina! Ang'lina! You came back! I cried and cried when you went away."

Distressed at the sad pronouncement, Angelina found confirmation in the minister's expression. She bent to hug the little girl. "Oh, Noely, I'm truly sorry. I was only trying to help. I thought you would be fine with these kind people."

The child's lower lip protruded. "But I wanted you. Don't go away again. Say you won't. Please, please." A slight lisp enhanced her plea, as did a harder hug.

"There, there, sweetheart. I don't live here, you know. I had to go home to my house before there was too much snow to find my way."

Pastor Winters patted the curly head. "How about going back and finishing your supper, Noely? Miss Matthews and I need to talk."

"But then she'll go away again, and I don't want her to." A flood of tears made her doleful eyes swim as she turned her gaze upward and clutched Angelina's hand in both of hers.

"I'll stay for a little while, honey," Angelina promised. "But when it's time, I really must go to my own house. Do be a good girl and mind the minister. For me."

Noely stood firm for several seconds before finally relenting. Her lips in a definite downward tilt, she trudged back to the dining room table, where the pastor's kindly aunt helped her up onto the pillowed chair she'd vacated.

Angelina tipped her head and smiled at the plump older woman, then limped after Gabe Winters, observing things on this visit that she had missed the previous night. She took a seat on a wine-colored settee, whose rich hues were picked up by the multicolored braided rug occupying much of the plank floor.

"I'm glad you came by," he said quietly, lowering his bulk to one of the wing chairs flanking the hearth.

"I do hope Noely wasn't an awful bother," Angelina began.

He raised a large, broad hand. "No, no, not at all. She was fine. She was upset to discover you weren't here, of course, but Aunt Clara managed to get her settled down again. A warm bath and some hot food, and she was asleep before she knew it."

The news was comforting. "Did she say where you might find her parents?"

His countenance sobered. "From what she told us, there are none. Her mother 'got sick and went away' as she put it, some time ago. Then her father became ill also. Noely said when 'some people came and took him away' yesterday, she ran as fast and as far as she could so no one would get her and never bring her back. Then she couldn't remember the way home. She doesn't know of any aunts or uncles or other relatives." He smiled. "Noely thought you were an angel come to save her. In a way, I would have to agree."

Angelina would have smiled if she could. But the information was far more dire than she had hoped. Her heart went out to the little waif. "Please, Reverend. . . don't put her in the asylum," she pleaded in a whisper. "It's no place for—"

"You needn't worry about that," he assured her. "There are any number of families in my congregation who might be in a position to take her in. I'll bring the matter up at service tomorrow and see what transpires."

"But what if—?"

He shook his head. "I'll do everything within my power to find Noely a good home, a loving family. You have my word, Miss Matthews."

"Thank you," Angelina breathed, finally able to relax against the burgundy upholstery.

The minister's aunt came into the parlor just then, a gracious smile crinkling the pleasant features beneath a coronet of salt-and-pepper braids. "We'd love to be havin' ye to supper, miss, if ye've a mind to stay. I'm sure little Noely would like to have ye visit for awhile."

Angelina bolted upright. "Oh, thank you. But I mustn't impose. I should get home before it's too dark."

"Stuff and nonsense," she declared with a wave of her hand. "Me nephew would be more than willin' to see ye safely home. Ye wouldn't want to disappoint a wee lassie."

Meeting a pair of huge, hopeful eyes in the next room, Angelina could do nothing but accept. "Well, this time, perhaps, if you're quite certain I'm not putting you out. But I don't intend to make a pest of myself after this."

"There's no danger of that, miss, to be sure. This house could use a few more young faces around from time to time."

Angelina had no sooner nodded her acceptance than the minister stood and offered her a hand. The homey meal did smell delicious. . .something she had tried not to notice in view of having to go to her own cold, dark house in the very near future.

As Reverend Winters seated her at a newly laid place setting, his aunt served a plate heaped with roast beef and mashed potatoes—fare Angelina never troubled to cook for herself.

"I kept yours warm in the oven," the woman said, returning her nephew's partially eaten portion before him. "Now, I'd say grace is in fine order again, don't ye think, Noely?"

"Yes!" She lisped, clapping in childlike delight. Then she grew serious and clasped her fingers, her head bowed.

"Our Father," the pastor prayed, "we do thank You most kindly for sending our friend Miss Matthews to visit us this evening. We pray Your gentle hand will be always upon her for her kindness to our little Noely, and ask Your blessing upon this bounty before us. This we ask in the name of Your Son, Amen."

The simple, heartfelt prayer warmed Angelina inside in a way she had never before experienced. The man prayed as if the Almighty were his personal Friend. And somehow, she believed God truly listened to the requests that came from such a sincere heart as his. Raising her head, she met the minister's merry blue eyes, and she felt a flush heat her face.

"I'm happy you're here, Ang'lina," Noely said, beaming from ear to ear, her upper lip lightly coated with milk from the glass she had just set down.

"I am too, sweetheart," she heard herself say. . .and lost herself in the delectable tastes of the Irishwoman's cooking and the pleasant company about the table. That was far less awkward than imagining herself being escorted homeward soon by this man she'd barely met. . .who, she had to admit, seemed to possess a refreshing, gentle manner for someone so large. Sensing his gaze on her, she quickly turned to smile at Noely.

Chapter 3

"Is Ang'lina coming to church?" Noely asked, her voice echoing in the stillness of the sanctuary. Soft pastel light diffused by the stained glass windows cast irregular patches of color across her blond curls.

Clara O'Malley tugged the child comfortingly nearer on the hard wooden pew. "I've no way of knowin' that, darlin'. She may have her own church, ye know. We can't be makin' her come here."

Noely pouted. "But I miss her."

"I know, dearie. She's a fine, fine friend, to be sure. And she'll be back to visit us, wait and see. But ye must be quiet now, in the House of the Lord." Seeing an obedient nod, Clara patted her little charge's knee. Noely looked quite nice in the somber but stylish dress that had turned up in the Poor Box. Gabe had even managed to unearth a fairly new pair of sturdy shoes and a warm coat, so with her meager undergarments washed and mended, the child was very presentable, if Clara did say so herself. Now one could only hope a suitable family would step forward when Gabe presented Noely before the congregation. Clara tamped down her trepidation and waved to the first arrivals trickling in to worship.

As each one took a seat, she felt a resurgence of doubt.

The Stuarts did need help with chores, since the mister's heart was weak, but she was sure they'd specified a boy. And the Butterfields certainly couldn't feed another mouth. As Noely fidgeted beside her, Clara gave her a tiny hug.

Gabe took his place in the platform's middle chair as the organist played the opening notes of "Joy to the World," and beefy-shouldered Dell Taylor stepped to the pulpit. "That's a fine song to get us into the season," the jovial man announced. "Let's turn to page forty-nine in the hymnal and join in on the next run-through." He beat the tempo with one hand as he sang. "Joy to the world! The Lord is come. . . ."

Unable to concentrate on the words, Clara only half participated in that carol or the following one. And what was even more disturbing, for the first time in her life, personal concerns precluded her enjoyment of her nephew's sermon. She barely heard the text announced, let alone kept track of the points Gabe made in rendering the account of the Good Samaritan. All she could think about was the needy little girl beside her who so quickly had stolen their hearts. Surely the Lord had a special place in mind for Noely, a family who would love her and care for her as if she were their own. Breathing a prayer on the child's behalf, Clara was surprised when Gabe closed his big black Bible so soon and stepped alongside the pulpit.

"Folks," he began, "before we close the service in prayer, I have a rather important matter to bring to your attention." He turned to her and nodded. "Aunt Clara?"

Her heart beating double-time, she stood, took Noely's hand, and led her to the platform. The tiny fingers gripped hers so tightly they all but cut off the circulation as Noely sagged shyly against her. Clara thought she felt the child tremble.

"This is Noely Carroll," Gabe said, with a warm smile her way. "Sad to say, she has recently suffered the loss of both her parents. And as far as we have ascertained at this point, she has no relatives to take her in."

Scanning the faces in the audience, Clara spotted Lucinda Blackwell, Hortense Witherspoon, and Miranda Keys—the three Old Crows, as she irreverently referred to the black-clad biddies on widow's row—who sooner or later managed to find fault with everything and everyone at the church. The threesome hiked their scant eyebrows and exchanged significant looks. Clara averted her gaze.

"All we ask, dear friends," Gabe continued, "is for you to search your hearts. Perhaps one of you might be willing to make room in your family for this little one. Make it a matter of prayer this week—and come by the parsonage and get to know Noely. You won't be sorry, I assure you."

Several murmurs passed in the ranks, along with shrugs, nods, and shakes of the head.

None of them deterred him. "She is a very mannerly child, even quite helpful," he went on. "I'm sure anyone who would open his heart to her would be extremely thankful the Lord had sent such a dear little girl into his home. Thank you, sweetheart." Patting Noely's shoulder, he smiled at Clara and indicated for her to be seated.

"Now, let us close in prayer. . ."

❧

"*Another* story?" Gabe, in feigned shock, adjusted Noely's weight to his other knee.

She nodded sleepily. "Please?"

Never one to resist a girlish lisp, he leafed through the big picture book he'd loved as a child, settling on the story of Noah. "Once there was a man who loved God," he read. "The people all around him, however, were far too busy to bother with building altars or making the sacrifices the Lord wanted. But they weren't too busy to make fun of Noah and his family. In fact—" Gabe looked down at Noely, only to discover her eyes had closed. He smiled and laid the book aside.

"Poor tyke's tuckered out," his aunt declared from the rocker across the room, her knitting needles clicking away.

"It's been a long day."

"And not a soul came by to see her *or* us."

Gabe tipped his head in thought. "Well, not every member of the church attended services. I'll take Noely on my visits this week. Something's sure to turn up. In the meantime, I'd best tuck this little gal into bed." Gathering her easily into his arms, he stood and headed for the stairs.

"And I'll be puttin' on some tea," Aunt Clara offered as he passed. "While the water heats, we'll pray for the little dear. She makes a body wish hearts didn't wear out. I'd gladly live me life over again, just to watch her grow up."

Gabe could only agree with his ailing aunt's sentiments.

She seemed in her glory around children, and had the clumsy oafishness of his youth not dampened both of the relationships he had hoped might lead to matrimony, Aunt Clara could be showering all that love on his own little daughter by now. But his hopes had been in vain. Oh well, he was approaching thirty already. . .much too old—and apparently *unappealing*, as an outspoken member of the opposite gender had once informed him—to inspire that sort of lasting bond. Now resigned to bachelorhood, he expended his energies in serving the Lord.

Flipping the layers of warm blankets aside, he gently placed Noely on the bed and covered her up. His gaze lingered on the peaceful innocence in her expression, and his heart crimped. She'd been noticeably subdued today, waiting and watching at the window for Angelina Matthews, but the young woman had never come. Granted, the distance was a substantial enough for someone with her infirmity to walk unnecessarily. Perhaps she had spent the day resting at home. Tomorrow after work she'd be more likely to come by the parsonage. At least he hoped so. . .for Noely's sake, he quickly assured himself.

Angelina, her leg propped up to keep it from aching, sipped the warm broth from her spoon as best she could in her awkward position, then gingerly tipped the spoon into the bowl of soup again. The wrapped bricks she'd heated at the fireplace usually soothed bouts of reoccurring pain, but this time they hardly made a difference. The slightest movement caused agonizing jabs almost beyond her ability to endure.

Well, it was her own fault for being more hasty than cautious in her eagerness to visit Noely. She should have expected icy spots. The hard fall had severely wrenched her twisted leg. But at least it was Sunday, so she could rest.

Tomorrow her leg had to be better. She couldn't afford to miss a day's work, any more than her employer could have her do so. After all, Mistress Haversham had taken her on with the assurance that Angelina would be faithful in coming to work regardless of her withered leg. So far, the promise had been kept.

Today Reverend Winters had planned to present Noely to his congregation. Angelina couldn't help wondering how the event had gone. She hadn't much use for church herself since childhood circumstances had raised serious doubts regarding a loving God. But all the same, she knew that many folks set a lot of store by their faith. Maybe among his flock of do-gooders someone would step in to provide a home for a destitute little girl. If Noely had a loving family, Angelina's own spirit would find rest.

In any event, she'd get to work tomorrow, then go home by way of Second Street. And she'd do the same every day after that, until the good Reverend or his aunt asked her not to. . .as long as that sweet little orphan child needed her. *If* she still needed her.

Finishing the remainder of the soup, Angelina braced herself for the painful journey upstairs to her bed.

Thankfully, morning brought measurable improvement, though her limb was far from feeling its best. With care, she could manage the long walk to work—and she would, if it was the last thing she ever did. With that determination, she dressed warmly and allowed extra time to hobble the long blocks to Front Street.

The day dragged as she and Ruby labored over the endless stack of party frocks. And her leg, which had seemed improved that morning, began its relentless aching by midday. When at last closing time arrived, Angelina was only too happy to set aside the butternut velvet gown and take down her coat.

Picking her way along the streets, she watched carefully for any icy patches and headed toward the parsonage of Second Street Baptist Church. It would be so good to see Noely again. She rapped on the door. Then rapped again.

Just as she turned to leave, the pastor answered the summons, a grin of vast relief spreading across his lips. "Miss Matthews! Come in, come in. I was about to be pressed into service by Aunt Clara—to help fit Noely with a dress! She'd be far better off with a woman's help. I have some letters to write anyway." He ushered her inside and took her coat.

"Certainly," Angelina said. "I'll do what I can."

He led her into the brightly lit kitchen, then inclined his head and retreated to the parlor.

A wondrous assortment of copper pots glinted from their hooks on the wall next to the big cookstove whose warmth quickly began to wrap itself around her sore limb. Observing a few unfamiliar and curious devices whose purposes she could only surmise, Angelina realized she had never seen such an efficient kitchen. And in the middle of it all was a wooden chair, with Noely standing like a statue on its seat.

"Ang'lina!" The child grinned from ear to ear, and looked on the verge of hopping down, but the older woman kept tight rein on the little one's skirt.

" 'Tis good of ye to come by," she gushed. "Dresses from the Poor Box always seem to need lettin' down or takin' up, I daresay, if not let out. Gabe's come up with three that still have a good bit of wear."

Examining one yet to be altered, Angelina held it up to Noely and nodded approvingly. "This shouldn't take much to fix."

"Not if ye lean toward such talents," the older woman commented, deep dimples appearing with her smile. "Some of us, on the other hand, discover our strengths blossom better before a cookstove. I haven't even started supper."

"Then I'd be only too happy to take over this chore, Mistress O'Malley, while you tend to yours."

Without hesitation, the older woman relinquished her pincushion and moved to the vegetable bin, where she began gathering potatoes to peel.

While Aunt Clara's back was turned, Noely smiled playfully and bent to administer a quick hug to Angelina, then just as swiftly straightened again.

"How have you been, sweetheart?" Angelina asked, assessing the portion of hem already pinned. After making a few minor adjustments, she continued around the remainder.

"You didn't come to church," the child announced flatly.

"And I'm sorry. I, well. . .almost did. It just didn't quite work out." She cut a questioning glance toward the

Irishwoman. "Was there—I mean, did anyone—?"

The braided head wagged slowly. "Nary a soul. But Gabe hasn't quit tryin'."

The pronouncement brought mixed reactions of relief and disappointment, each equally strong. What if someone offered to take the child with the intention of putting her to work, instead of providing a loving, happy home? Or what if the couple already had children of their own who would resent a newcomer's usurping attention which rightfully belonged to them? The morose thoughts crowded out the small hope Angelina still harbored for the sweet little one with whom she had so quickly become enamored.

"Are you gonna eat supper here?" the childish voice asked.

"Course she is," Aunt Clara piped in before Angelina had time to answer. "She's welcome anytime, and that's a fact."

"Oh, good."

"You're much too kind," Angelina told the older woman. Finished pinning the first garment, she eased it carefully over Noely's upraised arms, then turned the second wrong-side out and slipped it over the child's head.

"After supper, Pastor Gabe reads to me," Noely lisped, sliding her arms into the sleeves. "From the Bible book. It has pretty pictures. Will you stay for a story?"

"We'll see." Unbidden scenes flashed to mind of the huge minister with a little girl curled on his lap, his big head bent over hers. Noely's tiny form would be absolutely swallowed in those long arms. The imaginary picture brought a smile.

Angelina caught her breath. Her solitary existence for the past six years had her enjoying the loving atmosphere of this home too much—and becoming far too attached to the charming family she had met mere days ago. These people were fine Christians, certainly, living up to their own code of standards. But once Noely had been placed, there'd be no further reason to return. Still, if she truly felt welcome, an inner voice reasoned, what harm could there be in visiting while she could?

"The more the merrier," came the reverend's booming voice from the doorway.

Having been unaware of his presence, Angelina turned away to hide her blush. Her embarrassment only strengthened her resolve not to expect more from this association than what was on the surface. After all, these visits to the parsonage were for Noely's benefit—and *only* Noely's. She would enjoy whatever friendship might be offered here as long as it lasted, and then let go. . .no matter how much it might hurt when the time came.

"I'll stay."

Chapter 4

Watching Angelina Matthews ease up from the dining table, Gabe was certain he detected new lines of pain around her dark brown eyes. Earlier, when Noely had inadvertently bumped against the young woman on her jump from the chair, he'd even caught a sheen of moisture across her eyes, but she had quickly blinked it away. In an elaborate gesture of chivalry overdone, he made a grand bow and offered her his elbow. "Might I escort your ladyship to the royal parlor?"

"Oh, but I should help clean up."

"Fiddle-faddle!" his aunt said. "You young folks go on ahead. I'll see to the supper things. Off with ye, now."

The seamstress actually grinned, a dazzling smile which somehow made Gabe even more sure she was expending excessive effort to appear natural. With the merest hint of a curtsey she accepted his help. " 'Twould be my pleasure, milord."

He felt a rush of gratification when she joined in with the game. . .but then, she *was* trying to help entertain Noely. The little girl giggled and skipped alongside them, then made a beeline for the picture book.

Gabe settled their guest on one end of the settee. Then,

taking the other end, he drew the curlyhead onto his lap. "What will it be, princess?"

She scrunched her girlish face in thought.

"Well," he coaxed, "there's a very special day coming. How about the story of the first Christmas?"

"Oh, I like that one!"

Opening to the proper page, Gabe cleared his throat. " 'Once there lived a Prince who ruled the whole world. Many of His people didn't know Him, and that made Him very sad. They were forever muddling things up, going here and there like sheep without a shepherd. They did many bad things, and He knew that one day every one of them would have to stand before His Father, the Mighty King and be judged. The Prince knew the only way He could help them was to become one of them Himself, so that's exactly what He did. . .' "

Even as he went on to the simple account of the Babe being born in a manger in Bethlehem, Gabe was aware of Miss Matthews' intense interest. She had never spoken of her personal beliefs, and yet she neither interrupted his reading nor reacted scornfully to the story. Once he glanced at her and saw she appeared faraway, as though lost in a memory. His heart breathed a prayer that whatever her needs, the Lord would meet them.

" '. . .and now we remember the birth of the Christ Child once a year,' " he read, " 'on Christmas. And in giving each other gifts, we demonstrate how God gave His very best Gift to all of us, in His Beloved Son.' "

Noely smiled and lay her head back on his shoulder. "I really, really like that story, Pastor Gabe. It's my favorite."

"Mine too, pumpkin. Christmas is the most special time there is. But it's getting late now. Time to dress for bed."

"Can Ang'lina tuck me in, this time?" she pleaded.

"Don't see why not—unless she doesn't like stairs," he added quickly, looking for her response.

"I can manage. . .but I've never tucked a child in for the night, sweetheart. You'll have to tell me what to do, so I can get it right."

"It's easy," she lisped, sliding off Gabe's knee. "I'll show you." All smiles, she held out a tiny hand.

Gabe watched after them, and tried not to notice the halting, careful steps Miss Matthews took with each rise. Though she hadn't complained, her limp was much more pronounced today. His heart went out to her.

"And now I kneel and say my prayers," Noely advised as Angelina fastened the last button on the castoff man's shirt the child slept in. "But big people usually just sit on the bed."

"Fine." Relieved she didn't have to try and kneel, Angelina took her place as the youngster sank to her knees at the bedside. Noely laced her fingers and reverently bowed her head. "Dear Lord, thank You for bringing Ang'lina today. I miss her when she doesn't come. And thank You for Jesus and the Christmas story. Please take care of my mommy and daddy, and bless Pastor Gabe and Aunt Clara, and help me to be a good girl. Amen." Opening her eyes, she scrambled into bed. "Now you cover me up and kiss my cheek."

"Is that everything?" Angelina asked, following

instructions to the letter.

"Mm-hmm. And I hug you, like this." With a surprisingly strong squeeze, she smiled. "Good night. I love you."

The unexpected remark made Angelina's eyes sting. When had anyone last said those words to her? Brushing a curl from the child's forehead, she straightened. "Good night, sweetheart." Tiptoeing to the door, she stole one more look at the little girl, then slowly made her way downstairs.

Seated in a wing chair with his open Bible, the minister glanced up on her approach.

"I shall be going home now. Thank you for supper."

"Wait, please," he said. "No need to hurry off." He gestured toward the settee. "I thought we might talk."

"About what?" Nerve endings in her spine tingled as she lowered herself to the upholstered seat and perched stiffly on the edge, wondering what was coming.

"Nothing," he said. "Everything. Anything. It's been rather a pleasure getting to know you, that's all. May I get you a cup of tea?"

"Yes, that would be nice, thank you." She knew the pastor and his aunt were merely extending the hand of friendship to her as they would anyone else. The assurance helped her to relax as homey sounds drifted from the kitchen.

He returned moments later with the refreshment. "Noely sure is happy whenever you come," he said, handing her one of the two cups he carried. He settled back in his chair with the other.

"She's a dear little thing," Angelina admitted. "I haven't

been able to get her off my mind since the night of the blizzard." With a shake of her head, she went on. "In a scant few days that little child has captured a large part of my heart."

"And ours. It is a wonder." He sampled his tea. "We all expected you to come yesterday."

"I. . .nearly did. Then I could not."

He gave a nod. "You're in pain, aren't you?"

Angelina blinked at the blunt question. "I'm always in pain."

"But not like today."

"How would you know that?"

"I read people."

It was a peculiar remark. She averted her eyes from his and took a sip of the hot liquid in lieu of replying.

"Sorry. I don't normally pry into my friends' lives." His voice were husky, as though he were embarrassed.

"Are we friends?" she couldn't help asking.

He grinned. "We're approaching it. And what my aunt told Noely happens to be true. You *are* welcome here—whether Noely continues to live with us or not."

Hesitant to linger over the ramifications of that particular statement, she centered on the important part. "Have you found someone who'll take her?" she murmured.

"Not yet. But I haven't exhausted all my resources."

Angelina nibbled the inside corner of her lip. "I only hope someone will want her. Will love her." Memories of visiting days at the orphanage cut into her consciousness. She recalled so many endless partings as, one by one, her friends were adopted. . .and she recalled her own hopeless waiting, the people shaking their heads, turning away. She didn't want that for Noely.

"I won't rest until Noely becomes part of a loving family," the minister vowed. "If I have to move heaven and earth to accomplish that, I will."

His sincerity made Angelina smile. "Were you ever an orphan?" she finally asked.

He shook his head. "I grew up with my parents, lived with them until I graduated from theological school. The last outbreak of cholera took them both within days of each other. It's what they'd have wanted. Now they're with the Lord."

"That's something I'm quite curious about," Angelina confessed. "That some people aren't afraid to die. . .yet how can they believe God is so loving, when He'll take parents away from a little girl?"

"As He did yours?"

She frowned. "Am I so very transparent?"

"Not at all. I just got that impression from the plea you made regarding not sending Noely to an orphan asylum."

Finishing the last of her tea, Angelina rose carefully to her feet. "Well, I really must get home. I have work tomorrow."

"Of course." Having stood at the same time as she, the pastor retrieved her coat from the hall tree and assisted her into it. Then he reached for his own and pulled it on.

Angelina peered up at him in puzzlement.

"Thought you could use some assistance this evening."

She flushed. "That's not necessary. I'm used to getting

about on my own."

"I'm sure you are. But this once you won't have to. You have a friend to help. Aunt Clara," he called, "be back shortly." With that, he opened the door.

Angelina preceded him into the starry night, and he closed the door behind them. But before she took a step she felt herself being whisked off her feet and into his strong arms. "What do you think you are doing?" she railed, mortified at the situation and the informality of it all. She hadn't known the man but a few days!

"Helping a friend," he said evenly.

"A friend who can walk on her own," she countered, craning her neck to make sure they weren't being observed.

"If she had to—which she does not. Besides, I haven't done my good deed for the day."

Unsure whether to laugh or cry, Angelina settled for the former—not that she had much choice in the matter. "Surely you don't intend to carry me all the way home! I'm too heavy, and it's too far."

"Heavy!" he snickered. "I've carried sacks of coal heavier than you!"

"Really, Reverend," she began.

"Do you think you could possibly call me by my Christian name, as my other friends do?" he teased.

"Certainly not! It isn't. . .proper."

A chuckle rumbled from his chest. "You actually prefer that sort of stilted friendship?" he asked, not even winded as he strode over the cobbled street. "My forever calling you Miss Matthews, and your referring to me as Reverend Winters? Times *are* changing, you know. Honestly, little Noely's the only one who's got the whole thing in perspective."

Angelina laughed again. It had never entered her mind to be so familiar she'd resort to using his Christian name. *Gabe.* Gabriel. It did suit the man—he was so much bigger than life.

She hadn't had a true friend for many years. Ruby, though chummy to a certain extent, had a husband, a life of her own. Gabe Winters was the first person in a long time who offered real friendship. What harm could there be in accepting it—at least while they both shared a concern for Noely?

Sooner than she'd have expected, the minister set her down on her stoop. "Friends, then. . .Angelina?"

She almost couldn't breathe. "I—I suppose."

"Good. We really do want you to come by the parsonage every day—or whenever you can. I've had my fill of stuffy church business, starched deacons and elders, proper protocol. You and Noely have been like a breath of spring to Aunt Clara and me."

"That's nice to hear."

He nodded, and his gaze remained fixed on hers. "Look, it's bound to be dark and cold in there," he said in all seriousness, motioning with his head toward her house. "Would you like me to get your fire going? Bring in extra wood or coal?"

"Certainly not!" she gasped. "We've probably caused scandal enough as it is. And anyway, aren't you forgetting? You've done your good deed for the day."

He grinned. "So I have."

"And I can manage. Truly. But thank you for offering."

"Gabe," he prompted.

"Gabe," she whispered, waiting for lightning to strike her dead. When it did not, she expelled a pent-up breath and dug into her pocket for her key.

He took it from her and unlocked the door, nudging it open. "Well, take care, then. Will we see you tomorrow?"

"Most likely. Your aunt told me you'll be taking Noely around to some of your parishioners' this week?"

"That's right. We'll see that she gets a good home, I promise. Good night."

"Good night, my friend. Thanks for seeing me home."

With a nod, he backed away, and Angelina stepped inside, closed the door, and leaned against the jamb. How many people in the world could boast of having an angel for a friend. . .for if ever one walked the earth, he had to be a lot like Gabriel Winters. Her heart felt strangely warmed with the knowledge. And she had no trouble at all *thinking* of him by his given name. Reaching for the box of matches, she lit the parlor lamp and then the wood she'd laid earlier.

An indescribable peace flowed through her regarding Noely. Gabe would keep his promise. . .to both of them. Could she help it if a tiny part of her hoped he wouldn't find a home for the child too soon?

Gabe rolled over and punched his pillow, trying to get comfortable. He hoped he hadn't been too forward with Angelina. Overfriendliness had always been his greatest fault and rarely endeared him to the fairer gender—in fact, one or two refined lasses had proclaimed him an oaf to his face! Well at least he'd finally managed to overcome the tendency to trip over his own big feet or bump his head going through shallow doorways, but maintaining proper protocol would forever be a trial.

The trouble was, the profound loneliness in Angelina's dark eyes reminded him of his own, and he desperately wanted to ease her heartache. He knew someone so beautiful as she would never look twice at a big ox like himself—and after the way he'd pushed her tonight, he should count himself fortunate that she even agreed to be his friend!

Then a darker thought surfaced. Once Noely was out of the picture, would Angelina take her leave as well? Releasing a slow breath, he rolled onto his back and laced his fingers beneath his head, staring up at the ceiling.

Chapter 5

Her arms full of fabric scraps, Clara entered the back door of the church. Gabe had already stoked up the furnace for today's gathering of the mission society, and the pervading warmth helped erase the chill. If all the women showed up, the many nimble fingers would easily finish another quilt by day's end. Never fond of stitching, much less possessed of such talent herself, Clara contributed by tearing donated materials into strips or cutting needed shapes for the various quilt patterns, an arrangement which seemed to suit everyone.

She descended the stairs to the basement supply room and piled her burden into a large basket, together with needles, thread, and several pairs of scissors. Then she took the items up to the side room where the activity was held. To her surprise, she heard voices. Some of the ladies had come early.

"You can't tell me there's not something scandalous going on," came Lucinda Blackwell's distinctive high-pitched pronouncement. "And under our very noses, no less."

Clara stopped in her tracks. The Old Crows' Society. Not one to eavesdrop, she nevertheless paused and waited for an opportune moment to enter.

"Saw it with my own eyes, I did," Miranda Keys affirmed. "Pretty as you please, him carrying that hussy in his arms, right past my house for all the world to see! Near brought me to heart failure right then and there, I daresay. That woman's at the parsonage every single night and stays till past dark. And not even a member of the church, at that! I suppose the rest of us are expected to believe she goes there to see that urchin. Hmph! It's downright sinful, if you ask me. Mark my words."

Hortense Witherspoon went into her usual fit of coughing. Clara could just picture the other biddies thumping her back with their scrawny fists. "Why, it's a sheer disgrace," she croaked after the coughs subsided. "That's what."

"Never did approve of calling such a young preacher to our church," Widow Blackwell told the others. "I let the board know my opinion in no uncertain terms, as if it mattered—they voted him in anyway. Well, if you ask me, it's high time a special meeting was called. We'll see what the high and mighty elders think of these goings-on."

"True, true," Mistress Keys said. Clara could envision the old gal's nod of assent. Miranda had little backbone of her own, and usually went along with anything her cronies said.

Tucking a strand of stray hair into her coronet, Clara reached for the latch.

"Wait, girls," came the annoying nasal voice again.

There were far worse sins than listening in, Clara reasoned, detecting a sinister change in Lucinda Blackwell's tone. She settled back onto her heels.

"Maybe we shouldn't stop with the Board of Trustees," the widow went on.

"What are you saying?" the others asked as one.

"Just this. I've never approved of that child-placement sideline of his. Philadelphia isn't a fledgling colony anymore. The city has institutions to handle that sort of thing. People paid to deal with riffraff. I'll wager the authorities would be mighty interested to hear of the preacher's dabbling in affairs beyond his calling. That orphan brat belongs in a proper asylum, and I intend to see she gets there."

Clara's hand flew to her throat. In the pregnant silence that followed, she could almost see the sly conspiratorial smiles spreading from one self-righteous face to the next. Determined to squelch this nonsense before it went any farther, she opened the door and entered.

The maleficent expressions became amazingly guileless as the three bony women turned. "Why, good day, Clara," Widow Blackwell gushed. "You're looking spry. I was just remarking to the girls about how well our little church is functioning under the fine hand of your nephew."

"Indeed." The outright lie stole any more deprecating response Clara might have made. Moving stiffly to the storage closet, she took down the folded in-progress quilts and spread each out on the long tables with precise deliberation.

Hortense Witherspoon broke into another spasm of coughs.

Clara, still searching for the exact words to put the presumptuous busybodies in their place, opened her mouth, but the arrival of two more members stayed her tongue. She knew it was for the best, seeing as how it spared her from having to repent afterward. But all the same, Gabe should know about this. And know he would, as soon as she got home.

"Don't tell me you took that folderol seriously!" Gabe looked incredulously at his aunt over pie and tea as Noely played with clothespins and buttons on the parlor rug.

"Of course I did. And so should you."

He forked a chunk of the dessert and stabbed at the air with the utensil to punctuate his words. "Those meddlesome widows have been nitpicking ever since we got here, Aunt Clara. If it isn't about one thing, it'd be another—whatever their idle imaginations can conjure up and pass on to itching ears. It's not worth losing sleep over."

"But ye didn't hear them, Gabe. They won't stop until they've done as much damage to your ministry as they possibly can, to say nothing of—" She glanced in Noely's direction. "It was all I could do not to be tellin' those troublesome biddies off, and in no uncertain terms."

"And what would that have accomplished?" he asked quietly. "We're all equally capable of wounding another person with the sharpness of our tongues. Only through His grace can those women's cruelty be tamed, and our words tempered and used to praise rather than crush. I'm glad you remained quiet."

"I'm not sure I am, to be quite truthful." She crossed her arms and rested them on the table.

He gave a comforting pat to her worn hand. "You and

I both know there'll never be a perfect church until the Lord Himself comes to establish His. No matter how hard His servants labor for the kingdom, or how selfless and faithful their service, there's bound to be some devil's advocate right in the thick of things, stirring up trouble. All I can do is my best to remain faithful and continue to seek and do God's will. Meanwhile, He will handle those *Old Crows*—as you so aptly termed them."

"I only pray He will," she said quietly.

"What crows, Pastor Gabe?" Noely asked, coming to the table and draining the last drops of milk from her glass.

"We're just talking about some grownup matters, pumpkin," he said gently. "Nothing for your little head to worry about." He studied the young child as she returned to her play, then exhaled deeply. "I have more pressing matters to occupy my mind, Aunt Clara. No point worrying about idle threats. Dress Noely up real pretty this afternoon. I've a few calls to make."

Angelina often noticed a slight improvement in her weak limb during milder weather, and even more so after having been spared a long walk in the night chill.

She hardly felt the smile that crossed her lips as she thought back on it. Never would she have imagined she could relax and be herself in the presence of a virile, compelling man like Gabe Winters. Of course, having established the boundaries in her mind, she would never presume anything beyond friendship.

Besides, she had resolved years ago never to set herself

up for another heartbreak. She had learned that particular lesson well on the first try, when a young man she thought loved her took her home to meet his parents. Nothing matched the cruel sting of that humiliation. . . the raised brows, the faces beginning to redden slightly, the oh-so-polite stammered excuses which rendered swift death to the blossoming romance.

And no one needed to point out that for all the interested first glances she received from young bachelors who crossed her path, there rarely came a second. But she had come to terms with her solitary destiny. Yes, Angelina resolved inwardly, friendship was blessing enough, for a cripple.

"Any news about that homeless tyke?" Ruby's query interrupted Angelina's musings. Removing her eyeglasses, the willowy girl wiped them on her work apron, then resumed stitching a ruffled gown of sapphire taffeta.

"No. Nothing's turned up for Noely as yet, I'm afraid. But Reverend Winters is still trying to find her a home. At this moment she's probably accompanying him on his pastoral calls so folks can meet her." Angelina clipped a little extra trim for the remainder of the neckline on the coffee satin frock, then turned the raw edge under and tacked it. She snipped the thread.

"Then she shouldn't be on her own much longer, I'd expect."

"No." The sad reality disturbed Angelina greatly.

"Well," her coworker mused, "with Christmas comin', she should have a nice new family to call her own. Case she doesn't, though, will you be givin' her a present?"

"I hadn't thought about it," Angelina admitted in

dismay. "I really should get her something to remember me by, I suppose."

"Or make her somethin'. A doll, mebbe."

"Do you think there's time, Ruby? Oh, I should have thought of it myself, only I've been so busy!"

Ruby gestured toward the remnant bin in the corner. "Dig through that when we're done. Might be Mistress would let you have whatever you need. It don't take much to do a doll."

For the first time in years, Angelina felt a measure of joy at the thought of the approaching holiday barely a week away. She'd been contemplating the story Gabe had read to Noely regarding the significance of the event, and as she lay in bed, long-buried childhood memories had surfaced. She could recall taking part in pageants, being filled with the wonder of the birth of the Holy Child, the One destined to suffer a cruel death on a cross so that all who believed on Him would one day live with Him in Heaven. And she recalled uttering a simple girlish prayer that He might come to dwell within her own heart. So long ago that had been. She wondered if God still remembered her.

"Will you look at that!" Ruby declared suddenly. "It's the last one! We've finished them all!"

"Why, so we have." Angelina laughed. "At least, those needing to be done for the holidays. Tomorrow we'll start back to work on the more ordinary garments."

"Yes, those." Grimacing, the auburn-haired girl hung the newly completed gowns, then began tidying the work table in readiness for going home. "Don't forget to look through the remnants, Angie."

But Angelina had already started rooting through the various fabrics in her eagerness, absolutely astounded that there were so many to choose from. Wouldn't Noely be surprised!

Her feet fairly floated over the cobbles that evening, limp and all. Her employer had been wonderfully generous. Patting the soft bundle of materials in her pocket, Angelina visualized them made into a Christmas doll. A shorter visit might be prudent this evening to allow time at home to work on the project.

Though she felt surprisingly at ease when Gabe welcomed her at the parsonage, she found the mood there somewhat subdued. Several peculiar glances passed between the minister and his aunt during supper, and Noely, overtired from her long day, fell fast asleep at the table and was whisked off to bed.

"I take it you were unsuccessful," Angelina remarked when Gabe returned from tucking the little one in.

"That's an understatement." He sank wearily into a parlor chair. "My three best possibilities, and not one was the least bit interested in taking on a three-year-old."

"Well, she can't remain three forever," Angelina said, trying to raise his spirits. "In fact, do you even know her birthdate?"

He raked his fingers through his hair. "Actually, yes. I came across it when I checked the birth and death records of the only Carrolls known to be in Philadelphia. Noely will turn four on April tenth."

"Would either of ye be wantin' more tea?" Aunt Clara asked, stacking supper dishes on a tray.

"Not just now," Gabe answered.

Angelina rose. "Nor I, thanks. I'd best be on my way."

"Already?" he asked, getting up also. "You've only just gotten here."

"Yes, but I have something urgent to do at home."

"Need my assistance?"

She barely stayed her blush. "Actually, I'm much better this evening. But if you could spare the time to walk with me part of the way, I really would like to talk with you."

"As you wish." Fetching her coat, he helped her into it, then put on his own, and they took their leave.

The night was chilly, with blue-white clouds drifting across a velvet sky and a partial moon. The arm he offered aided her greatly as they strolled toward Elfreth's Alley.

Gabe broke the silence. "What did you want to discuss?"

Not quite certain how to put her thoughts into words, Angelina peered up at the minister, feeling quite at ease with him, drawing strength from his presence. "It's. . .well, it's about the story last night. The Christmas one."

"And? What bothers you about it?"

She shrugged. "Nothing, really. It's just—" Pausing, she drew a deep breath and released it. "It's been ages since I'd been reminded of the significance of Jesus' birth. After you read the account last night it brought back long-forgotten experiences from my own childhood. And I was wondering. . .that is, do you think—" Angelina swallowed.

Gabe gave an encouraging pat to her gloved hand in

the crook of his arm.

"Do you think God would still remember me?" she finished in a near whisper.

He stopped and smiled down at her. "Of course He remembers you, little friend. He sees you when you lie down and rise up again. He knows the number of hairs on your head and everything else there is to know about you. And He loves you as He does all His children."

"Even if I haven't spoken to Him in years?"

"Even then."

They had reached the end of her street. Angelina was almost too overcome to speak as she gazed up at him. "Thank you. That's what I wanted to know. I can go the rest of the way home on my own."

Somehow, as she left him behind, she knew he wasn't merely counting stars when he lifted his face to the sky.

Chapter 6

Angelina stitched far into the night on the surprise doll for Noely. Though she had never attempted making anything in the nature of a child's toy, her basic sewing talents made the project much easier than she had dared to hope. In a burst of inspiration she decided to use straw-colored yarn for the hair and embroider eyes of blue, so the little plaything would resemble its new mama. That would make it all the more special.

However, as she assembled the front and back sections of an indigo muslin dress similar to one Noely wore, the thoughts which meandered to the parsonage on Second Street did not always remain on the young orphan.

The new friendship she shared with Gabe Winters seemed truly precious. For the first time in ages, she felt free to be herself, so much of her loneliness was fading away. The minister possessed the ability to put her completely at ease and never treated her like a cripple. . .nor had he belittled her for what must have sounded like a childish question.

Angelina tried to picture the sandy-haired pastor standing behind the pulpit of his church, encouraging his little flock to be faithful to Almighty God. Did he read his sermons, as had the few ministers who had come to give services at the orphanage, or merely speak from his heart? And did all his prayers fall as naturally from his lips as those she had heard at the table?

Somehow she imagined his messages—no matter how deep their subject—would be delivered in the simplest of ways, so that anyone who heard them would be able to understand. To someone with as big a heart as Gabe Winters', that would be of the utmost importance.

It was still a struggle for her to call him by his Christian name, but perhaps as time passed it would become easier to be casual about such things. After all, as he'd said, times were changing. People were turning from the old stiff rules to more relaxed ones.

A deep sigh evolved into a yawn. Glancing at the clock, Angelina discovered it was half-past midnight. She'd best put away the Christmas doll and get whatever sleep remained before time came to go to work.

Gabe knelt at his nightly prayers, lingering longer than usual as he upheld his church members before the Lord, along with the various concerns of the church itself. On visitation rounds he always accumulated a growing number of requests for prayer, and he did his best to remember them all.

Then there was Angelina. He'd felt compelled to pray fervently for the beautiful seamstress since she had appeared on his doorstep the night of the blizzard. He pleaded ceaselessly that God would allay the suffering she endured from her frail leg and lighten any other cares she might have. He was intensely gratified that she'd felt free to discuss personal spiritual concerns with him, and he hoped her mind had been put to rest. *And Father,* he added, shifting position on the braided mat at his bedside, *I ask You to keep my thoughts and motives pure regarding her. Never let me take advantage of the friendship we've only just begun. You know my tendency to rush and bungle things, the many relationships I've managed to sour single-handedly. Please restrain me from doing anything that would make Angelina take flight. If I can just be a true friend to her, I will not presume to ask any more.*

And then there was Noely, who barely resembled the timid, ragged urchin who had arrived at the parsonage in Angelina's arms. *Dear Lord, the little one is becoming more attached to Angelina, Aunt Clara, and me with each passing day—as we are to her. You know this could make her adjustment into yet another family every bit as painful and devastating as the loss of her own parents such a short time ago. Please help me to find a solution to this problem. Soon.*

Gabe rubbed his temples as he sorted through his jumbled thoughts. It galled him to admit that Noely had some very definite points against her. She wasn't a newborn baby, and folks tended to look more favorably on an infant of either gender than a child of nearly four. She wasn't a boy, and the latter remained much more in demand after the long years of Civil War had exacted such a high toll among the male population. And she wasn't heart-stoppingly pretty or possessed of delicate features, but rather plain and sturdy instead. That particular prejudice was hardest of all to justify.

His mind went over the sweet charm Noely had

about her. Once past her initial shyness, she tugged at a person's heartstrings and moved right in to take over the whole heart. She seemed, in some uncanny way, able to sense when to be quiet—or when a jubilant hug might be in order. Her musical giggle never failed to bring a smile. And anyone could see that the dear face which now seemed so grownup for such a young child would one day blossom into a lasting and stately beauty which would not quickly fade, but become all the more handsome with the passing years.

Oh, Lord, what will become of this little one? Why hasn't there been even one ray of hope for her? If Aunt Clara weren't prone to recurring heart seizures, we could try to seek permanent custody ourselves. But You know she's much more frail than she lets on. Were something to happen to her, I wouldn't have an inkling about how to nurture a little girl on my own. I don't know where else to turn. Or what else to pray. I cast this burden at Your feet and ask You to do with it what You will. Provide an answer which will bring glory to Your Son, in whose name I pray.

At the end of himself, Gabe climbed into bed and pulled the blankets and quilts snugly about his neck. . . but sleep eluded him for some time.

A summons at the door rendered an end to the peace of mid-morning. With Aunt Clara bathing Noely in a tub in the kitchen, Gabe answered the knock.

Dell Taylor, turning his hat around and around in his work-hardened hands, stood on the stoop, along with two other deacons from the church. "Reverend," Dell mumbled, shifting uneasily from one foot to the other.

"Gentlemen," Gabe replied with a nod, already beginning to suspect why they were here. A niggle of dread coursed through him. "Come in."

The beefy tradesman shook his head. "Might be best if we could speak over at the church office."

"If you don't mind," rawboned Harris Thresher quickly added, appearing every bit as ill at ease as Mr. Taylor.

Small, highbrow Randall Bent had yet to meet Gabe's eyes as he hunkered into the collar of his dark wool coat.

"Certainly," Gabe replied, plucking his own wrap from the hall tree. He led the others to the house of worship next door and ushered them into his tidy, book-lined study. He motioned toward three chairs and took his place behind the worn mahogany desk, trying to ignore the signs that an axe was about to fall.

The deacons exchanged furtive glances before Dell spoke up. "We, er, that is, a rather disturbing matter has been brought to our attention—one that's probably just so much rumor and gossip. But anyways, we thought we'd best lay it all out on the table right here, before it grows into something more serious, requiring a meeting of the whole board."

Thresher and Bent gave nods of assent.

"What is it?" Gabe asked, glancing from one grim face to the next, finally settling on Dell Taylor.

Dell flicked an imaginary speck of lint from a trouser leg, then met Gabe's gaze. "It concerns a certain young woman who's been frequenting the parsonage of an evening." He reddened and averted his attention to the floor.

Gabe relaxed a bit. "Is that all? Well, allow me to put your minds at ease. Miss Matthews happens to be the person who found Noely freezing on the street and brought her to us. She's been coming by to visit the child —who, by the way, formed a singular attachment to her rescuer. There's nothing more to the matter, I assure you."

Thresher cleared his throat.

"I'm afraid there is, Reverend," Taylor went on. "It's been reported that, er, you've been seen—" His color deepening, he tugged at his starched collar, then managed to continue. "You've been seen conducting yourself in a fashion most. . .unseemly, in public." That said, he exhaled a long breath as if greatly relieved to have the problem off his chest.

For a moment Gabe stared, dumbfounded. Then the evening he had escorted Angelina home in his arms popped anew in his memory. He felt his ire start to rise and fought to keep his tone even. "I don't suppose it was also reported that the young woman suffers from a serious infirmity which renders walking quite difficult. Or that sometimes she is in such pain she requires assistance."

"No, sir, it wasn't." Some of the color left Dell's face.

"Well, then, you can see the charges are erroneous. I can tell you here and now, my conscience is entirely clear before the Lord and before my church. I hope this sets the record straight."

"Only on one of the charges, Reverend," Thresher announced, gesturing for Mr. Taylor to elaborate further.

Dell swallowed. "About the orphan. . ."

Completely baffled, Gabe didn't respond.

"Certain folks in the church think," the deacon went on, "that your concern for her is taking up time which might be better spent in matters directly related to your ministry."

"Is that a fact?" Gabe responded, his anger barely contained. "And does the Bible not tell us it is the duty of every Christian—minister or layman alike—to aid a person who comes seeking need? Someone who cannot lift a finger to help herself?"

"There are institutions for that very purpose," meek Mr. Bent finally piped in.

"I see. Let someone else do it? Well, I have reasons not to agree with that particular conviction, and the primary one has to do with love. Noely is a dear, sensitive little child who happens to be in dire need of a family to love her, not an institution where she'll be one of a throng of homeless children in her same position. . .though I'm sure her continued presence at church probably inflicts a measure of guilt upon people who have refused to help her. But if she happened to be your grandchild, would you not be a lot more concerned about what becomes of her and feel as strongly about her as I do?"

The man had the grace to nod in agreement, and as the other deacons did the same, the tension lightened noticeably.

Gabe softened his tone. "I have every reason to believe I'll be successful in placing her in a Christian home in the very near future—perhaps among the congregations of other churches. And until that time I intend to continue striving toward that end. . .as I believe God would have me do."

"Yes," Dell conceded. "Put that way, I would share your feelings." He stood, and the other men joined him. "We'll be on our way, then, and pass on the results of this meeting to the wom—I mean, folks who brought it all up. We hope you won't hold this against us, Reverend."

"Not at all. I know people like to be sure things are being handled in a manner which behooves a minister of God. And," he could not restrain himself from adding, "you might advise them their added prayers would be of greater benefit in all of this than their criticism."

"I heartily agree." With a sheepish grin, Dell Taylor extended his hand.

Gabe shook it warmly, and did the same with the others, then showed them to the door. "God be with you, gentlemen."

As they exited the study, Gabe returned to his chair and bowed his head in a prayer of thankfulness. Aunt Clara would be glad to hear that nothing came of the hornet's nest stirred up by the widows who perched ever so piously on the more prominent church pews. He smiled inwardly and headed home.

When he related the discussion he'd had in the church office, his aunt placed a hand over her heart as if to quiet the agitation the news had caused. "I knew those biddies wouldn't quit until they started trouble for ye."

Gabe touched her shoulder. "Oh, now, I wouldn't worry over it, Aunt Clara. As I told you, I managed to put the minds of the deacons at rest, so I can't see anything else coming of the accusations." But he could see she was clearly disturbed about it and retained considerable doubts.

The better part of that day and the following one were spent in what had quickly become routine, calling upon church members who for one reason or another had not been attending services regularly. Not one to give up hope easily, Gabe resorted to asking these parishioners for the names of any other prospects they might know who might be interested in taking in Noely. But even those efforts failed to pan out.

On the third afternoon a purposeful rap sounded on the door. Gabe set aside his Bible and commentary and went to answer. This time he found two unsmiling strangers attired in crisp black suits and felt hats. "Good day, gentlemen. How may I be of service?"

"You're the Reverend Gabriel Winters?" the taller of them inquired, peering at him through a gold-rimmed monocle.

"That's correct."

"I'm Harland Smeade, of the Agency for Displaced Persons. This is Mr. Townsend, of the Nesbitt Orphan Asylum."

A jolt of alarm slithered up Gabe's spine. Glancing over his shoulder at Noely at play with the button box, he stepped out on the stoop and closed the door behind him.

"We have been informed that you are presently providing sanctuary to a dispossessed minor, one Noely Carroll."

"That is correct. But—"

Before Gabe could finish, Smeade reached into an inside pocket of his waistcoat and drew out some folded documents and presented them. "You are hereby ordered to deliver said minor into Mr. Townsend's custody within forty-eight hours. If you do not comply with this order, we have been authorized to remove the child from these premises. Good day." With a curt bow of the head, the two turned and departed.

A suffocating heaviness deprived Gabe's lungs of air as he stared after the officials. He leaned back against the door, his eyes searching the heavens. *Dear Lord, why this? Why now, when I've been trying day after day to find little Noely a Christian family and get her settled in before Christmas?* But no answers blazed across the brilliant December sky.

He had let them down. All of them. Noely. Aunt Clara. And most of all, Angelina. How would he ever find courage enough to tell her he had failed?

Chapter 7

Forty-eight hours! Two days. Oblivious to the winter cold, Gabe slumped despondently against the parsonage door. Never in his life had he felt so utterly inadequate or powerless. All the effort he had expended. . .was it all for naught? He could parade Noely before his flock again tomorrow at service, but should that action prove fruitless, there would be only one final morning to find the orphan a home.

How insanely cruel to uproot a youngster right before the holiday! Gabe couldn't bear to dwell upon the memory of an unsmiling, fearful little girl who huddled by herself in the corner, or of her wrenching sobs that first night at the parsonage. . .and now to think of her being torn from this home, too, and cast away with more strangers. There had to be some way to keep it from happening. Maybe he could obtain a few days' extension from the authorities, precious time to place her himself. . .or at least postpone the inevitable until after Christmas. Surely they would see the benefit of that, wouldn't they? *Please, Father,* he pleaded. *For Noely.*

Expelling a ragged breath, he shored himself up and went back inside. . .where the sound of a little girl's giggles ripped at his heart.

Angelina relaxed over her morning tea. Out the window she could see gathering clouds dulling the Philadelphia sky, and the draft seeping around the window frames and doorjamb gave evidence of a quickly dropping temperature. Thank heaven there was no longer a need to report to the shop on Saturdays. It was a little early to call at the parsonage yet, but perhaps after her noon meal she'd go to visit Noely. In the meantime she would continue working on the child's gift.

The doll was adorable, Angelina had to admit, assessing the toy at arm's length. She didn't know when was the last time she had derived such joy from making something—and she'd finished the project with days to spare! With Christmas still four days off, there was no reason the dolly shouldn't have an entire wardrobe. It was easy to envision an array of sweet dresses, undergarments, a tiny flannel sleeping gown, even a wool cape. Smiling, she spread out a remnant of apple green calico and began cutting out a second dress.

The first huge feathery snowflakes began swirling to the ground on a gusty wind in mid-morning, a sight Angelina found particularly depressing. She could nearly always manage to get where she needed to go, as long as she allowed extra time for caution. But watching the snow gradually increasing in density and the layer of white beginning to smooth out the uneven cobbles in the street, she emitted a sad sigh. And she was all too aware that the worst of winter still lay ahead. It might be prudent to stay inside until the storm abated. Well, she would make the best of it. Squaring her shoulders, she eyed the remaining materials, then set to work.

Thoughts of what she would miss at the parsonage—one more treasured visit with Noely, a lively conversation with Gabe and his aunt, and that over another scrumptious supper—were made bearable as a small stack of doll clothes began to accumulate.

But one disappointment could not completely be dismissed. Angelina knew slippery conditions would keep her away from services at Second Street Baptist Church on the morrow. She had planned to start attending worship each week and become part of what surely must be a wonderful and loving Christian family. As she'd lain in bed the night before, she had tried to imagine Gabe's expression when he stepped to the pulpit, surveyed his congregation, and discovered she was there. Just thinking of surprising him had brought a smile that refused to go away. Oh well, the worst that could happen would be a postponement of her plans until next Sunday. But that seemed a month away.

❧

"Ye seem a bit off your feed," Aunt Clara remarked, helping herself to a small second portion of roasted chicken.

"Hm?" Gabe let go of the fork he'd been turning absently in his fingers and swung his gaze to his aunt.

"Not hungry?" she asked.

He hadn't realized his meal sat untouched before him. "I have a lot on my mind is all. Would you care if I save this for later?"

"Not a bit."

"I finished everything on my plate, Pastor Gabe," Noely boasted with her light lisp. She rested her forearm on the table, the fork in her fist standing straight up.

"I'm real proud of you, pumpkin," he told her, giving her wrist a squeeze.

"Do I haveta go see more people again today?" she asked, blue eyes wide.

He shook his head. "I have an errand to run by myself. You can keep Aunt Clara company."

"Oh, goodie! Then I can help make gingerbread cookies, huh, Auntie?" A pretty little grin disclosed her anticipation.

"That ye may, darlin'. 'Tis much more fun with two of us doin' it, to be sure." The older woman lifted a questioning glance to Gabe.

Preferring not to dump extra worries on his aunt's shoulders, he offered as much of a smile as he could work up, then blotted his mouth on his napkin and stood. "I'll be at my study for about an hour, after which I must pay a call on someone," he told her, then ruffled Noely's curls. "Just thinking about fresh-baked gingerbread makes my mouth water. Sure hope it'll be done before I get back."

She giggled. "Me, too."

The bright expectation in her eyes made him all the more aware that his own hopes were diminishing like sand through an hourglass.

In the solitude of the church office, Gabe fell to his knees before his leather chair, needing to pour out his heart to God, yet finding no words. He dared not imagine tomorrow morning's appeal to his congregation would be unsuccessful, nor could he allow himself to think past it. He had to believe God had things under control and was working out His purpose in the very best way for all concerned. Hadn't he preached those lofty ideals often enough? Well, if the promises in the Bible were true for one person, they were true for everyone, and if that were the case, then they'd work for a little defenseless girl like Noely, too. And right now, he would do everything within his power to be sure they did.

Gabe hadn't managed to acquire many influential friends in the city during his years at Second Street, but God had mercifully provided him with one man who had offered wise counsel on several occasions. Rising from his knees, he pulled on his coat and strode purposefully out the door into the falling snow.

Harrison Lawrence, an aged justice of the peace, now retired from most civic duties, had befriended Gabe when he'd arrived in Philadelphia and sought directions to his first pastorate. Evenings spent with the elderly man and his gracious wife during the first several months in the city were among some of his most treasured memories. Though the aging pair were affiliated with one of the more prosperous churches in Philadelphia, they had nevertheless welcomed Gabe into their stately home and treated him like the son they had never had. He regretted allowing the visits to taper off to almost nil.

Reaching the four-story mansion fronting Fourth Street, its fountains and well-maintained gardens now dormant and covered with snow, Gabe inhaled a fortifying breath and rapped on the door.

A soft-spoken butler ushered him across a marbled entrance hall flanked by huge urns of fragrant evergreen boughs and into an immense library, where books of every size and color lined floor to ceiling shelves on three walls. There the white-haired gentleman sat in a wheelchair behind the elaborate carved oak desk, a plaid woolen shawl draped about his stooped shoulders.

"Gabe, my dear boy," he said, extending a blue-veined hand. "I was just thinking of you the other day. How are you, lad?"

"Fine, sir. Just fine." Almost speechless at the toll taken on the once hearty man since his last visit some months ago, Gabe tried his hardest not to crush the feeble hand in his own grip. "I'm afraid I've neglected you far too long. But that was unintentional," he added, trying not to be obvious about his surprise at seeing the wheeled conveyance.

The keen hazel eyes astutely read his expression. "Don't let this contraption get to you, son. I took a tumble down the stairs a few weeks ago and broke my leg. The doctor —tough old sawbones that he is—insists I stay off it till he says different."

Relieved that the man retained his sense of humor and still spoke with surprising vigor, Gabe grinned. "Well, I hope your recovery is speedy, sir, and that you'll be up and around very soon."

He nodded his thanks. "How's that church of yours coming along these days?"

"Very nicely, actually. It's grown quite a bit over the last year or so."

"I'm glad to hear that. I pray for you and your ministry every day." The white head tipped slightly. "What brings you by?"

Gabe released a nervous breath. "Some of that insightful counsel of yours, actually. I've always been thankful for the friendship and encouragement you and your dear wife, rest her soul, gave me when I first came to Philadelphia. Welcoming me into your home, praying with me, helped me over some of the rough spots. Not every minister fresh from his theological studies is fortunate enough to have such wonderful mentors."

"Yes, those were grand times. Margaret thought the world of you."

With a smile, Gabe continued. "I only wish I'd kept in better touch. I might have been able to help after your accident."

"Oh, pshaw!" he exclaimed with a wave of one hand. "I've got servants a'plenty, lad. I know a growing church keeps its pastor occupied. I'm just glad you came by today. Now, how can I help you?" His snow-white brows flared wide.

Gabe shook his head. "I don't know where to start. What I need most is an ear to confide in, a shoulder to lean on. And I thought the two of us might pray about a matter that's weighing heavily upon me just now."

"Always a wise step, seeking the Lord's intervention. I'm more than glad to offer my support."

Pausing, Gabe grouped his thoughts. "Not long ago—in that last blizzard we had, to be precise—a young woman brought an orphan to the parsonage, hoping we could find the little girl a new home. It seemed of considerable importance to her that the child not be sent to the asylum."

"I see."

"I've turned all my efforts since then into trying to fulfill that request and find a family willing to take the girl in. But so far, no one has come forward. Meanwhile, someone at church reported the matter to the authorities, and they've swooped in like vultures, intent upon following proper legal procedure to the very letter. They want to take the child away. Day after tomorrow, in fact. Today being Saturday, there's nobody I can go to and slow things down."

Mr. Lawrence kneaded his thin jaw in thought. "I can see your concern. Once those sharp-nosed authorities get wind of something, they latch onto it like English bulldogs. If I know those buzzards right, they're more interested in the fee they'll get paid to house one more orphan than they are in the child's welfare." He frowned. "Pity you've never taken a wife."

Gabe shook his head. "Not that I haven't considered it, mind you," he admitted sheepishly. "I do have my widowed aunt still living with me, but her health has been failing. She had quite a bad spell this past fall. So needless to say, I'm not in a position to take legal custody of Noely myself, no matter how much I wish I were."

"Hm. That's too bad. If you only had a wife, they'd have no reason to bother anybody."

With a lopsided smile, Gabe shrugged.

"Well, I'm sure none of this catches Almighty God by surprise," the older man said, his eyes glinting. "But His ways are far above ours, and sometimes what seems wrong in our own judgment turns out to be wise beyond our ability to understand. Let's lay the matter at His feet and let Him work out His will."

As the white-haired gentleman bowed his head, Gabe knelt by the desk.

"Our Gracious Father," Mr. Lawrence prayed, "we thank You for Your constant and abiding presence in our lives, for the unceasing blessings You shower upon us every day. We praise You that through Your Son we can come boldly into Your presence at any time, knowing You are concerned with all our circumstances. And now, Lord, we bring before You this little orphan and her needs. We ask You to stay the hands that might carelessly bring harm to her. Grant wisdom to young Gabe as he deals with this matter, and show Him Your perfect will. This we ask in the name above all names, Jesus Christ. Amen."

As always, Gabe found himself drawing immense and immediate strength as much from his mentor's unshakable faith as from the man's fervent prayer. Renewed peace began to flow through him as he smiled and stood. He reached for the man's gnarled hand and held it warmly in his own, trying not to acknowledge its almost transparent papery skin. "I do thank you, sir, for listening to me. Somehow, though I can't explain it, I always feel better after coming to you."

"I trust things will turn out for you."

"I'm sure they will. I must get back now, spend whatever time is left with Noely and Aunt Clara."

"Well, don't be a stranger, son. Let me know what happens. Meanwhile, I'll continue to keep all of you in my prayers."

Gabe felt a new spring in his step as he headed home after the visit. The city always looked so pretty with a new blanket of snow, especially at times like this, with the clouds drifting away and the sunshine adding its glory.

And hearing one of his own convictions reinforced by Mr. Lawrence somehow revived his spirit. If Noely had parents to look after her, the authorities would have no reason to bother anybody. And an almost outlandish idea began to take root.

Chapter 8

Angelina was ecstatic when sunshine flooded her parlor in the middle of the afternoon. A glance outside revealed almost two inches of new snow, but at this time of day she could manage walking through it easily enough without fear of slipping. Putting aside her sewing, she limped upstairs to freshen her face to go visiting. Shortly after, in an emerald gabardine nicer than her typical work attire, her hair brushed and shining in its soft waves, she made her way up Elfreth's Alley toward Second Street.

The world glistened anew in white splendor as huge cloud puffs in the brilliant sky reflected blue-violet shadows across the snow. Angelina could not restrain a thankful prayer that she hadn't been confined at home for long. Reaching the parsonage, she tapped lightly with the knocker.

The door opened within seconds.

"Angelina." A curious spark in Gabe's blue eyes made her heart trip over itself as he stepped aside to allow her in. "I was hoping you'd come by." He took her coat and scarf and hung them while she removed her boots.

"It's lovely outside, isn't it?" she remarked casually, certain that the curious tension in the air had to be her imagination. "I was lonesome for Noely." She glanced around, becoming aware of an abnormal quiet in the parsonage.

"Aunt Clara took her out to frolic in the snow for a little while. They'll be back shortly. Come sit down." Gabe gestured toward the settee. "We need to talk."

A prickle of apprehension fluttered up Angelina's spine.

"By the way, there's fresh tea. I was just about to have some. Join me?"

She nodded. "Thanks."

In moments he returned and handed her one of two cups he carried. "Sugar? Cream?"

"Black is fine, thanks." She sipped some of the soothing warmth as she watched him lower himself to the wing chair he seemed to prefer. Without even a hint of childish laughter anywhere in the vicinity, the ticking of a grandfather clock was the most prominent sound in the house. How far away had Gabe's aunt taken Noely? "Any new developments?" she finally asked.

He cocked his head. "I have gone to every possible home I could think of—and to a few where I had never met the people before."

"And no one wanted her?"

"Well, actually, there is someone quite interested."

Angelina felt a lump rise in her throat at the announcement. The familiar combination of relief and sadness flooded her. "Is—is it someplace where Noely will be happy, do you think?" Schooling both her expression and her emotions to remain even, she took another sip of tea.

"I sure hope so. It took me a lot of prayer to even find

this solution, and if it's going to work, it will probably continue to require prayer for a while. But something tells me this may be God's will."

There is no way to argue against that, she told herself. If God had found a home for dear little Noely, it had to be the best one for her. But it was hard to think of her being passed on to strangers after all she had been through. . .and even harder to imagine never coming back here to visit again, never seeing the child who had become such a part of the three of them. She surmised Aunt Clara and Gabe would battle a similar attachment when they had to let go. Noely was such a presence, such a sparkle. The reality of how much she herself would miss the little girl made Angelina's spirit deflate.

Trying to breathe over the heaviness, she became aware that Gabe was staring at her. She raised her lashes and met his gaze.

"Of course," he said quietly, "I haven't had the nerve to approach the party as yet and bring up the matter."

Something in his voice made Angelina's cup rattle slightly in its saucer. She tightened her grip, then carefully set the cup on the lamp table beside her as the sandy-haired giant rose to his feet and crossed to the settee.

He sat down next to her, and his huge hands captured one of hers. Her heart stopped. She could not draw away . . .nor was she certain she would have, had she the strength. Her pulse picked up again, making it increasingly difficult to breathe as the rush of it throbbed in her ears.

"Please look at me, Angelina," he pleaded softly.

Knowing exactly how much she wanted to do just that

made it all the more difficult. But she slowly obeyed, and warmth flooded her cheeks.

Gabe's eyes held hers. He didn't speak for a moment, and she saw him swallow. She thought she detected the hint of a tremor in his touch. "I've. . .exhausted every other possibility. I haven't mentioned this to Aunt Clara yet, but unless Noely is placed in a home immediately, the authorities are going to take custody of her. On Monday."

"Oh, Gabe!" she gasped. "Right before Christmas? But I thought you said—"

"That someone wants her," he finished. "It's true."

"Well, then, I—I don't understand."

A muscle worked in his jaw, and then he smiled. "Noely needs a home. She has one here. She needs love, and she has that here, too. And she needs parents. A man and a woman who love her as if she were their own. . ." He paused, and his face turned a dark red. "I think she. . ." He cleared his throat. "I think she has a man and woman who love her right here too."

Angelina's lips parted at the implication she could read in his eyes.

"I know this is sudden, Angelina, but there's nothing I can do about that. If only there were more time, I could court you properly." His forehead wrinkled. "Heaven knows a beautiful woman like you could do far better than a big ox like me."

To her dismay, Angelina felt tears well up in her eyes and spill over her lashes. She fought to stem the tide.

Gabe's head bowed and his shoulders slumped. "I knew you'd find the very suggestion repulsive. Forgive me." He released her hand and turned away. "You were my last hope. I thought that since we're friends—good friends who can be honest and open with one another—maybe we could have a chance. Could make a home for Noely somehow." He grimaced and shook his head. "I guess that was stupid of me. I'm sorry."

Mustering all her resources, Angelina touched his forearm. "Sorry?" she whispered. "You think I'm repulsed by you?"

"Well, you're crying. . ." His voice was hoarse.

"Only because I thought *I* would be unattractive to someone like you. Someone. . .perfect."

He lifted his head and stared at her, amazement filling his face. Then slowly he began to smile. "Believe me, sweet Angelina, I am far from that, I assure you." He cupped her face in his palm, and his thumb gently brushed away a tear. "And there is nothing about you I would ever consider less than beautiful, not even that weak leg of yours. I'm sorry that it pains you—but it does nothing to mar your beauty. You will never have to hide it from me, I promise you that."

Angelina could not speak past the ache in her throat.

His gaze never wavered as he searched her soul. "But with Noely's welfare to consider, we can't afford to take the time to do this properly. I must ask you now." He paused, as if choosing his words very carefully, and she thought she heard a tremor in his voice when he continued, "Could you find it in your heart to marry a humble pastor? I vow I will spend the rest of my life courting you. But I have to tell you, we must do this today. Tomorrow at the latest."

Today! Angelina thought in shock. *Tomorrow at the latest!* There wasn't time to list advantages and disadvantages, to reason things out, to find another—perhaps better—solution. A little girl needed them, needed them both, and needed them now. And Christmas was coming. Could either of them bear to break her heart on that day of all days?

"Yes," she heard herself murmur. "I'll marry you."

His strong arms enveloped her and ever so tenderly drew her near.

Any second thoughts Angelina might have expected vanished as Gabe's heart pounded against hers. She knew they were rushing things, that a lifetime commitment such as marriage should be entered into after great deliberation—yet she was consumed by the greatest peace she had ever felt in her life. She had felt drawn to him and to Noely since the first time their paths had crossed. Surely God had brought them all together. . .and He wanted them to stay together always.

Gabe never imagined the world could contain this much joy. He had no idea how on earth he had gathered courage enough to propose to this enchanting young woman who had so recently become such a part of his life. He had tried to ignore the attraction he had felt for her from the first, had tried to deny it even as it grew stronger with each meeting. Somehow she seemed to have always been there, just beyond his dreams, part of himself that he had never hoped to find—and yet she was reality.

Angelina's courage in suffering had touched him more deeply than anything else about her, even more than the loneliness lurking in her beautiful eyes. Everything about her made him want to protect her and keep her safe from anything that might bring her further pain. And to think she had actually accepted his offer of marriage! He grinned to himself and shook his head. Mr. Lawrence was surely a mighty man of prayer.

Of course, Gabe's own prayers had been no less fervent, he had to admit. Both Angelina and Noely desperately needed someone to look after them. To love them. Maybe they needed him just as desperately as he needed them and their love.

Love. Dared he speak that word aloud again after having had it thrown back in his face by someone else he had once thought he loved? Looking back, he could see the feelings he had known then paled in comparison to what filled him now. Letting his gaze devour Angelina's features, he decided to take the chance.

With the edge of his finger, he tipped her face upward. "I—" He swallowed and sucked in a breath. "I know you love Noely. You want to do what's best for her, and so do I. But I wanted you to know that this isn't just about Noely. I know it's too soon to expect you to— Well, what I mean is. . . " He rubbed a big hand across his face and then said in a rush, his voice barely louder than a whisper, "I just wanted you to know—I love you, Angelina. With all of my heart. More with every passing day."

He hardly dared to look at her, but when he did, he saw that her tears had come again. . .but this time, with a sense of wonder, he recognized them for what they were.

"And I love you," she whispered with a misty smile.

❧

Clara, with Noely in hand, stood beside Angelina and Gabe as the pair faced Mr. Lawrence in the gentleman's parlor later that evening. Having returned home from an hour's play with the exuberant child, the news of an impending wedding was almost more than Clara's old heart could contain. But observing the couple, seeing the breathless smiles and exchanges of expression, she could do naught but thank the Lord for His wondrous working—and for the influential justice of the peace's abilities to make swift arrangements.

Her nephew had seemed much more settled since these two dear ones had shown up on the doorstep. Noely had provided a new avenue for his attention, one that was separate from his ministry, one far more personal which put his faith into action. And Angelina, precious soul that she was, had brought to the fore a gentle, caring side of him which Clara knew he had buried deep inside long ago. They would be good for each other. All of them.

"You may kiss your bride," she heard Mr. Lawrence say.

Gabe smiled down at Angelina with heart-stopping tenderness, and she, with shining eyes, melted into his embrace. Their lips met. . .tentatively at first, then again with the greatest of joy, and they embraced for a long moment.

Noely leaned against Clara with a big grin, and Clara gave the child's tiny hand an encouraging squeeze.

Who would have thought this foundling would bring together two people who once considered themselves undesirable? Strange what love could do—and right before Christmas, too.

Christmas. Ever so special. . .ever so precious. From the very beginning the most wondrous of days.

And all for the love of a Child.

Sally Laity

An accomplished writer of contemporary and historical romances, Sally's novel, *Dream Spinner,* contained in the *Inspirational Romance Reader–Historical Collection No. 2* (Barbour Publishing), is a best-seller. She recently coauthored an inspirational romance series set during the Revolutionary War entitled "Freedom's Holy Light" (Tyndale House Publishers). Sally makes her home in Bakersfield, California, and is married with four children and nine grandchildren. She enjoys writing inspirational romance because it is an avenue for her to openly share her faith.

Miracle on Kismet Hill

Loree Lough

Prologue

Fort Fisher, North Carolina
January 15, 1865

Blood oozed from the colonel's left temple as a dozen of his men knelt in a protective semicircle around his battered body. Daubing the officer's forehead with the corner of a dingy neckerchief, Trevor Williams caught the eye of one soldier and demanded, "Where's that water I told you to fetch?"

"What's the point, Sarge? He's bleedin' like a stuck pig. We ought to be fetchin' a shovel, instead, and start diggin' his. . ."

"Quit talkin' a fool," Trevor growled. "The Colonel's strong as an ox. He'll pull through this."

Shrugging, the private rolled onto his belly and, using his elbows to propel himself forward, dodged flying debris as he headed for the water trough.

"Be a cryin' shame iffin that boy dies tryin' to save a dead man," came a coarse whisper from the back of the group.

Trevor stood, fists clenched at his sides, oblivious, it seemed, to the constant barrage of cannon fire exploding around him. Glaring at each man in turn, he said through clenched teeth, "Get back to your posts. Anyone who has any other ideas will be talking to the front-end of my musket!"

Without another word, the small crowd dispersed.

"You were a might hard on 'em, don't you think?"

On one knee again, Trevor studied his colonel's black-bearded face. "Good to see you're awake," he said, ignoing the question. "Billy'll be back with some cool water any minute."

The colonel waved the offer away. "Don't need water. What I need is. . ." Arching his back, he winced with pain. "How long was I out?" he gasped when the agony released him.

"To tell the truth, Colonel, with all that's been goin' on, coulda been an hour. . .or a couple a minutes. All's I know is, a block of stone knocked you cold when the east tower came down." Trevor nodded at the colonel's bloodied pant leg. "Hurt much?"

Richard Carter forced a half-hearted snicker. "Hurts plenty," he managed to say. He'd been hit enough times to know this was no mere flesh wound. It would be bad—the sticky dampness in his boot and the unending throbbing told him that much—but how bad, he wouldn't know until he mustered the courage to look. Summoning all his strength, Richard levered himself onto one elbow, took a deep breath, and focused on his right foot.

The sight sent waves of nausea and dizziness coursing through him.

His once slate-gray trousers leg now glistened with the deep maroon of his lifeblood, and the squared toe of his boot was missing. . .along with three of his toes.

Whether his light-headedness came from what he'd just

seen or loss of blood, Richard didn't know. He slumped wearily back onto the brass-buttoned jacket his men had wadded beneath his neck. A rasping sigh slipped from his lungs as the image of the mangled foot flickered behind his closed eyes. Even if the injury healed, he'd walk with a limp for the rest of his life. And if gangrene set in. . .

But he couldn't allow himself to dwell on the grisly possibilities just now. He focused on his men—mere boys, some of them—who were counting on him to lead them to safety. "What're the damages elsewhere, Sergeant?"

With quiet efficiency, Trevor Williams gave his commander a run-down.

The assault that began in the early afternoon had continued until Union General Terry aimed his navy's guns to targets inside the fort. As the Yanks at sea struck the north facade, two thousand troops stormed the seaward wall. But armed only with cutlasses and handguns, the Bluecoats were no match for Fort Fisher's soldiers, and after hours of bitter hand-to-hand combat, the Northerners retreated. When they returned, better-armed and more determined than ever to win, they forced the Confederates to fall back.

"We lost hundreds of men," Trevor continued, his voice soft with reverence, "and hundreds more will likely die of their wounds." Hanging his head, he took a shaky breath. He frowned deeply, and his eyes and lips narrowed with fury and disgust. "The Bluebellies're loadin' up every Reb who's breathin'. " He rubbed the furrow between his brows, his hand casting an even darker shadow across his sooty face, and snarled, "Well, I ain't goin' to no Yankee prisoner of war camp!"

Richard surveyed the surrounding terrain. Lifeless bodies of boys and men lay alongside the wounded, the blood of Blue- and Graycoats puddling together on the rust-red North Carolina clay. The smoky air thickened overhead, trapping the stink of gunpowder and burning wood—and death—beneath it. The boom of exploding Colombiad cannonballs echoed within the fortress as horowitzers, carbines, and musketoons discharged deadly lead balls.

Amid the melee, Richard remembered the Albermarle. He'd been on board the sturdy boat when it attacked Plymouth. The North hadn't been prepared for its enemy's ingenuity, and the shallow-draft gunboat, secretly constructed in a cornfield beside the Roanoke River, defeated a squadron of eight Union gunboats, giving the South reign over the western end of the Sound. None of the North's vessels could match the ironclad's power. . .until Cushing's torpedo sank her. Afterward, Richard and a handful of stalwart survivors were quickly reassigned to Fort Fisher. . . .

"Worst of it is," Trevor was saying, "they've cut us off from reinforcements."

Richard acknowledged the seriousness of the sergeant's statement. The North was better armed. Better fed. And in many ways, better led. Still, Richard refused to believe the South would be defeated. After all, no one, least of all northern forces, had expected the Albermarle to succeed. Yet she had. . . .

"We're not licked yet," Richard grated. Then, with a fortitude that surprised even himself, he wrapped his bloody fingers around Trevor's forearm. "There's a letter," he began, "in the pocket of my coat. If I don't. . ." Clamping his teeth together, he hesitated. "If I don't make it through this one, I want you to see it reaches my family."

Trevor grimaced. "Ain't like you to talk this a way, Colonel. What is it you're always tellin' us? 'You lose only when you give up.' Seems to me you oughta take a little of your own good advice."

Eyes wide with fear and desperation, Richard tightened his hold on Trevor's arm. "Get the letter," he hissed.

Gently, Trevor slid the coat from beneath Richard's head and rummaged through the pockets until he found an envelope, addressed to the Carter family in Spring Creek, Virginia. He held it up for the colonel to see.

"Put it somewhere safe," Richard insisted.

Trevor stuffed the envelope into his shirt and patted it. "Snug as a bug in a rug," he said, feigning a lighthearted grin.

Only then did Richard release his death grip on Trevor's arm. His relieved smile disappeared as a coughing fit devoured his remaining strength. Eyelids fluttering and arms flailing, he reached blindly for Trevor. "Is it getting dark, or. . . ?"

"Ain't got a watch," the sergeant interrupted, squinting into the powder-gray sky. Giving the older man's shoulder an affectionate squeeze, he added, "You ain't gonna die, Colonel. Least. . .not if I have anything to say about it."

But Trevor's assurance fell on deaf ears, for Colonel Richard Carter had once again blacked out. His sleeplike state rendered him dumb to the fact that his men were being seized. Somewhere, from deep within the fog of unconsciousness, he pictured his beautiful brown-eyed daughter Brynne. His burly son Edward who he'd heard had been wounded in Nashville. His loving wife Amelia. *Oh, how I miss her sweet smile. . .and that way she has of fussing over me,* Richard thought. *How are they faring, with me gone three long years?*

He seemed to recall seeing Trevor, picking his way through the ruins of Fort Fisher, ducking and dodging, weaving and bobbing. . . . He'd always admired the young man. Like himself, Trevor believed in leading by example. *He'll be a fine officer someday, if he doesn't. . .*

Richard's buzzing brain would not allow him to complete the grisly thought. *Take care,* was his silent message to the sergeant. *Take care, and get that letter to my Amelia.*

The very thought of her comforted and calmed him. The vapor in his mind cleared just enough for the hard-voweled voices of two Union soldiers to break through. "This one'll never make it," the first said as he and a mate roughly slung Richard onto a dirty wagon bed.

"Doesn't matter," said the second. "We were told to take every one that was breathing, and this one's breathing."

"Maybe so," replied the first, "but he won't be breathing long."

Richard hadn't talked to God in a very long time. Hadn't had time to do anything, really, but attempt to survive this miserable war. But the smoky haze cloaking his mind felt cool and comforting. It stanched the throbbing in his foot and the ache in his head, too. In the white mist, he smiled, feeling whole and healthy and pain free, as boyhood imagines of heaven echoed in his memory.

Lord Jesus, he prayed, *if You decide to take me home*

to Paradise, let them bury my bones on Kismet Hill, near that stubborn little pine. . . .

Chapter 1

February 1865

Brynne had been working since dawn, trying to put the house back together after the last Yankee raid, when a persistent rapping at the front door interrupted her work. She had played hostess to enough Yankees to recognize their "calling card" when she heard it.

She had to admit that, by and large, the regular troops of Bluecoats passing through had been gentlemen, but a few ragged stragglers were another story. As a result, half of her father's cherished book collection had disappeared, along with her mother's wedding rings, and the cameo Brynne had inherited from Grandma Moore. They'd also helped themselves to chickens and sheep, cows and horses, bushels of potatoes and sacks of flour.

If the two- and three-man parties that regularly showed up without warning had known she'd gladly have shared the family's quickly dwindling food supply, would they have stolen heirlooms and keepsakes anyway? And if they'd been given advance notice that she considered it her Christian duty to tend their wounds and mend their uniforms, would they still have found it necessary to break windows, trample flowers, destroy fine upholstered pieces that had been in the Carter family for generations? Brynne's cynical answer, after years of dealing with these blue-coated marauders, was yes.

The very first time Yankees had approached Carter soil, Brynne hid her father's pistols and hunting muskets. The weapons, as yet untouched by Northern hands, still nestled beneath the parlor floorboards.

Now, Brynne climbed down from the stepladder and knelt to pull up the plank nearest the fireplace, where Richard's rifle lay wrapped in a bedsheet. Balancing it on palms that trembled with fear and rage, Brynne stared at the weapon. *Do you have what it takes to use it?* she wondered, biting her lower lip.

As she searched her heart and mind for an answer, Brynne recalled what a raiding party had done to her neighbors to the east: The Smith house had stood majestically on Spring Creek soil for nearly a hundred years before the drunken infantrymen burned it to the ground—with the family trapped inside. And no one would ever forget what the next group had done to the Warner's twin daughters. . . .

Before the war, had anyone asked Brynne if she could aim a gun at one of God's children for any reason, the answer would have been a quick and resounding "No!" But now. . .

"Please, Lord," she prayed under her breath, "don't let them give me a reason to use this. . .because we both know that if I must, I will."

Had her mother been home, she'd have reminded Brynne in not-so-gentle tones that it was not Christian to take up arms against her fellowman. "A true lady leaves the fighting to the menfolk," Amelia would have scolded.

But her was mother not at home. As Spring Creek's only midwife, she'd been at the Andersons' since dawn, helping bring their first baby into the world.

Brynne hoped the soldiers would be satisfied with a bite to eat and a cup of weak coffee, because she had little else to offer, and she would not be satisfied leaving the fighting to the menfolk any longer!

She tucked the hem of her full blue skirt into her black belt and slipped into her boiled wool jacket. Hoisting the rifle, she tiptoed through the house and sneaked silently out the back door. Crouching low in the shadows, she worked her way around to the side of the house, doing her best to time each step to coincide with the soldiers' knocks. *There's no telling how many of them have descended upon Moorewood this time,* she cautioned herself. *You mustn't reveal your position. . . .*

Once she rounded the corner and peeked over the winter-browned honeysuckle, she halted in surprise: just one soldier stood on her porch. He appeared to be a young man, tall and lanky, with broad shoulders that slumped a bit under the oppressive weight of war.

He carried no weapon that she could see, but experience had taught her the wisdom of the old proverb, "An ounce of prevention is worth a pound of cure." Creeping alongside the forsythia hedge that led to the front door, she made it to the bottom porch step. . .and rushed him. "Turn around slow, soldier," she snarled, the rifle barrel mere inches from his blue-coated back, "real slow."

He did as he was told. “No need to be afraid, ma’am,” he said in a soft Southern drawl.

“You’ve got that right,” she snapped, giving him a gentle poke with the end of her gun. “No need to be afraid if you have enough firepower.”

If someone had been pointing a gun at her, she’d be shaking in her boots. That he could stand there, calm as you please, amazed her. What amazed her more was that he wore neither the arrogant smirk nor the malicious grin of those who’d come to Moorewood before him. The expression on his bearded face seemed genuinely gentle, seemed. . .

Stop it, you little ninny! she warned herself. *Could be he’s just a good actor, like your precious Ross Bartlett. Could be he’ll grab this gun and point it at you if you’re not careful!*

“I’m on your side,” he said quietly.

Brynne knew better than to judge all Yankees by the behavior of a despicable few. Still, she refused to be fooled by this one’s friendly demeanor. “The last bunch of your buddies didn’t leave much behind,” she said, sneering, “but they generously left my eyesight, and I can plainly see that you’re wearing blue. You, sir, are not on my side!”

Looking down at the brass buttons on his jacket, the soldier nodded. “I know this looks bad, ma’am, but I can explain. Y’see, I knew I’d be traipsin’ through enemy territory, so I sort of, uh, I borrowed this here jacket from a Union soldier.” Moving nothing but his pointer finger, he gestured toward the haversack at his feet. “My coat’s in there. Ain’t too perty after the last fight, but. . .”

She was scowling by now. "Oh, please. Give me credit for having some sense."

Shrugging, he sighed. "Reckon I can't blame you for bein' suspicious, ma'am. But you're more'n welcome to check it out."

No doubt if she did, Brynne would find a Confederate jacket in the bag. *But that doesn't mean it's his.*

Suddenly, something he'd said earlier gonged in her mind. "You. . .you stole that coat from. . ." Brynne swallowed hard. "From a dead man?"

Wincing, he said, " 'Fraid so, ma'am." In a more serious tone, he quickly added, "But I never kilt him; he was dead when I found him."

The mental picture of him peeling the uniform from a corpse sent a shiver up her back. Blinking rapidly, she took it all in: his shaggy blond hair and beard, the badly scraped boots, trousers that likely hadn't been washed in an age, cuts and bruises on the backs of his hands. . . hands that had touched a fallen comrade. He'd wrapped those same hands around the handles of his bag. . .

Wrinkling her nose with disgust, Brynne used the weapon as a pointer. "You open the bag. And take care not to pull any stunts," she warned, narrowing her eyes, "this gun has a hair trigger. . ."

She watched carefully as he crouched, unbuckled his knapsack, and withdrew the contents, item by item. First, a gray fez. A small and well-worn Bible. A pair of holey socks. And a bonafide Confederate jacket. The soldier stood slowly and held it out for her inspection. "In the inside front pocket," he said, "you'll find a letter from your pa."

A letter from Papa? Brynne repeated mentally. She whispered the words out loud, as though their meaning had some sacred significance that demanded hushed tones of reverence. Why, the soldier had said it as casually as he might have said, "Nice weather we're havin', ain't it?" Her heart began to hammer so hard, Brynne could count the beats in her ears. She wanted that letter, and she wanted it now.

But she had only two hands. How would she search the jacket and keep the soldier at gunpoint at the same time?

Frustration got the better of her. "Here," she said, handing him the rifle. "Hold this while I have a look-see."

The soldier obligingly exchanged the gun for the jacket. She paid no mind to the grin that split his face as she excitedly dug through the pockets. "It is from Papa," she sighed, holding the envelope at arm's length. "I'd know his handwriting anywhere!"

Quick as it appeared, the joy that brightened her face dimmed. Flustered and furious at the same time, she grabbed the rifle from him and shoved the letter into her apron pocket. "How did you get this?" she demanded. "Did you pick through his pockets the way you went through that dead soldier's. . . ?" Brynne simply couldn't finish the question. "If you harmed him," she grated, "I'll, I'll. . ."

He'd relaxed some when she handed him the gun. Now, as her agitation escalated, the soldier's arms slid slowly skyward again. "Harm him! Why, I'da sooner been gut shot!" He shook his head. "Last words he said to me were 'See that my family gets the letter.' When my unit was captured by the Yankees, I slipped away. Coulda headed south, to be with my wife an' young'un." The soldier frowned. "Came here instead, on account-a I gave your daddy my word."

Brynne tucked in one corner of her mouth. His voice, his face, even his stance communicated sincerity. The man was either a very good actor or telling the truth. It was all she could do to concentrate on keeping him in her gunsights. She wanted nothing more than to tear open the envelope. She wanted to shout for joy, for no one had heard from her father in so long that the family had begun to think. . . A sob ached in her throat as the blood pounded in her ears. Brynne tightened her grip on the rifle's burled wood stock.

"The Colonel told me he hadn't heard a word from home in nigh on to a year," he continued, "but that didn't stop him from writin' y'all ever' week. Weren't no easy feat, let me tell you, what with pencils and paper in such short supply, and one confounded Yankee or another tryin' to blow us to smithereens at ever' turn."

Brynne said nothing. As he talked, she felt her resolve ebbing away. Still, she trained the gun on him.

The soldier looked toward the shrub to the right of the porch. "Forsythia ought to be buddin' soon." Meeting Brynne's eyes, he added, "Your daddy said spring is your mama's favorite time of year. Your brother's, too." He brightened some. "Speakin' of Edward, did he make it home all right? Last the Colonel heard, the boy had got himself shot down in Nashville."

Brynne's brows drew together as she attempted to make sense of all he'd said. If he was the type who could steal a coat from a dead man, he was the type who could use force to extract personal facts from a dying man. “How do you know so much about my family?”

Despite his raggedy uniform and haggard face, he stood taller to say, “Fought alongside your daddy ever’ day for a year. We had time a-plenty to talk ’bout families. Got me a son back home, name of Ezra, like in the Bible.” His eyes took on a faraway look as he smiled wanly and added, “Weren’t even walkin’ when I left, but he’ll turn four in a month.”

Brynne watched as tears glistened in his eyes. He shook his head, as if to summon his former control. He spoke with the dulcet tones of a southern gentleman, she couldn’t deny that. But what if like Ross, he’d been born with a gift for emulating accents? And where was his gun? Edward had told her that no self-respecting soldier went anywhere without his standard-issue six pounder. “Where’s your rifle, soldier?”

He nodded toward the end of the long, winding drive. “Hid it in the bushes ’longside the road,” he said, grinning sheepishly. “Didn’t think it’d be smart to come down here, wearin’ a Union coat and brandishin’ artillery!”

Something told her he was everything he professed himself to be. *Lord,* she prayed, *if he isn’t a Southerner, show me a sign; help me protect Moorewood.*

When a minute ticked silently by, and no such proof materialized, Brynne lowered the gun. “Tell me, soldier, when was the last time you had a decent meal?”

Patience had never been one of Brynne’s strong suits. If the letter had been addressed to Amelia Carter instead of the whole Carter family, she would have waited to read it until her mother returned from the Andersons'. But this was Mary Anderson's first baby, and Brynne knew how long it sometimes took to bring a firstborn into the world. Her mother might be away for hours, yet.

She lit a flame under the big kettle on the cookstove to heat up the vegetable soup she'd cooked for supper last night. Without any meat to flavor it, it was thin and watery, but she figured it would make a fine snack for the hungry soldier after his bath. Pouring herself a cup of tea, Brynne sat at the kitchen table and began to read.

December 1, 1864

My dearest family,

I can only hope this reaches you. It seems the only messages getting through these days are from general to general!

No doubt you've tried to contact me since I left Moorewood in '62, but only the letter dated December 22, 1863 reached my homesick hands. I have read it so often, I could recite every word by heart.

December 5, 1864

Fell asleep at the General's writing table, and was awakened by artillery fire to the south. This is the first opportunity I've had to get back to the writing.

I'm sure you've heard by now that supplies are scarce for our side. I won't insult you by denying it, but I will assure you I am fine. "Every cloud has a silver lining," or so the sages say. One bright side of this dismal war has been that I've learned to appreciate cornmeal mush. Think what a good example I'll set for our little grandson when at last I'm home again!

I'm told the blame for our food shortage rests squarely on the shoulders of the governors, who demand "protocol" be followed to the letter. I have half a mind to run for office myself if this miserable war ever ends, and as my first official duty, I'll pass a law making arrogance and self-importance illegal!

Colonel William Lamb has been an able leader. Fort Fisher is the strongest fortification constructed by either side. We are nearly two thousand men strong and have fifty powerful guns at our disposal. All landward approaches are protected by palisades, with land mines buried around the perimeter. As I told you in one of my earlier letters, the only way the Yanks can get us here is if they should attack by both land and sea.

Often, I find myself comparing our situation to that of our forefathers. When the Minutemen stood up against the British nearly a hundred years ago, they, too, lived off the land. Some of our boys are calling themselves "The Savages" instead of "The Confederates," because they've taken to trapping varmints and eating them raw so the shooting and the cookfires won't give away our position. I can almost picture you, my sweet Brynne, wrinkling your nose at that one!

January 1, 1865

Now, where was I?

If we're to believe the latest scuttlebutt, Southern agents are overseas, begging for shoes, clothing, medicines, ammunition, and firearms. If you ask me, this war is serving no purpose other than to make the French and the English rich! But enough talk of politics.

I hope all is well in Spring Creek. I think of Moorewood and everyone there often. But it is you, my darling wife, that I remember most. In the dark of night, when all is silent, I picture your beautiful eyes. If I close my own eyes in the light of day, I can imagine myself touching your velvet-brown hair. When the skies darken with storm clouds, I have only to think of your smile, and I see blue skies. You are my heaven in the hell that is this war.

Oh, how I yearn for the day when I return. That is the tonic that warms me when cold winds blow. And neither the cannons' blast nor the rifles' report can blot your loving voice from my memory.

Your love has sustained me thus far, my

darling, and it will keep me safe until this dreadful fight is won. I promise to move heaven and earth to come home to you. Please never stop believing that I will come back to you.

Well, the bugler is blowing, and I must muster the troops. There's a rumor afloat that the Union has sent ships to test our mettle. If that's true, the Yanks are in for a rude awakening, for they'll be "welcomed" by a fierce defence of the Stars and Bars!

Sleep deeply and well, Amelia, and know that as you do, I'll be dreaming of you. All of you are in my prayers—Amelia my dear wife, my beloved daughter Brynne, my brave son Edward and his sweet wife Julia, and last but not least, my little grandson Richie.

All my love, eternally, to all of you,
Richard

Chapter 2

Hours later, snuggled deep in the cushions of her window seat, Brynne drew up her knees. With trembling fingers, she held the pages on which her father had created a link between the scarred battlefield and his home. She brushed them against her cheek, as if the feel of them could replicate the gentleness of her father's touch.

Her dark eyes drank in every word that described the torment and suffering of war, as she hoped against hope that he would survive it, as her brother had. Yes, Edward had hobbled home on crude wooden crutches, but he would walk on his own again, eventually.

Something told Brynne she ought to put the letter away the moment she began reading the loving words her father had written to her mother. Tall and powerfully built, no one—not even his only daughter—would have guessed that inside this burly man beat the heart of an incurable romantic. Captivated by his endearments, by his confessions of the deep and abiding love he felt for her mother, Brynne read on, despite the fact that doing so made her feel a bit like an interloper.

Will a man ever love me as Father loves Mother? she sighed dreamily.

Quickly, she got hold of her emotions. *Not very likely,*

she told herself, tucking the letter back into its soot-rimmed enveloped. Ross Bartlett had been the only one to woo her, but he had tossed her aside for a fancy Boston-schooled girl.

Like her father and brother, Brynne's fiancé had gone off to war. But unlike Richard and Edward, Ross had decided to live by the code of the jungle: "Survival of the fittest" became his battle cry, and he sold himself to the highest bidder. With nary a backward glance, he turned on Virginia—on all the South—by putting his talents for mimicking accents to use as a double agent. Ross's spying paid off quite handsomely, she'd heard. And one of his rewards had been the hand of a wealthy general's daughter.

To add insult to injury, Brynne learned of his marriage from Camille Prentice when the girl returned from Massachusetts where she had been visiting relatives when the war started. If Ross had given her the news in a letter, that would at least have been preferable to hearing it from Camille's smirking lips.

Common sense told her that her wounded pride would eventually heal, but her shattered spirit would not. Much as she yearned for it, Brynne believed she would never know love as her mother knew it. Because, to put it plainly, she didn't trust her judgement when it came to men.

Laying her father's letter aside, she thought of her conversation with Trevor earlier. Because Richard had described Brynne as a strong young woman, Trevor had felt free to tell her the truth, with no frills or soft touches.

"I did my best to bind his wounds," Trevor had said quietly, reverently, "but he was bleeding badly. Last I saw of him, the confounded Bluebellies were loading him onto a wagon."

Trevor said that he'd hidden in the trees until the Yankees headed north. His intent was to follow them, and when they bedded down for the night, he'd set his comrades free. But he hadn't eaten in days, and he carried a Union lead ball in his own leg. Bleeding and near starved, he'd hadn't been able to keep up, he admitted dismally, and he lost their trail.

The tears she'd blinked back earlier flowed freely now. Her wounded, weakened father had been roughly carted off to a prisoner of war camp. She'd heard about those places, so crowded and dirty that even younger, healthier men had died within their confines. He was dead, and suddenly she couldn't continue to pretend otherwise.

Brynne threw back her shoulders and lifted her chin. Drying her tears on the backs of her hands, she took a deep breath and rose from the window bench. *Grieve Papa's passing later,* she told herself. *For now, you must be strong and brave, for Mama.*

No doubt when Amelia returned from the Andersons', she'd be exhausted. With one last sniff, Brynne marched toward the kitchen and started supper. After the rest of the family heard her news, only little Richie was likely to be hungry. But cooking would give her something to concentrate on besides her father's letter.

"Why so glum?" her brother said from the kitchen doorway.

No point in telling the story more than once, she decided. Hopefully, by the time their mother returned, Trevor would have awakened from his nap, and he could explain to all of the Carters at the same time.

She felt him studying her face for a moment, and she worried he might want to know why she'd been crying. She prayed he wouldn't ask.

God saw fit to answer her brief prayer, for Edward lifted the lid of the pot she'd just sealed. "Mmm, smells delicious." Then, wrinkling his nose, he added, "What is it?"

"Potato soup."

"How many potatoes are in there? One?"

"No, two. But there's a piece of an old turnip too." She gave the back of his hand a gentle pat with her wooden spoon. "Now put the lid back on so the flavors won't escape. I'm rationing the herbs and spices, you know."

Edward affectionately mussed her hair. "Anything you say, sister dear. . .provided I'll get a bowl when it's time."

The day Edward left to fight, Amelia had insisted that his wife and son move into the big house with her and Brynne. "What will we do with all this space, just the two of us?" she'd asked in her typical lighthearted way. "Besides, I wouldn't sleep a wink, worrying about Julia and my grandson, alone over there on the other side of the knoll with all these Yankees prowling about."

Brynne had come to think of Julia as the sister she'd never had, and of four-year-old Richie as a young brother. If her brother and his family ever moved back into their own home, Brynne thought she'd die of loneliness.

"Of course you'll have a bowl." She wiggled her eyebrows and winked. "And maybe, if you fetch me a bucket of water for my dishpan, I'll dip you up a second bowl. . . ."

Grinning, he dampened her cheek with a noisy kiss. "What will two buckets get me?"

"Sparkling clean dishes, that's what," she responded, grinning right back. "Now get on out of here before I take the broom to your backside!"

Edward stood at attention and saluted. "Yes'm," he said, and headed for the door.

It still broke her heart to watch him walk—but not as it had when first he'd returned from Nashville in November of '64, minus his left leg.

Edward had always been proud and stubborn. Why, even as a boy, he felt duty-bound to outlift, outrun, and outshoot every other boy in town. Everything was a game, everyone a competitor. No one was surprised then, when within a week of his return, Edward began hobbling about on the crude wooden crutches the army sent home with him. She'd been so proud of the way he refused to be pitied and insisted upon trying to do his share around Moorewood. By mid-January, his grit paid off, for the gnarled stump that had been his leg had healed enough to strap on the peg he'd whittled for himself. Seeing his drive and determination dwindle each time the prosthesis slipped and caused him to fall nearly broke Brynne's heart. But it had given her a drive and determination of her own. . . .

Late one night, after everyone had gone to bed, she tiptoed into the room he shared with Julia and took the peg from where it leaned near the door. Sitting at the kitchen table, she'd turned it over and over in her hands, trying to puzzle out a way to connect it to a brace, a holster. . . something that would secure it to Edward's body.

The idea struck like lightning, and Brynne had barely been able to contain her excitement. She'd lit a lantern and headed for the shed, where her father had kept an old leather wagon tarp.

Night after night, Brynne worked by lamplight, sewing straps to the body of the brace. Day after day, someone demanded an explanation for her swollen bloodied fingers. She couldn't very well tell them she'd done the damage trying to drive the needle through the deerskin, lest one of them let the cat out of the bag and spoil Edward's surprise. "I'm trying to get the blackberry hedges under control so we'll have a hearty crop next summer," she'd say, smiling as she hid her aching hands behind her back. She was working on the blackberry hedges during the day, but that wasn't what was turning her fingers red and sore.

And then one night, after three weeks of secret struggling, Brynne completed the brace. The sky turned the deep purple shade that signalled the dawn as she added the padded liner that would protect Edward's scarred stump from the hard wood. She'd slipped the peg and its brand new brace into Edward and Julia's room, thanking God he'd never noticed it was missing, and then Brynne returned to the kitchen to wait. . .and pray the brace would fit.

It did, Brynne discovered just after sunup. She'd been at the stove, tending the biscuits she'd baked up, when she heard an unfamiliar sound. The *step-slide-clomp, step-slide-clomp* began at the front stairs and echoed down the hall.

Edward thumped into the kitchen, beaming. "When did you do this?" he'd asked, his voice foggy with emotion. "How did you do this?" Wiggling his brows, he smirked wickedly. "I'm stumped, sister dear!"

It had been good to see him standing there on his own, grinning like his old self, with no crutches to support him. So good that Brynne couldn't answer. Instead, she'd covered her face with both hands and wept softly.

He'd limped over to where she stood and took her in his arms. "Brynne, Brynne, Brynne," Edward had sighed, stroking her hair. "I know why you're such a good teacher—because I've never known a gentler, more kindhearted woman." There had been tears in his own dark eyes when he'd held her at arm's length to add in a raspy whisper, "I haven't felt much like a man since I got home. . .till this morning." He'd kissed her forehead. "Thank you, Brynne. And God bless you."

She watched him now, moving about at almost his old speed, and smiled ruefully. When he'd walked into the room, she'd tried to sidestep his question, but she had seen the telltale eyebrow arch that was proof her quick change of subject hadn't fooled him in the least.

She wondered how long he'd wait before demanding an answer to his question. Wondered, too, how she'd phrase her response.

Ah, to be a child again, she thought, sighing, *like Richie, and never have to worry about protecting others from bad news, always able to believe in happy endings.*

Because right now, she'd give anything just about anything, to believe that her father was still alive.

Chapter 3

March 1865

"Cullen Adams, this is the third time in a week you've come to school late," Brynne scolded gently. "What do you have to say for yourself?"

She didn't expect the boy to respond, for Cullen hadn't said a word since his parents died in a Yankee raid on Petersburg. Why Clay, his older brother, made the child come to school at all seemed as big a mystery to Brynne as Cullen's silence. If sitting in her makeshift classroom all these months had made a difference in his behavior, Brynne would have been the first to insist that he attend. But he sat alone in the last row, staring blankly ahead, never speaking, barely moving. It was time to discuss the matter with his brother.

First thing next morning, she set out to do just that.

Brynne had heard much about Clay Adams, but though she had seen him around town, she hadn't exchanged more than polite nods with the somber-faced man. Once, in response to something Buster the postmaster said, she'd seen Clay smile. Until that moment, she'd guessed his age to be thirty or thirty-five—but the smile had so completely transformed his face, that she decided he was closer to twenty-five after all.

She felt a strange interest in this man who was now the guardian of her silent student, an interest that had first begun to grow when she had talked with his parents about him. The Adamses had moved to Spring Creek from Louisiana in the summer of '59, and as their younger son's teacher, Brynne had had occasion to talk with the parents, first at school functions and then at numerous church gatherings. Ernest and Claudia had been so proud of their eldest son who was attending a Boston college. When he graduated, they said, he planned to put his education to use improving their tobacco plantation.

The war killed the plans of thousands like the Adamses. Clay, his mother tearfully told Brynne one Sunday morning, felt duty bound to defend his beloved South and had enlisted in the Confederate Army the moment he heard about what had taken place in South Carolina. He fought long and hard. . .until an injury suffered during the Franklin-Nashville Campaign in November of '64 sent him home, just weeks before his parents became victims of the slaughter in Petersburg. The war had put a heavy hand on Clay's family, just as it had on Brynne's. Maybe that was why she felt this strange sense of kinship with him. . . .

Since childhood, Brynne had made a hobby of tracing the meaning of folks' names. Her own meant "the heights," a fine name for a girl with her head in the clouds, Brynne told herself, but not at all appropriate for a young woman like herself, with both feet planted firmly on solid ground.

Clay's name meant "of the earth." Now there's a name, she'd told herself, that fits like a comfortable shoe. He stood tall and broad as a mighty oak, with hair the color of acorns and eyes as blue as a summer sky, and he looked as though his feet, like hers, were planted solidly on the earth. She just wished that one day she could see him smile again. . . .

As she guided her two-wheeled buggy over the bumpy road toward Adams' Hill, Brynne wondered how he would react when she told him to keep his brother home from school. The time, she'd say, would allow the boy to heal privately from his emotional wounds. Would Clay be the kind of man who'd understand that her idea had been born of concern for his brother—or the type who'd tell her to mind her own business?

She pictured the determined set of his jaw and the deep furrow that lined his brow. "I have a feeling he'll be a bit of both," she told herself.

He'd been so engrossed in repairing the pasture fence that Clay never heard the buggy's approach. When he finally caught sight of it from the corner of his eye, he nearly hammered his thumb. *Cullen's teacher,* he acknowledged, grimacing as he drew a sleeve across his perspiring brow. If she had come this early on a Saturday, it couldn't be good news that brought her.

Jamming the hammer handle into the back pocket of his trousers, Clay tucked in his shirt as she smiled and waved in friendly greeting. "Good morning, Mr. Adams," she called, bringing the buggy to a halt at the end of the drive. "My, but you're up and at it early."

He cocked one dark brow and tucked in a corner of his mustachioed mouth. "What can I do for you?"

He winced with guilt at the startled expression his gruff tone had etched on her pretty face, but thankfully, she recovered quickly. Wrapping the horse's reins around her left hand, the pretty young teacher adjusted the bow of her wide-brimmed hat. "I need to speak with you about your brother," she said, squaring her shoulders and lifting her chin.

He'd been casually leaning on the fencepost, but now he straightened in response to her statement. "What about him?" Clay crossed both arms over his chest. "He givin' you some sort of trouble?"

She blinked several times, as if trying to read the reason for the anger in his voice. "Quite the contrary. Cullen is the best-behaved boy in class." Pursing her lips, she added, "Trouble is, he isn't learning a thing."

"That's impossible," he grated, shaking his head. "I see to it he does his lessons, every night after supper."

She raised a brow in response to the heat of his words, then leaned forward slightly to say, "I realize this visit is impromptu, Mr. Adams, but. . ."

He watched as she bit her full lower lip and tilted her head. *I like a woman who thinks before she speaks,* he thought, hiding a smirk. *It's a right rare commodity these days.*

"I seem to have completely forgotten my manners," she said, holding out her hand. "I don't believe we've ever been properly introduced. I'm Brynne Carter, Mr. Adams."

Frowning, he focused on the tiny, lace-covered hand for a moment. He tried to shake off the gentle feeling growing inside him toward her. *She's just more of what I've had too much of lately. . .trouble,* he told himself. "I know who you are," he growled, meeting her eyes. "What do you take me for, some kind of simpleton? Spring Creek has but one teacher."

When she realized he had no intention of taking her hand, she made a fist of it, then rested it on her hip. After a moment of intense scrutiny, she climbed down from the buggy seat and tethered her horse to the post Clay had just repaired. Tapping a fingertip to her chin, she gave his dusty work boots a cursory glance. "It appears you're putting most of your weight on your right foot, Mr. Adams." She met his eyes. "Would you mind very much shifting it to your left?"

Clay's brow wrinkled with confusion. He hadn't moved a step. How could she have noticed his limp? He looked at his feet, then focused on her face. "What?"

Mischievous light danced in her dark eyes. "It's the most sensible thing to do, since we seem to have gotten off on the wrong foot."

"The wrong. . ." When understanding dawned, Clay chuckled softly and shook his head. Extending his own hand, he said, "Pleasure to make your acquaintance, Miss Carter."

The power of her grip amazed him even more than the way her hand all but disappeared in his. And the way she stood there, blinking up at him, made his heart lurch. The sunlight glinting on her hair reminded him of ripe chestnuts.

Clay's ears had grown hot. His cheeks, too. He turned her hand loose and tried to recall why she'd come here in the first place. "Now, tell me about this trouble Cullen is giving you."

She glanced toward the house. "Where is he?"

"In the barn, mucking out stalls. Why?"

Brynne untethered her horse and climbed back onto the buggy seat. "I don't think he should overhear our conversation." Pausing, she swung her gaze to his eyes. "Do you suppose we might go on up to the house?"

"You're not a woman who beats around the bush, are you?" he asked, grinning slightly.

Brynne grinned right back. "I find bush-beating a terrible waste of time. . .and unnecessarily hard on the shrubbery." Smiling, she patted the seat beside her. "You're more than welcome to drive," she added, offering him the reins.

He hesitated, but only for a moment. "Well," he grumbled, "I reckon the sooner we get this over with, the sooner I'll be able to get back to work." Clay climbed up beside her and relieved her of the reins. He didn't say another word until he parked near the front porch. Neither did Brynne, and something told Clay this was not typical behavior for the lovely little teacher.

Though he'd stared straight ahead as they made the ten-minute trip from the road to the house, he could see from the corner of his eye her every reaction to the sights around her. As they rode over the narrow drive that curved like a gently flowing river of crushed stone, her eyes had widened. A little smile curved her lips as they passed beneath stately magnolias that lined the entire length of the drive.

He'd had the same eye-popping reaction the first time

he'd seen the big house, with its black-shuttered, many-paned windows that offset wide double doors on the first floor. A dozen red brick steps led from the drive to the massive portico. Tall columns supported either side of the porch roof, crowned by a second, equally grand porch, enclosed by a white picket rail.

A sense of well-being had wrapped 'round him like a mother's hug the first time he caught sight of those four imposing chimneys, silhouetted against the blue, sun-bright sky. And the two gigantic oaks that flanked the porch. And that sea of velvety white crocuses. . .

"White crocuses," she sighed. "They're my mother's favorite flowers." Brynne turned a bit on the buggy seat to face him. "How did you avoid the Yankee raids here at Adams' Hill?" she asked, incredulous. "Why, they completely burned the Smiths out. And it'll likely take us years to repair the damage they did at Moorewood."

Clay shrugged. "Don't rightly know," he admitted, stepping down from the buggy.

She was watching him, he knew, and making note of his limp. *Dear God,* he prayed, *don't let her feel sorry for me. I can take just about anything from her but that.* Just in case pity was shining in her eyes, he avoided her gaze as he reached up to help her from the buggy.

But Brynne wasn't having any of that! "Mr. Adams," she said brightly, forcing him to look at her, "you are a true gentleman indeed."

He didn't see a trace of pity on her face, which only made her all the more beautiful to him. He clamped his hands around her waist—a waist tinier than any he'd ever seen—to lift her from the seat.

"Now, don't strain yourself, Mr. Adams."

He bristled for a moment, but the gentle look on her face told him her comment hadn't been motivated by pity. "Why, I've hefted sacks of wheat and corn that weigh more than you, Miss Carter," he said, putting her gently onto the ground. She seemed so small, so vulnerable. And yet, if all he'd heard about her in town was true, she'd more or less single-handedly run Moorewood while her father and brother were fighting. Suddenly, Clay didn't want to let her go. He wanted, instead, to draw her close and wrap her in a protective hug.

"Forgive my boldness, Mr. Adams, but do you have anything warm to drink inside? I know the sun is shining bright as can be, but I'm afraid I've caught a bit of a chill. . . ."

The question broke the trancelike connection that had fused his eyes to hers. He quickly unhanded her, and with a grand, sweeping gesture, invited her to precede him into the house. If he led the way, she'd have to walk behind him and watch him shuffle along like a three-legged dog. "Could be there's some coffee left from breakfast," he said.

She lifted her skirts and dashed up the stairs. "That'll be just fine." She stopped suddenly and faced the barn. "You're sure Cullen won't overhear?"

Clay held open the front door. "Not if we get this matter settled before sunset."

Brynne pursed her lips. "Well," she huffed, smiling only with her eyes, "you're not one to beat around the bush, either, are you, Mr. Adams?" And with that, she breezed past him and into the house.

"Do you mind talking in the kitchen?" he asked, closing the door behind them.

"The kitchen is my favorite room at Moorewood." She leaned forward as if telling state secrets. "Kitchens are the coziest rooms in any house, where people can gather around the table and have a companionable conversation and. . ."

If he had to stand there and listen to her chatter like a magpie for another minute, he was likely to sweep her off those tiny feet and give her a big kiss, just to shut her up. Clay grinned and quirked a brow. *Not such a bad thought,* he told himself.

". . .the very best place to discuss the day's events. Don't you think so?"

"Yes, yes," he agreed, though he hadn't the foggiest idea what she'd been babbling about. "The kitchen's right down that hall."

She headed in the direction he'd pointed and helped herself to a white mug from the shelf above the cookstove. She hadn't even taken her gloves off yet when she touched a palm to the coffeepot. "Good. It's still warm." And as though she were the lady of the house rather than the guest, Brynne smiled. "May I pour you a cup?"

Clay had to admit she looked lovely standing there at the stove, his mother's coffeepot in one hand, his father's favorite cup in the other. More than that, she looked as if she belonged. He shook his head to clear his mind. "I, uh, I'd just as soon get down to business, if you don't mind." He nodded toward the yard, visible through the window beside her. "There's that fence to finish repairin', and. . ."

"Then I suggest we sit," she broke in, settling herself in a ladder-backed chair. Brynne placed her mug on the table and wrapped her hands around it. "Tell me, Mr. Adams, how long since Cullen has spoken?"

Clay turned his chair around and sat across from her, leaning both arms across the seat back. "My folks were killed in Petersburg in December," he said matter-of-factly. "When I told Cullen about it, he said, 'You're lyin'. Ain't no way they're dead!' " Clay frowned, linked his fingers. "Then his eyes filled up with tears and he ran out to the barn." He met her eyes. "Hasn't said a word since."

Brynne clasped both hands under her chin. "Oh, how dreadful," she sighed, shaking her head. "I heard how your folks volunteered to travel south, to interview the seminarian who would replace Pastor Zaph."

Tears shimmered in her eyes as she absently stroked a scratch on the tabletop, the nonchalant action, it seemed to Clay, an intent to hide her tender side from him. It touched him deeply that she would cry for his losses when she'd suffered so many of her own.

"So much death and destruction. So much suffering," Brynne was saying, more to herself than to Clay. "I wonder if, when it's over, either side will think it was worth it."

He had heard what happened to her father. To her brother Edward. To her precious Moorewood. Yet there she sat, head up and shoulders back, determined to take it on the chin. What and who she was showed in her determined smile, in her warm brown eyes. Brynne Carter was a woman who cared deeply. What more proof did he need than the concern for his brother that brought her here today?

Clay didn't know what prompted him to do it, but he blanketed her hand with his own. "Now, about Cullen. . ."

She looked at their hands, and he was pleased that she didn't draw away. He was still more pleased when she put her free hand atop the stack of fingers. Brightening a bit, she smiled. "As a matter of fact, I have several ideas I'd like to discuss with you."

Grinning, Clay gave her hand a gentle squeeze. "I had a feeling you might."

Chapter 4

June 1865

When Sergeant Trevor Williams had left Moorewood in late February, he made two promises to Amelia: "Yes, Miz Carter, I'll take good care of myself, and don't you worry, if I hear anything about the Colonel, I'll get a message to you."

Almost four months had now passed without a word from him—or any army official, for that matter. Not that Brynne was surprised. Amelia still insisted that her husband would return to them, but in Brynne's heart, she knew she'd never see her father again. Sometimes, when the pain of her grief seemed too heavy to bear, Brynne wished that, like her mother, a little childlike faith beat in her heart.

Because, oh, how she missed him! Not a day went by that she didn't think of him, for there wasn't a man like him on earth and likely would never be. *If Papa were here,* she thought, shaking her head at the irony, *he'd know how to make Mama face the truth. . . .*

Brynne had been taught both at home and in Sunday school that worrying never solved any problem. "Prayer, faith, and patience," her father had always said, "are the ways to ease a troubled mind."

Well, she'd prayed morning, noon, and night that God would give her the words to help Amelia deal realistically with what had happened to Richard. And she'd clung to her faith, hoping the Almighty would answer those prayers. But day by day, it grew more obvious that Amelia could spend the rest of her life clinging to the hope that her husband would return. If only God would show the poor woman a sign!

Having been born and bred in Christian fundamentals, Brynne couldn't make herself believe the Lord had simply turned His back on her family. Compared to the war, Amelia's delusions were a small problem; surely the Lord had plenty more important prayers to answer. . . .

Still, it had shaken her faith a bit that the Lord had not provided a solution to her mother's problem. Brynne was feeling a bit lost. A little less trusting in the God who had promised peace to all those who put their troubles at the foot of the cross. . . .

Not once in her life had Brynne spoken a disrespectful word to her mother. But one evening, four months to the day after the Andersons' baby was born, the day Trevor had brought them her father's letter, all that changed.

Amelia had visited little Jake at least a dozen times since bringing him into the world. "Just seeing the little tyke grow and thrive makes me feel better." Just back from yet another visit, she hung her hat on the peg near the door. "It's proof that life goes on, even as this horrible war rages on all around us."

Brynne wanted to point out that death was very much a part of life, because of the war. But she held her tongue.

The subject of Richard's survival was by now a sore point that both mother and daughter scrupulously avoided. Brynne could not understand how, after so many months with no word from her father—or about him—Amelia could still be so certain he was alive, that he would return.

Her mother had not shed a tear, not while reading the letter Trevor delivered, not as she'd stuffed it back into its envelope. Instead, she'd held up her chin in stubborn denial of the obvious and shook her head.

She was looking at Brynne that same way now, and Brynne didn't know if she possessed the strength of character to continue pretending she shared her mother's faith. Life had taught her that such naivete could only bring pain and disappointment.

"Don't wrinkle your brow at me, young lady," her mother scolded. "You're not too big to turn over my knee, you know."

Brynne sighed. "I mean no disrespect, Mama. It's just. . ."

"Just nothing! Remember what Jesus said: 'If you have faith as a grain of mustard seed, you can say to that mountain, move, and it will move.' "

"Papa isn't Lazarus, Mama," Brynne said dully, "Christ isn't going to bring him back to life."

Amelia planted both hands on her hips. "If your father was dead, don't you think I'd know it?" She pressed a fist to her chest. "He's. . .he's. . ."

Her mother's hesitation surprised Brynne, and she sat in stony silence as Amelia stared at an unknown spot beyond Brynne's shoulder.

For a time, soon after Richard's letter had been delivered, she'd tried to share her mother's unwavering optimism, but whenever her mood darkened, reality set in, and when it did, her father died anew in her tortured mind. And so she'd turned loose the dream that could never come true, and clung instead to the tried and true: Expect the worst, and when it comes, you can say "I told you so!" And if the worst never happens, it'll be a blissful surprise.

While Brynne had been daydreaming, Amelia had gathered her former resoluteness. " 'Christ isn't going to bring Papa back to life,' " she quoted Brynne. "Well, the disciples spoke just as plainly of Lazarus's death." She gave her words a moment to sink in. "And they were just as wrong."

Nodding, Brynne stared at her hands, folded in her lap. She knew the verse well, for she'd read it a hundred times since her father's letter had been delivered: "And Martha fell at Jesus's feet and said, 'If you had been here, Lord, my brother would not have died,' " Brynne quoted the Book of John. She met Amelia's dark eyes, unaware of the rage that rang in her voice. "Jesus wasn't on that battlefield. If He had been, Papa wouldn't be—"

"I'm surprised, Brynne," Amelia interrupted, "that I need to remind you the Lord is with us always, everywhere."

Expelling an exasperated sigh, Brynne closed her eyes in an attempt to summon patience. "If that's true," she said slowly, her voice quiet and cool, "how do you explain all those who died fighting, and your own son, who came home wounded beyond repair? How do you explain the destruction of the South and our beautiful Moorewood?" *How do you explain the way Ross turned his back on his own people, on me, and. . . ?*

Amelia wrapped her daughter in a hug and sighed. "I can't explain it, Brynne, because I don't understand it my-self. But it isn't our place to understand such things. God calls us to believe, nothing more." Smiling gently, she cupped Brynne's cheek. "I only know that God promises to give us the strength to bear up under any burden. 'He will not let you be tested beyond your strength, but with the test, he will provide the way of escape, so you may be able to endure it.' He knows our limits better than we do."

In a blinding flash, Brynne realized that Amelia needed to believe in the impossible every bit as much as Brynne needed to stare the truth straight in the eye. Could her mother's heroic demeanor be a disguise that hid her true fears? If so, her mother needed loving support.

"Your father will come back to us. I'm certain of it!"

What harm can it do to pretend you share her sunny view? she asked herself. "Of course he will," Brynne said, feigning a smile. "Now I really must get to bed. I have a busy day planned for my class tomorrow."

Amelia pressed a gentle kiss to Brynne's forehead. "I was so proud when you suggested to Pastor Gentry that the congregation use our barn as a temporary church and school after the Yankees destroyed the church and school. The shed will be plenty big enough for Bessie until the new church is built."

Once, Bessie had been one of dozens of dairy cows that stood side by side in the big wooden structure.

Now, she stood alone in what was little more than a ramshackle lean-to behind the house. "True, but Bessie is awfully spoiled," Brynne said, heading for the door. "I hope she doesn't decide to stop producing milk, just to get even for being reassigned to such tiny quarters."

Smiling sadly, Amelia shook her head. "Goodness, Brynne, when did you become such a pessimist?"

When our great nation was divided by a ridiculous war, Brynne wanted to say. *When Edward came home mangled. When the list of the dead soldiers on the post office wall doubled, then tripled. When Ross chose money and social position over doing the right thing. When Papa's letter came and. . .*

But remembering her decision to be loving and supportive for as long as her mother needed it, Brynne grinned and affectionately patted her mother's hand. "I promise to try and keep my negative comments to a minimum, starting now." She gave her mother a quick hug and a peck on the cheek. "Good night, Mama. I love you." She hurried to her room, hoping that a good night's sleep would help her continue the pretense tomorrow, and the next day, and the next.

Brynne's pessimism, as it turned out, had not been completely unfounded. Though Bessie dutifully continued to pour out an ample supply of milk, European support of the South dried up. Everyone, it seemed, was hungry and, according to all reports, desertion in Lee's army had increased alarmingly.

The Yankees were bored. There was little else for them to do but pillage and rampage and complain about the war that would not end. Rumor had it that Lee's remaining veterans, despite their skilled—if not grim—determination, had spent the last of their fighting strength.

Rumor became reality mid-month when word came by way of a fleeing Rebel soldier that on April second, the Confederate government, guarded by a stalwart few, fled Richmond by way of the railroad. By the fourth, said an article in a special edition of the Gazette, President Lincoln arrived, unescorted and unannounced, to inspect the grand old city, now under Union control. "Let 'em up easy," he was quoted to have told General Grant. "Let 'em up easy."

But there was no letup, and by May tenth, the war that would not end officially ended.

The suffering in the South did not end, however. Hunger, homelessness, illness, and poverty afflicted people who, before the war, had never experienced physical or monetary discomfort. The Carters, like their neighbors all around them, attempted to get back to living life as they had prior to April 12, 1861, when the ten-inch mortar that screamed over Charleston Harbor blasted Fort Sumter.

Brynne held tight to a hope of her own. Colonel Richard Carter had died a hero's death and deserved a hero's burial; someday, perhaps, his family could bury his remains in his favorite place. . .at the top of Kismet Hill, beside the scraggly pine that had somehow grown in a bed of rock.

Chapter 5

July 1865

It wasn't an easy hike to Kismet Hill, and Brynne had decided to spend the night there rather than making the long trek back before nightfall. She started out late in the afternoon and walked along the stream, as her father had taught her. Part of the beauty of this country, he'd always said, was that it never changed. Brynne recognized trees and trails she'd marked as a little girl, using her father's big hunting knife as he supervised with a watchful eye. Finally, as the sun slid down the backside of Moore's Peak, their special place opened up to her.

Brynne sat on a fallen tree trunk, hands resting on her knees, and drank in the territory like a woman lost in the desert might suck at the wet lip of a canteen. This was where her father always came when he sought to escape life's hectic pace or yearned for the privacy to thank God for his blessings. She'd been honored that he'd shared his secret place with her. Over time, it had become a place of respite for her, too. Since he'd left to fight for Moorewood, it had become a place to hide.

Not until a cardinal peeped in a nearby tree did she rouse from her memory and begin setting up camp. The temperature here could dip low at night, even in summer, but Brynne had come prepared. Nature couldn't do anything to her up here to equal what the war had done! She constructed a makeshift tent from an old blanket and several ropes, strung from low-hanging tree branches. If it rained, she'd climb inside. Otherwise, she'd sleep under the stars.

Staring up at the shimmering darkness, she felt Richard's presence. He'd been nothing but the poor son of a pig farmer when he met Amelia. "She fell for him like a lumberjack's tree," Grandpa Moore often said with a wink and a grin. "And so did the rest of the family. I saw brilliance peekin' out from under that bent straw hat he wore, and decided to take a chance on it."

Richard, Grandpa insisted, had been born with a head for business. Less than two years after marrying George Moore's only daughter, he'd tripled the worth of Moorewood. "It's only fittin' that it become yours when I leave this old world," Grandpa had written in the letter accompanying his last will and testament.

Brynne had often acknowledged her father's intelligence, but it was his heart that she admired most. Yes, he'd slaughter pigs and sheep and cows to put meat on the table, and yes, he'd sell whole herds to assure there'd always be money to care for his family. He was a crack-shot hunter, too, but Brynne understood better than anyone how it pained him to take a life for any reason.

They'd been here, on Kismet Hill, overlooking the valley when he'd spied a doe and two fawns in the distance. "Look there," he's whispered. "Isn't it the most beautiful sight?"

Puzzled by his awestruck expression, young Brynne

had frowned. "But Papa," she'd said, "you're here to kill them."

He'd taken her face in his hands to say, "The Lord created every creature on earth for man's benefit—some for food, others for coats and hats. . ." An eagle screeched overhead just then, and he'd said, "And some, we're to admire from afar." Gently chucking her under the chin, he'd winked. "It's up to us to know when and how He means for us to use what He gave us." Only then did he raise his rifle and fire.

Brynne missed Richard more at that moment than in those first hard days after he'd left home. She and Clay Adams had been going for some long walks together. At first, they had discussed Cullen and his problems, but lately their conversations had ranged far and wide. On their last walk, Clay had held her hand, and Brynne had been filled with confusion ever since. If she'd come to her father for advice on the thoughts she'd been thinking about Clay Adams, he'd have known exactly what to say. . . .

Am I being foolish, she'd ask him, *giving my heart away so soon after Ross's betrayal? And do you think Clay will ever give his heart to me?*

She snuggled under the blankets she'd brought and smiled. Papa and Clay would have gotten along famously, she acknowledged, missing them both more than she cared to admit. Brynne remembered her first meeting with Clay, when she'd spelled out ways they might help Cullen learn to talk again.

He hadn't rejected a single one of her suggestions. Instead, Clay had nodded in agreement with everything she'd said, right down to and including her idea that he start attending church services again.

"Haven't been inside a church in a while," he'd admitted on a heavy sigh, "but if you believe it'll help the boy, I'll give it a try."

"Someday, perhaps you'll tell me why you've stayed away so long," she'd said.

An array of emotions had flickered over his handsome, bearded face in response to her simple request. Like storm clouds that blot out the sun, his secret reasons dimmed the light in his brown eyes. The furrow between his brows deepened, and the corners of his mouth turned down. His soft, rich voice took on a hard cold edge, like a blade scraping across a dry stone. "Don't hold your breath," he'd grated. But his hand had still been sandwiched between hers when he'd said it, as if he hoped that "someday" would indeed come.

With her heart and head full of these memories, Brynne slept deeply for the first time in months. When she woke at dawn, she felt as though she'd slept six nights instead of one. She sat up to stretch and breathe in the sharp pure scent of pine.

She got onto her knees and faced the sun. "Dear Lord," she prayed, hands folded and face tilted toward the heavens, "thank You for a night of peaceful slumber. Thank You for this glorious morning and this beautiful view and everything else You've given me. Bless this day, and see that I do Your will throughout it. Amen."

When she was finished, Brynne set about the business of having breakfast. Poking at her smoldering campfire, she carefully placed dried leaves and sticks atop the coals and blew gently until they glowed red. When the tiny flames licked at the twigs, she added larger limbs, until the fire blazed hot and bright. Now Brynne dumped a handful of coffee grounds into the bottom of a blue-speckled pot and poured fresh mountain spring water over them. While she waited for it to bubble, she tore off a chunk of bread and popped it into her mouth as she looked out over the valley beyond.

Tears stung her eyes as she surveyed the pristine scene. "How could anyone plant their boots on ground like this and not believe in God?" Richard had said. Brynne couldn't help but agree, for only a powerful and mighty Being could have created anything so vast and magnificent. The vista was an explosion of color and scent, from the sun-glinted hilltops to the twisting aqua river below, from the pale azure sky to the pillowy green of faraway treetops.

Wiping her eyes with the back of a hand, she slid her father's letter from her skirt pocket. Most of the time, her mother kept the letter with her, in her pocket, but she had let her daughter borrow it, and now Brynne stared down at the blackened paper. Her father's handwriting, like the man itself, bespoke power and determination. He had promised to move heaven and earth to come home to them, but even Richard Carter didn't possess that kind of strength.

He'd left them in May of '62 and hadn't gotten a letter through until July. In it, he told his family there had been a lot of activity near the Rappahannock River. As his unit continued to push south to block the enemy, it had grown smaller and smaller. "You know that I believe in the truth," he'd written, "and so I shall never lie about my situation." He'd closed that letter with a promise to return, too.

They didn't hear from him again until November of '63. This time, he wrote that the fighting had escalated in the area. They were thinking of building a secret weapon, he'd told them. But he hadn't said what sort of weapon, and since the family hadn't heard from him again, no one knew if it had been a success. All they were left with was his second promise to come home.

The next letter described his move to Fort Fisher. "The Yanks will never defeat us here," he had promised. "Not unless they should be foxy enough to come at us both by land and sea. But I believe the Northern generals are not as clever as the Southern." And then again he had promised, "I promise to be home as soon as I am able."

If this, his final correspondence, had not been delivered in person by the young sergeant, it would have been easy to believe that maybe Richard could keep his promise. As it was, Trevor's description of the colonel as he'd last seen him made it only too clear there was little hope her father had survived.

Head in her hands, Brynne sobbed and remembered those last precious moments with her father.

"Why must you go?" she'd demanded. "No one expects it of you, not a man with all your responsibilities. . ."

"I expect it of me," he'd said, buckling his haversack. "What kind of man would I be if I didn't do my share to protect what's mine?"

She'd read newspaper accounts of the fighting that had already taken place. And she'd done her Christian duty, standing among neighbors and friends as they buried sons and brothers and husbands. Brynne wanted no part of any obligation that would have her saying a final farewell to her father! "But Papa," she'd pressed, "we need you here. Why not leave the fighting to the younger men?"

He'd put both hands on her shoulders and given her a gentle shake. "I realize I seem ancient to you, daughter, but there's plenty of fight left in me."

She'd wriggled free of his grasp and stood at the window, hugging herself to fend off the cold chill that had wrapped itself around her. "What if. . .What will we do if. . . ?"

Resting his chin atop her head, he hugged her from behind. "Nothing is going to happen to me, sweet girl."

"You can't be sure of that," she'd said, facing him. And with the last of her hope, she'd added, "Can you?"

" 'No man is sure of life,' " he quoted from the Book of Job. "But you can be sure I'll do everything in my power to come home." Drawing her into a comforting embrace, he'd added, "Home is what I'm fighting for, remember?"

Now, Brynne folded the letter and returned it to the worn envelope and resigned herself once more to the inevitable. She had hoped that in coming here, to their special place, she might find reason to share her mother's optimism.

Here, he'd told her breathtaking stories that simplified the miracles of life. Her favorite was his explanation of how one lonely scrub pine had been able to grow from a fissure in a boulder at the top of the hill.

"Some time ago," he'd said, "a tiny seed parted from its mother plant and soared through the heavens in God's palm, searching for a place to rest. From on high, God pointed to a minuscule crevice. 'There?' the little seed asked. 'But Lord, nothing can grow in solid rock!' And God said, 'You can grow there, if you believe enough in Me.'

"So the seed coasted to earth on the breath of God, and nestled deep in the darkness of the crook where nothing else had had the courage to go.

"God smiled upon that brave little seed, and because it had trusted so completely in Him, He saw to it there was soil enough, and water enough, and the seed took root and grew, and it survived."

Though she had always loved the way he told tales, with wonder and awe rumbling in his deep voice, Brynne had never understood its application to her own life. It seemed to her the little pine had endured many hardships by blindly doing as God asked it to do. For one thing, it stood completely alone all these many years, without grass or flowers or another tree to keep it company. And the wicked wind had blown cold for so long that the spindly thing had needles on only one side, and leaned hard toward the rocks, as though seeking shelter from the constant blasts of tempestuous air.

It had been here for as long as Brynne could remember, yet the tree stood barely taller than she, while pines that had rooted in the forest's loamy soil for half as long had developed trunks as big around as barrel hoops and needly branches that raked the undersides of the clouds.

Well, she told herself, *it's a nice story, all the same.* She didn't have to learn a lesson from every tale he told, did she? And Richard had taught her many valuable lessons here, like how to find her way through a dense forest, where to find drinking water, how to tell which berries and mushrooms were poisonous so she could survive in any locale.

Much to Brynne's dismay, though, she realized her father had overlooked the most important lesson of all: He hadn't taught her how to survive the loss of him.

Chapter 6

The community of Spring Creek had finally built themselves a new church building where they could meet to worship God. Clay chose the same seat in the new building every week, hoping that as few people as possible would notice him and his brother.

"Sit front and center," had been Brynne's advice, "so Cullen can hear God's Word, loud and clear!" Third row from the altar, at the end of the pew nearest the stained glass windows was as close to front and center as Clay intended to get.

He found himself daydreaming during the services, a practice that would have earned him a heated scolding from his mother, even at his age, had she lived. Try as he might, he could not focus on the music or the words filtering around the tidy chapel, for just as he had chosen this seat near the wall each week, Brynne found her own favorite spot every Sunday, too: in the pew right in front of his, but in the center, right where he couldn't help but see her pretty profile.

Like an earthly angel, he thought, smiling inwardly as he watched her sitting there, looking serene and beautiful as she stared ahead, hands folded primly in her lap. Her students, he'd noticed in weeks past, scrambled and shoved for the opportunity to sit beside her. Mary Scott and Sammy Barber had won the contest this week, and though neither child had yet seen a tenth birthday, each sat almost as tall as their teacher.

She moved with the grace and agility of a doe, and something told him that despite her fragile-looking bone structure, Brynne was anything but delicate.

He remembered that day when she'd ridden out to the farm in her dainty two-wheeled buggy to discuss Cullen's emotional problems. Her diminutive size and stature had given him a powerful urge to wrap her in a protective embrace. When she bounded toward his front door, he couldn't help but grin, for everything about her, from the smile that lit her eyes like a beacon to the surefooted way she moved, forced him to see her as larger than life.

The congregation rose in unison. "Please turn to page one hundred twenty-one in your hymnals," the preacher said, nodding to the organist. Smiling, Mrs. Henderson nodded back, leaning hard on the ivory keys as the first melodious strains of song filled the new church.

"Sing praise to our Creator, O son of Adam's race," the parishioners sang.

Clay stood, open hymnal balanced on one palm, head bowed and eyes closed. After years of loss, he had something to sing praise about again, he realized. Brynne's suggestion that he bring Cullen to church, for starters. Before, the boy barely lifted his chin from his chest. Now, at least, he made eye contact from time to time. He sent a heartfelt "thank You" heavenward.

"God's children by adoption, baptized into His

grace," the song continued.

He regarded Cullen from the corner of his eye. The boy was staring hard at his songbook. Though he'd turned to the right page, he stood as silent as a statue. Clay sometimes wondered what might be going through his brother's head. Was he picturing the explosion that killed their parents? That would certainly explain the shadows that so often dulled Cullen's dark eyes and twisted his face into a tortured scowl.

Granted, it had been a difficult piece of news to hear. Still, despite the slight improved Cullen had shown, until Brynne had confronted him, Clay's patience had been wearing thin. After all, Cullen had turned thirteen on his last birthday, older than some of the boys Clay had fought with in the war. They had performed many tasks to assist their older comrades, from handing rifles down the front lines to reloading muskets. They filled canteens and sewed rips in the men's shirtsleeves. Sometimes, in the quiet of the night, their soft angelic voices could be heard in the distance, singing sad old ballads that lulled the tired soldiers to sleep.

"Praise the holy trinity," the congregation continued, "undivided unity. . ."

Lovely as it was, the hymn couldn't begin to compare with those simple tunes created by the youngsters on the battlefield. Those boys had walked side-by-side with the foot soldiers, straight into the bowels of battle. They'd seen all manner of death and destruction, yet managed to keep their fears at bay as the unit marched toward the next skirmish, and the next.

Clay remembered one in particular. As second

lieutenant, Clay had been ordered to report to General Hood's quarters for a top-secret conclave. The officers were bending over the map table, studying their options, when the youngster barged into the tent and stood at attention. "Dale Allen Jones, reporting for duty," he'd said in a loud, official-sounding voice. "I can play a fife and drum; I know how to shoot. And I'm an orphan, so it don't much matter iffin I get back to Chattanooga alive or not." Looking straight ahead, he'd concluded his little speech with a snappy salute: "Brung my own bedroll and canteen, too."

It was hard not to be impressed by a boy like that. Tough through and through, he more than made up for his smaller than average height and weight. "All spit and vinegar, that one," the men often said of Dale. The boy never complained, not when the blisters on his feet bled, not when his flute was destroyed by enemy fire. He didn't whine when the men who'd become his substitute fathers took direct hits, didn't cry when they died. Even when a Union cannonball exploded near him, pocking his puny frame with shrapnel, Dale did not whimper. He would have been quite a man, Clay acknowledged, had he survived that last battle. . . .

Dale, like so many boys who did their part for the South, understood that a man couldn't hide from pain any more than he could hide from himself. Clay had begun to wonder when Cullen would learn that lesson. Did he enjoy the pitying stares and whispers that floated round him everywhere he went? Had he no pride at all?

The voices of his brethren united in a resounding

tribute to the Almighty. "Holy God, mighty God, God immortal be adored."

"Please, be seated," the pastor said. Amid the din of shuffling feet and hymnals dropping into bookrests, the flock sat on the hard wooden pews.

"Bow your heads and ask for God's blessing," came Gentry's booming voice. "He will cleanse you of your sins, if you will only ask Him to." The preacher raised both arms and closed his eyes. "Does something trouble your heart? Give it to the Lord! Have you done a deed that separates you from His love? Give it to the Lord! Do you harbor a grudge that darkens His light in your soul? Give it to the Lord!"

A hush befell the church as members of the flock searched their hearts and minds for sins to confess. As their murmurs sought God's ear, Clay's heart pounded. For while these good people of Spring Creek had been compassionate regarding his brother's condition, Clay had not. Until Brynne had shared her opinions with him, he had believed that the boy didn't need sympathy and mollycoddling, but a firm hand. The trouble with Cullen, he'd told himself time and again, is life's been too easy. He's a spoiled, weak boy.

"Give it to God!" Pastor Gentry repeated.

I was ashamed of him, Lord, Clay prayed. *I thought he should be standing at the crossroads to manhood by now. . . .*

He watched as Cullen repeatedly folded and unfolded his hands. Clay shook his head. *Lord, how can I help him?*

". . .give it to your Father in heaven!"

"Give it to the Lord!" the congregation repeated.

I give it to You, Clay prayed, *and I beg You. . .bring Cullen around. Help me to forgive him for his weakness.*

❧

"So good to see you," Pastor Gentry said, smiling and nodding as he greeted each parishioner in turn. "Good morning, Brynne. Don't you look lovely this morning."

Blushing, she tucked a flyaway curl under her bonnet. "That was quite a sermon, Reverend. Why, I believe your voice will vibrate in my ears till well past dinnertime!"

"You have a gift for changing the subject," he said, taking her hand, "but I have one, too. My dear mama called it a stubborn streak." Patting the hand he held, Gentry leaned close to say, "You make it difficult for me to do my job."

Her eyebrows drew together in a confused frown as she took back her hand. "You job? I'm afraid I don't. . ."

Chuckling, Gentry grabbed her other hand. "It isn't easy preaching fire and brimstone when you're staring into the sweet face of an angel."

Clay stood at the back of the church, waiting his turn to descend the stone steps. He'd never been overly fond of the hand-shaking ritual that concluded every Sunday service. Today, he found it even harder to bear. Look at him! *Why, he's flirting shamelessly with her,* he fumed mentally. *Him, a man of God, and here, on the steps of the church!*

The conversation between the women in front of him captured Clay's attention.

"Pastor Gentry is quite a specimen, don't you think?" the Widow Jenson whispered.

"Mmm-hmm," her elderly sister agreed. "I've always been particularly fond of blond-haired, blue-eyed men." Winking, she added, "If I were a few years younger. . ."

The widow giggled. "A few years! Why, Annabelle, you're old enough to be his great-grandma!"

Her sister sighed. "Well, still, I wouldn't mind a few minutes in Brynne Carter's shoes right about now."

A heavyset gray-haired woman barged to the front of the line and shoved Brynne aside. "Pastor Gentry, I am appalled!"

"Ah, Mrs. Anderson," he purred, ignoring her angry tone, "Lovely day, isn't it?"

The woman tucked in her chins. "If you think you can sweet-talk me the way you sweet-talked her," she spat, casting a glare in Brynne's direction, "you've got another think coming!"

Gentry bowed slightly. "Can't have too many 'thinks,' I always say."

"Save your charm for someone who appreciates it," she snarled. "What sort of preacher carries on so shamelessly in the House of God?"

The pastor drew himself up to his full six-foot height. There wasn't a trace of a smile on his face when he said, "The sort who's tired of the bachelor's life." He directed his next comment to Brynne. "And if Miss Carter would agree, I'd like nothing better than to escort her to the church picnic next Saturday."

Mrs. Anderson huffed off without another word as Clay watched Brynne's cheek flush crimson. It seemed to him she didn't want to attend the picnic as the preacher's companion. "I'm afraid Miss Carter is already spoken for," Clay blurted. Marching to the front of the line, he pumped the pastor's arm. "She will be going to the picnic. . ." He cast a glance in her direction, and nothing could have pleased him more than the relieved smile on her face. ". . .She'll be going with me."

It was the reverend's turn to blush. "Oh. I, uh, I see." He tipped an imaginary hat in Brynne's direction and shot her a disappointed smile, then turned to greet the next person in line.

Clay offered Brynne his elbow and together, they headed down the flagstone walk. "Thank you for coming to my rescue," she said, grinning up at him, "but I know how you feel about church events, so you needn't feel obliged to. . ."

"Obliged?" he broke in, facing her. "Why, I'd be honored."

If she continued looking up at him, blinking those long-lashed dark eyes and smiling that way, Clay thought he might just be obliged to kiss that very kissable mouth. "I've been meaning to have a word with you," he started, "about. . ."

She walked through the gate. "And I've been meaning to have a word with you."

Clay felt like a schoolboy in the throes of his first mad crush as he stepped along beside her. "Oh? About what?"

"About the wonderful things you've done for Spring Creek." She stopped walking and faced the church. "Just look at what all the scrap wood you donated has created. It's a lovely church. A wonderful schoolhouse.

Better, even, than what we had before. Why, there was enough to build a new home for the pastor." Brynne met his eyes.

Clay tucked in one corner of his mouth. "The pastor's house," he grated, his eyes narrowing as he glanced at Gentry. "Maybe I should have been a little less generous." He met her eyes to say, "But how did you know I donated. . ."

Shrugging, she smiled. "The only person in a small town who knows more than the doctor is the schoolmarm. Children are filled with all sorts of delightful—and personal—facts." She leaned in close to add, "Billy Donnelly's pa is. . ."

". . .the fellow who designed the buildings," he finished, shaking his head incredulously. Clay heaved a sigh. And grinning, he said, "Well, I'm glad you let me in on your secret. It's a good thing to know if a man aims to be, uh, friends with the teacher."

She crossed both arms over her chest and tapped one foot. "Go ahead. You may as well confess the rest."

"Confess?" Clay's brow wrinkled with confusion. "The rest?"

Rolling her eyes with feigned exasperation, Brynne began counting on her fingers all she knew about him. "You not only donated the wood from the outbuildings on your property, you handed over windowpanes and hardware as well. And," she said with a tilt of her head, "you did quite a bit of the work yourself."

He was certain his cheeks were redder even than Gentry's had been moments ago. Clay took her hand and led her away from the church and didn't stop until they were shrouded by the low-hanging branches of a weeping willow tree. "I've been thinking a lot about you."

"Cullen's doing quite well, don't you think?" she injected.

He waved the comment away. "Mmm. Yes. A little better." He looked at her distractedly, then blurted, "I dreamt of you last night."

A small gasp escaped her lips as her eyes widened. Pressing a hand to her bosom, she glossed over his comment. "Did you see the A-plus Cullen got on his last arithmetic test? And did you know that I saw him following along as one of the other students read a passage out loud," she rattled, "his finger underlining every word in his history book. He was even moving his lips! And—"

Clay grabbed her by the shoulders and pulled her to him. "I'm glad Cullen has finally decided to come out of his confounded self-induced, self-pitying trance. It's high time he started behaving like a man, if you ask me," he said through clenched teeth. "But—"

"You shouldn't be so hard on him, Clay. He's barely more than a boy."

Boy, my foot! he wanted to counter. But then he remembered what he had prayed during church, and he felt his impatience being washed away as he looked at her. The way she stood there, hands pressed against his chest and trusting eyes searching his face, made his heart beat fast.

Clay was a man who never did anything without first devising a careful plan. He hadn't planned what he might say if he got her alone. Hadn't planned to get her alone! But now that he had, he wouldn't let opportunity slip by.

"Brynne," he rasped, "have you any idea what a difference you've made in—"

"Helping Cullen was just part of my job," she interrupted.

Clay smiled as his hands slid slowly from her shoulders to cup her cheeks. "And what about the difference you've made in my life? Is that part of your job, too?"

"Your life?" Her lips parted with surprise as Brynne glanced left, then right. "I suppose. . .I guess. . .It's only natural," she stammered, "that any positive effect I've had on Cullen would also. . ."

His thumbs followed the contours of her jaw. "The effect you've had on me has very little to do with what you've done for my brother," he grated. "I've been watching you, almost from the moment I limped back from the war, and—"

"How did it happen?" she interrupted, straightening his tie with a wifely nonchalance that made his face burn.

"How did what happen?" he asked, confused.

"Your wound, of course."

"Mortar shell." Clay shrugged one shoulder. "Blew a chunk of my thigh away." He searched her face for any trace of sympathy.

As though she could read his mind, she lifted one brow and grinned. "Well, you'll get no pity from me, Mr. Adams." Nodding at his injured leg, she added, "Your leg got you here, alone with me under this tree, didn't it?"

"That it did," he said, smiling.

Still grinning, she put a hand on a hip and narrowed one eye. "Exactly why did you bring me. . .?"

Brynne never finished her question, for her words were swallowed up by Clay's insistent kiss.

Chapter 7

August 12, 1865

To the Carter Family
Spring Creek, Virginia

When I left your warmth and hospitality, I promised to find out what I could about the Colonel.

Well, I met a man who spent some time in the camp where they took the Colonel. He says he never met anyone name of Richard Carter. Could be he never heard of him because the Colonel was one of a dozen or so soldiers who escaped one night during a thunderstorm.

I am not one to believe in false hope. I can only say that I pray the Colonel was one of the lucky ones who stole their freedom that stormy night.

If I hear anything more, I will get word to you. My thoughts and prayers are with you.

Very truly yours,
Trevor McDermott Williams

Why does bad news always arrive right on the heels of bad news? Brynne wondered. Guilt hammered her heart as her mother flitted about the kitchen, giggling happily.

"I told you he was alive!" Amelia gasped, flapping Trevor's letter in the air. "Your father escaped from that nasty old prisoner of war camp, and right this minute he's making his way back to us!"

Brynne's heart ached with fear and dread—fear that her mother would find out that she'd been an unwitting accomplice in her father's death, dread that her father would never rest in peace, as she'd hoped, on Kismet Hill—thanks to the information she'd stupidly passed on to Ross Bartlett.

Over and over again, her mind replayed the memory that was torturing her: the day when Ross had wrapped his arms around her and he told her he'd be leaving on the morning train. He'd looked so handsome in his wide-brimmed black hat and many-buttoned uniform, a gleaming cutlass at his hip. She'd thought at the time it had been concern for her family that prompted Ross to ask where her father and brother would be stationed. If she'd known how he intended use the facts, she'd never have willingly shared what her father had written in an earlier letter: "The only way into Fort Fisher is by way of a narrow channel, so fear not, family, for I am safe, so long as the Yankees don't try a land and sea attack!"

It wasn't until she paid her respects to the Prentices last week that Brynne learned what Ross had done with the information. . . .

Joshua Prentice had also served—and died—at Fort

Fisher. After church, Joshua's sister Camille told Brynne a long story, all about how Camille's father, who had been an officer at Fort Fisher, explained the fall of the fortress: The Union army and navy had attacked simultaneously, and the South, though well-manned and well-armed, had not been equipped for the two-pronged attack.

"My daddy says he saw your ex-fiancé leadin' the Bluecoats in," Camille added with a baleful glare. "One minute, Ross was givin' orders to the Yankees, next minute the east tower was toppling over on my poor sweet brother." Her eyes narrowed. "And I wouldn't be surprised if your own father was there too."

Camille had paused to dry her eyes on a dainty hanky. "They nearly caught Ross, slinking away from the melee." All ladylike decorum was set aside as Camille made her final statement. "If that low-down polecat ever shows his face 'round these parts again, he'll wish they had hanged him."

Brynne had gone over and over it in her head, and try as she might, she could not escape one ugly fact: because of her loose tongue, hundreds of men—her own father included—had died!

She made an effort to pull her thoughts together and pay attention to her mother. "Mama," she said, a hand on Amelia's arm, "seems to me the sergeant made it clear there isn't much sense in holding out for. . ."

"Brynne Amelia Carter," her mother hissed, shoulders hunched and fists bunched, "I'll not have such talk in this house." Her eyes blazed with indignation. "Your father is alive, and he will come home." She shook the balled-up letter under Brynne's nose. "You promised once that you'd keep your negative comments to yourself. I'm holding you to it, do you hear?"

In all her life, Brynne had never seen her mother so angry. At least, she'd never been as angry with her. "I'm sorry, Mama. I never intended to hurt you. I only thought. . ."

"I know what you thought," Amelia bit out. "You thought if you were patient long enough, I'd stop behaving like a dotty old woman and come around to your way of thinking." She took a deep breath, then lovingly smoothed the letter against her stomach and put it back into the envelope.

Fresh tears filled her eyes. "I believe your father is alive, and I'll go right on believing it," she said past the hitch in her voice, "because your father can read me like a book, and I won't have him seeing a trace of faithlessness on my face when he walks through that door. Not after all he's been through."

More than anything, Brynne wanted to console her mother. But words and actions would seem empty and hollow to this woman who saw her daughter as a disloyal skeptic. Tears brimmed in her own eyes as she hurried to the back door. "I'm sorry, Mama," she repeated as she ran outside, "so sorry. . ."

Brynne didn't stop running until she'd reached the summit. There, she fell on her knees and looked toward the heavens. "Lord," she cried, "help me deal with this horrible secret. . .and to discern between false hope—and faith in what is possible."

Brynne did want to share her mother's steadfast

conviction, for she missed her father desperately. But, in the years since he'd been gone, she'd taught schoolchildren that two plus two equals four, C-A-T spells cat, Paris is the capital of France. Those facts were as undisputable as Ross Bartlett's acts of treachery and the ruination of her beloved South. Did her mother really expect her to accept the remote possibility that her father had survived the brutality of this awful war? Faith in God's might and power was one thing, but. . .

"Brynne?"

Immediately, she recognized the deep timbre of his voice. *But how did Clay find me here?* she wondered, dabbing her eyes with a corner of her apron. Ever since that day beneath the willow tree, she cared very much what he thought of her. He'd told her, when that first delicious kiss ended, how much he admired her strength of character. What would he think if he saw that she'd given in to self-pitying tears? What would he think if he knew the reason for them?

"Your sister-in-law told me I might find you here," Clay said, settling beside her and sliding an arm over her shoulders. "This is quite a view you have on the world," he said after a moment. "It's easy to see why you've kept it such a well-guarded secret."

"This was my father's favorite place," she said softly. "He came here often, when the trials and tribulations of life beset him."

He lifted her chin on a bent forefinger. "And what trials and tribulations have brought you here, my sweet Brynne?"

Silently, Brynne repeated his endearing words. *If*

you knew the answer to that question, you wouldn't be looking at me with such care in your eyes, she told him mentally. *I am here because I'm a faithless follower and a miserable excuse for a daughter. And that's the very least of my sins.*

He pressed a kiss to her temple. "Why is this place called Kismet Hill?"

"My father, like his father-in-law and Grandpa Moore before him, was often drawn to this place. Papa had read in one of his books that, in the far east, kismet means 'God's will.' It was God's will, he believed, that his father-in-law Grandpa Moore settled this land, and God's will that it remained in the family ever since."

Brynne brought Clay's attention to the stubborn little pine, growing from the boulder behind them. "Papa said this was God's will, too." She sighed. "It's been here for as long as I can remember, growing slow and steady, despite the constant wind and the bitter cold and the desolation of this place."

He took her hands in his. "Seems to me if God could make that pitiful little thing grow where nothing else could, He truly can do the impossible."

The impossible, Brynne repeated mentally. Could Clay's simple words be God's answer to her prayer? A hopeful smile lifted the corners of her mouth.

"What're you grinning about?" Clay asked, wiping an errant tear from her cheek.

"Just the fact that you seem to be a mind reader."

"I can't read your mind, Brynne, but I think I know what's in your heart."

The mere thought of it set her pulse to racing. Brynne

didn't want him to know the truth about her part in the devastation that befell Fort Fisher. . . .

He kissed each of her eyelids, her chin, the tip of her nose. "You're feeling guilty because you don't share your mother's optimism about your father's safe return. You don't think he survived the prisoners' camp, do you?"

Brynne focused on their hands. "I don't see how he could have." There was venom in her voice when she said, "The sergeant who delivered Papa's last letter described how things were the day the Yankees took my father away."

"You really hate them, don't you?"

She set her jaw. "I've tried not to. I've tried, instead, to hate what they've done. But sometimes it's hard to separate the vicious acts from the men who committed them."

Clay nodded. "I felt the same way for a long time." Unconsciously, he stroked his mangled thigh. "But I'm realizing that God can't come close to me, not when I hold such bitterness in my heart. I've had to let go of my anger and forgive. That's the only way I can feel close to God again. But it's not easy." On a lighter note, he added, "Still, God calls us to have faith."

Brynne harumphed. "In what?"

"Why, in Him, of course."

"I have plenty of faith in the Lord." *It's He who has lost faith in me,* she thought dismally. "Death is as much a part of life as birth. I think He also calls us to accept that."

"If you really felt that way, you wouldn't be here."

"How can you possibly know why I'm here?"

"I overheard your prayer. Deep in your heart, you hope your mother is right."

Brynne snatched back her hands. "You couldn't be more wrong! That wasn't why I was praying. It's my fault. All my fault," she spat, then bit her lip to keep back the words that would reveal her guilt. She choked, then continued more calmly, "But that doesn't change the fact that my mother may as well try to hold onto the air, for all the good her hope is doing her."

"She's holding onto the air every time she takes a breath. Seems to be doing a pretty good job, that air, at keeping her alive."

Who do you think you are, Brynne demanded silently, *coming up here, uninvited, telling me what I think and feel?* She leapt to her feet and began pacing a few steps from where he sat.

" 'When the Spirit of truth comes,' " Clay recited, " 'he will guide you. . .' "

Guide me to what? she demanded silently. *To tell the truth and face the hatred of everyone in Spring Creek who lost a loved one at Fort Fisher? No thank you!* "How is it you can quote the Book of John so easily, yet you can barely tolerate sitting through a Sunday service?" she snapped. "I may not believe in the impossible, but I haven't turned my back on God!"

"What makes you think I have?"

She took several steps closer to face him. "You stopped going to church."

Clay sighed. "I only stayed away to give myself time. . ."

"Your leg was healed long before your first visit to the Spring Hill church, Mister Holier-than-thou!"

He chuckled quietly. "I stayed away," he continued as though she'd never interrupted, "to give my head time to clear, so that when folks slathered me with pitying comments and sympathetic stares, I wouldn't respond with anger and resentment. I was angry with church—but that didn't mean I'd given up on God."

She understood only too well what he'd said. Brynne had yet to figure out a way to deal with those well-intended yet hurtful comments that came when people heard what happened to her father. What would they say if they knew the whole truth?

" 'O ye of little faith,' " Clay said, smiling slightly. " 'Do not be anxious. . .for your heavenly Father knows your needs.' "

If she and Clay had been anywhere else, Brynne might have kept a rein on her taut emotions, might have repressed the sob aching in her throat and the grief beating in her heart. But they were not somewhere else. They were high atop Kismet Hill, her father's favorite place. Never again would he enjoy the pristine view as the crisp winds fingered through his hair. Never again would he hear the screech of an eagle overhead, or the rushing river waters below. All because of her!

Brynne slumped onto the rock where the pine grew, and hid her face in her hands. Before the first tear slipped between her fingers, Clay was beside her, engulfing her in a reassuring embrace. She had allowed herself a few tears here and there since the war began. But here, in his arms in this special place, Brynne let herself mourn openly, for Edward, for Moorewood, for Virginia, for her father.

"It's all right," he whispered, stroking her hair. "It's going to be all right."

Too ashamed to admit her horrible sin to Clay and unable to trust herself to make up some other excuse to leave Kismet Hill, Brynne scrambled to her feet and, without a word, ran toward Moorewood.

She didn't get far before Clay caught up to her. "Talk to me, Brynne," he said, gripping her upper arms. "What did you mean when you said it was your fault? What's your fault?"

Too much had happened in too little time, shattering Brynne's control. "If. . .if I, if I tell you," she began haltingly, "will you leave me in peace?"

A faint smile glittered in his eyes. "I doubt it." He gave her a gentle shake. "Let me help you, Brynne."

She bit her lower lip to stanch the tears that burned behind her eyelids. "If you could help me, it would be a miracle," she sighed, her voice foggy with grief and sadness.

For a long moment, Clay didn't speak. "We're on Kismet Hill," he said at last, nodding toward the little pine. "If a miracle can happen anyplace, it's here."

Chapter 8

When she had finished her miserable story, he was silent for a moment, and she could not look at him; she was too afraid of the condemnation she would read in his eyes. "I love you," he said softly, and her eyes flew to his face. "Don't you know that by now?"

In the past few months, as they'd walked hand in hand down his magnolia-lined drive or sat side by side on her mother's porch swing, Brynne and Clay had discussed many things, from his brother's problems to world politics. Most of the time, though, he had kept a tight rein on his emotions.

But sometimes, when the breeze was soft and the birds were singing, Clay would hint that he loved her. Several times, she'd caught him staring at her, and she had been warmed all over by what she thought she saw in his dark eyes. If their hands accidentally touched as they exchanged Cullen's schoolwork, she felt the heat of his feelings for her. And every kiss since that first one, beneath the willow tree, had told her how much she had come to mean to him.

Still. . .he'd never said the words aloud.

"I'm a traitorous blabbermouth," she reminded him, "not a mind reader."

Clay held her at arm's length, his hot gaze boring deep into her eyes. "You knew that Bartlett was a double agent?"

Brynne's jaw dropped with shock. "Of course not! I only just found out."

He pressed a silencing finger over her lips. "Mm-hm. But if you had known, would you have told him what was in your father's letter?"

Shaking her head, Brynne's eyes filled with fresh tears. "Absolutely not," she whispered hoarsely.

"So it's just as I said. . .you're not responsible for what happened."

She turned away, unable to continue looking into his confidant gaze. Oh, how she loved this man! While Ross had been courting her, she had thought what she'd felt for him had been love. She couldn't have been more wrong, she realized now.

Sadly, she'd never taken the measure of the man, hadn't called Ross's character into question, hadn't weighed the positives against the negatives in his personality. He'd entered her life when her girlfriends were either married or engaged. It had seemed time to begin planning the future—a husband, children, a home—and so when he'd asked her to marry him, Brynne never considered any answer but yes. If she'd known what kind of man he'd been. . .

Brynne knew what he was made of now, not only by his own words and deeds, but in comparison to Clay, who had willingly gone off to war, prepared to die, if he must, so others might live. Once Clay had returned from battle, his leg damaged beyond repair, he avoided pity at all cost. He had been adamant about taking a stern, heavy-handed tactic to end Cullen's silence—and yet in the end his love for the boy had outshone his desire to have his own way. Because of his patience, Cullen was at last beginning to break free of grief's silence; in the past weeks he had begun to speak again.

Despite all these emotional burdens, Clay worked long, hard hours to keep Adams' Hill afloat—and yet he had put what little free time he had into helping rebuild Spring Creek's church and school. No, Clay was nothing like Ross.

The summer rolled by like a steaming locomotive as Brynne fell deeper and deeper in love with Clay. And, he continued to profess his undying love for her, despite her protestations that she was unworthy of it.

On Thanksgiving eve, the old-fashioned young man put on his best coat and tie and knocked on Amelia Carter's front door. To protect her from the clamminess of his palms, he didn't take her hand when Amelia opened it, and he cleared his throat to hide the tremors in his voice.

"There's something we must discuss," he said as Amelia stood back to let him in, "so if you have a moment. . ."

Over tea in her parlor, Clay told Brynne's mother, "Under ordinary circumstances, I would speak with the Colonel about this matter. But these are hardly ordinary circumstances."

Amelia nodded her agreement, her smile telling him that she knew why he'd come to see her. "I'm afraid

I'll have to do, then, since you haven't the patience to wait for Richard."

Clay met her eyes—and her statement—with straightforwardness. "I admire you, Mrs. Carter, for your steadfast belief that your husband will return, but there's no point beating around the bush, for as your daughter so aptly put it on the day we met, bush-beating is a waste of time that's hard on the shrubbery."

Amelia laughed softly. "That's my Brynne, all right!"

"Then we'll make a good pair, your daughter and I." He leaned both elbows on his knees and laced his fingers together. "This war has taught me that life is fleeting, at best," he began. "Call me foolish, or impetuous, but I haven't the time or the patience to wait for Colonel Carter to give his permission for Brynne to marry me. I'll take very good care of her and. . ."

"I'm sure you'll be an excellent provider, Clay," Amelia injected. She put her hand upon his sleeve. "But how does my daughter feel about this?"

He smiled sheepishly. "I didn't want to discuss marriage with her until I had your blessing."

She gave his arm an affectionate squeeze. "Do you love her?"

His heart beat double-time. "With all my heart."

Nodding, Amelia stood and walked to the French doors. "Have you a date in mind? For the wedding, I mean?"

Clay rose and joined her. "I thought I'd leave the details to you ladies."

Hands clasped at her waist, she focused on some distant spot known only to her. "You must promise me something, Clay."

"Anything."

She faced him, and in the late afternoon light that filtered through the bevelled panes, a silvery tear shimmered on her cheek. Amelia grabbed his hands. "Promise you'll never leave her, no matter what your male pride calls you to do." She blinked tear-clumped lashes. "Promise me you'll never break her heart the way. . ."

"I promise," he said, rescuing her from completing the sentence.

She lifted her chin and threw back her shoulders. "Well, then," Amelia said, "you have my blessing." She whispered conspiratorially, "So tell me, when do you plan to pop the question?"

Clay smiled. "Right now—if you'll be so kind as to tell me where to find her."

Amelia faced the horizon once more. "Where else?" she said on a sigh. "Kismet Hill."

Clay turned to leave, but her hand on his sleeve didn't allow it. "What are you and your brother planning for Thanksgiving?"

"Planning? A quiet meal, I suppose."

"Just the two of you?"

Clay nodded.

"Nonsense!" Amelia closed the curtains, blocking the light—and the view—with one snap of her arm. "You're family now. We eat at three, and we dress for dinner," she tossed over her shoulder, "so I hope you both have neckties."

Later that afternoon, Brynne watched as Clay walked away from her down Kismet Hill, his shoulders slumped with discouragement. Yes, she loved Clay Adams. But Brynne believed he deserved better than the likes of her, a silly woman who didn't know when to keep her mouth shut.

"I know what you're thinking," he had said softly, turning her to face him. "You're worried that if we were to marry, Cullen might have a relapse."

Brynne sighed heavily. That he'd considered his brother in the mix—while she'd focused on her own selfish needs—proved how wrong she was for him. "You deserve someone better than me," she admitted huskily. "That's what I was thinking."

Clay laughed. "Better than you? Darlin', there's no one on this earth more suited for me." He gathered her close and whispered into her hair. "You saved me, Brynne. Like the old song says, 'I once was lost, but now I'm found'. . .because of you. God used you so that I could learn to forgive. . .without you I would never have been able to forgive Cullen for what I thought was his weakness. Without the love I feel for you, I would still be nursing my anger at the Yankees. Your love has helped me to forgive. You're my miracle, Brynne, and I thank God for sending you to me."

Someday, she believed he would realize how wrong he was being. Until then, Brynne had to be strong enough to say no to his proposal. As much as it broke her heart, she couldn't marry him.

❧

"You haven't had much to say since Thanksgiving," Cullen said a month later, on Christmas Eve. "What's wrong—cat got your tongue?"

Clay good-naturedly elbowed his brother. "Look who's talking." He laughed.

"It's Brynne, isn't it? She's the reason you're so sad."

The older brother did not respond.

"If I were you, I'd find her, right now. Tell her how you feel. If she knew how miserable you've been, she'd marry you just to put a smile on your face!"

Clay said nothing.

Cullen frowned. "At least my silence had a good reason."

That brought Clay's head up. "What?"

The boy shrugged. " 'It is good that one should wait quietly for the salvation of the Lord. . .let him sit alone in silence. . .that there may yet be hope.' "

Cullen had quoted the Book of Lamentations, Clay acknowledged. "I don't get it."

"Ma and Pa went on down to Petersburg in the middle of a war to do church business, leaving us here to fend for ourselves. And you just home with a terrible wound! God couldn't have been pleased with them. I thought He might even be a little angry with them. So I decided to keep quiet, till I was sure He'd forgiven them. Turned out it was me that needed to forgive them, though. I was so angry with them—but once I'd forgiven them, then I knew that God would have forgiven them long ago. Way back when Jesus died on the cross, I guess. Nothing I could do could ever earn the forgiveness they needed for their prideful sin, because Jesus had already taken care of it. When you started taking me to church with you, that's when I figured it all out. And then I could begin to talk again."

"Prideful sin? Our parents? Cullen, you're not making sense."

"Yes, I am. They always took risks, without ever making provisions to protect themselves. If the body is His temple, He expects us to take care of it. Besides," Cullen continued, his voice hard-edged with anger, "we didn't need a new pastor right then. And even if we did, why couldn't someone else go and fetch him? Someone with no family obligations? They enjoyed the praises they got when they did good works. It wasn't faith that made them believe they could make that trip safely, it was pride."

"And stubbornness," Clay said dully.

Cullen gave his brother a slight shove. "You inherited it."

Clay frowned. "Which? Stubbornness, or pride?"

"Both."

He read the teasing glint in Cullen's eyes, and smiled. "Why, I oughta tan your hide, you ornery. . ."

"Sticks and stones will break my bones," the boy taunted, fists up as he hip-hopped like a boxer, "but proposals will never hurt me."

Just as he'd suspected, Clay found her at the top of Kismet Hill, bundled up like an Eskimo as she leaned into the biting wind. "What're you doing here in this miserable weather?" he shouted into the howling air currents.

Brynne pointed to the garden spade that lay at her feet. "I wanted to dig up the pine," she said, peeking out from under her fur-trimmed hood. "It would make a lovely Christmas tree, and afterward, we could plant it in the yard, as a memorial to my father."

"But. . .it's growing from a bed of rock."

"I thought I could hack away at it, bit by bit, until I freed the roots, and. . ."

Her voice floated away on a powerful gust as Clay looked at the boulder. She'd whittled away a considerable chunk of the rock. "Let me see your hands, Brynne," he said, taking a step closer.

She held them out. Gently, he slid off her gloves, and grimaced at the red, watery blisters that covered her palms. He wrapped her in a fierce hug. Rubbing her upper arms to warm her, Clay said, "Let's go back to the house and get the tools we need to do the job right."

"It's nearly noon. Do we have time?"

Cupping her face in his hands, he kissed her long and hard. "We're on Kismet Hill, remember. . .the place where miracles happen!"

They'd been hard at it for hours, Clay hefting the sledgehammer, Brynne holding the chisel steady, when the last bit of stubborn rock finally gave way, exposing the tree's gnarled roots.

Clay was amazed at the way the roots had burrowed into a hollow in the boulder. Over time, he surmised, the constant winds must have blown dust and dirt and leaves into the crevice, and the debris had nestled there, as though waiting for the little seed to float into its nourishing bed.

He stood and faced the valley, flexing his aching hands as Brynne led the horse and buggy as close as the rocky surface would allow. "Praise God that's over," he said, working the kinks from his neck. "I thought we'd need to blast it out, and I'm plum out of dyna. . ."

His voice faded away. The expression on his face made Brynne race to his side. "What is it? What do you see?"

Clay pointed to a form below them, half-mile or so away.

It was a man, walking alone, leaning heavily on a cane and dragging one foot behind him. His step-slide-clomp, step-slide-clomp echoed quietly over the rocks and floated to them on blasts of wintry wind. When he stopped and looked up at them, the blood froze in Brynne's veins.

Clay slid a protective arm around her waist and pulled her close. "My rifle is in the wagon," he said through clenched teeth. "I'd hate to have to use it on Christmas Eve."

Her pulse pounded in her ears as the distant stranger made an eerie eye contact with her. Something about him seemed familiar. But what? Brynne held her breath, watching, waiting.

The man raised his left arm, made a fist of the hand, and thrust his forefinger into the air. Only one man had ever waved that way.

"Papa," she whispered.

Clay's gaze swung to Brynne's dazzled face. "Are you sure?"

In place of an answer, she scuttled down the rocks and ran full-out until she stood no more than ten feet from him. Her joyous cry reverberated from every nook and cranny around them as she flung herself into his arms.

8:00 P.M., Christmas Eve, 1865

Richard was surprised that not one of the messages he'd sent by way of returning soldiers had reached his family. When their jubilant welcoming hugs and kisses subsided, he explained that in the seven months since President Johnson issued amnesty to those who'd taken part in the "rebellion," Richard had recuperated in the home of an elderly Yankee widow.

"We can harbor the Northerners no ill will," he warned, "because for every dastardly deed one of them did, another of them did a kindness."

The woman's son, Richard said, had been killed at Gettysburg, yet she'd risked the ire of friends and family to tend Richard's wounds, wash his clothes, feed him healthy meals. When he was able, he left her humble abode, hitching rides with returning Confederate soldiers, pausing in his journey only long enough for meals and rest.

After downing bowls of thick vegetable stew, the family set about decorating the pitiful little Christmas tree, each acknowledging, as they hung the ornaments, what they were thankful for.

Cullen gave thanks that not only could he speak again, but that anger and bitterness and grief no longer filled his heart.

Edward and Julia praised God for the child He'd bring them in the spring, a brother or sister for little Richie.

"I'm thankful for the miracle of having my husband back," Amelia said.

"And I'm thankful to be back," came Richard's reply.

His wife snuggled into the crook of his arm. "I always knew you'd come home."

"Believing in your faith and loyalty was my miracle." He focused on Clay. "What about you, boy? What are you thankful for?"

Clay's gaze sought out Brynne's. "There's so much, I don't know where to begin. Let's just say I'm grateful to have your daughter in my life. She is my miracle." He strode purposefully toward her, and took her hands in his. "If she'd consent to be my wife, I'd think I'd died and gone to heaven."

She met his eyes, and for the moment, they were alone in the universe. *Except,* she thought, *for "God also bearing them witness, both with signs and wonders and with diverse miracles. . .according to his own will. . ."*

She glanced at her mother, whose faith in the miracle of her father's return had never wavered. At her father, who admitted that belief in that faith is what gave him the strength to take each painful step home. At Cullen, who'd finally broken free from his prison of silence. At Clay, who'd called her his miracle. She took a deep breath, and she felt the burden of fear and guilt that she had carried slip off her back.

In the glow of the fire's light, Brynne's eyes misted. "I think we should start the year off right and be married on January first."

Epilogue

June 1866

When they reached the summit, Clay covered her eyes with his neckerchief. "You're sure you can't see anything, now?"

"Positive," Brynne said. "Now, what's all the secrecy about?"

He led her to the highest point on Kismet Hill and helped her sit on the boulder where the little pine had grown. The tree had brightened their Christmas and now thrived on the Carter lawn, where Amelia could see it each time she peered through the parlor's French doors.

"Ready for your surprise?"

Grinning with exasperation, Brynne sighed. "Clay, really. Stop teasing, or I'll. . ."

He whipped off her blindfold and directed her attention to the hole they'd carved from the big rock.

Clasping both hands under her chin, Brynne gasped. "I don't believe it. How do you explain a thing like this?"

He sat beside her and hugged her to him. "There's only one way to explain it." Gently, he touched the tiny sprig of green that would one day grow into a scrub pine. "It's a miracle." Pulling her into his lap, he said, "I love you, Mrs. Clay Adams."

Tenderly, she laid her right hand against his cheek. "And I love you."

He held her gaze for a silent, intense moment. " 'Thou dost show me the path of life, in thy presence there is fullness of joy, in thy right hand are pleasures for evermore.' I reckon that about describes what the Lord has done for me." He was taken aback when tears filled her eyes. "I had no idea the Book of Psalms had such an effect on you," he teased.

Brynne snuggled into the crook of his neck. "It's just that. . .well. . .I have a surprise for you, too."

"No blindfold?" he asked, chuckling. "I'm disappointed."

"I saw the doctor yesterday. . ."

Holding her at arm's length, he frowned. "The doctor? Why? You're. . .you're not ill, are you?"

Smiling serenely, Brynne shook her head. "Of course not, silly." Tilting her head, she said, "It seems we're going to have a baby."

Clay's eyes widened with awe and wonderment. "A. . . a baby?" He leapt up and danced a merry jig. "I'm gonna be a father!" he bellowed. His joyous shout echoed across the valley, and when it bounced back to him, he sat beside her again, and pressed his palm to her belly. "When, Brynne? When will our child be born?"

"Christmas."

"Christmas," he sighed. He gathered her close and whispered into her ear, " 'A man attested to you by God with mighty works and wonders and signs.' "

"Yes, Clay," she agreed. "Another miracle. . .on Kismet Hill."

Loree Lough

A full-time writer for over twelve years, Loree has produced more than 1,700 published articles, dozens of short stories that have appeared in various magazines, and two books for the American Adventure series for 8–12 year olds (Barbour Publishing). The author of fifteen inspirational romances, including the award-winning *Pocketful of Love* (Heartsong Presents), Loree also writes as Cara McCormack and Aleesha Carter. A prolific and talented writer, gifted teacher, and comedic conference speaker, Loree lives in Maryland with her husband, two daughters, and two constantly-warring cats.

God Jul

Tracie Peterson

Chapter 1

OSTAKA

(Swedish Pudding)

2 eggs
1 cup cream
½ cup flour
¼ tsp. salt
Oven at 400°F
2 quarts milk
½ rennet tablet
½ cup sugar

Beat eggs and ½ cup cream together, add flour and mix until smooth. Add salt. Heat milk to lukewarm and add mixture. Soften rennet tablet in a spoonful of water and add to mixture, stirring slowly until evenly mixed. Let stand for 10 minutes then bake in hot oven at 400°F for 30 minutes. Then turn oven down to 350°F and bake for 1 hour. Take out of oven and pour remaining ½ cup of cream and sugar over it and bake at 350°F for an additional 20 minutes. As the pudding is formed, the whey (milky liquid) may threaten to run over, so use a deep pan. Serve with sweetened berries.

Lindsborg, Kansas

Sigrid Larsson stared in stony silence at the pine casket. Inside, her mother's body lay in final rest and even now as the pastor spoke of the resurrection to come, Sigrid felt a terrible loss. She had built her life around her mother's needs and now she was gone, and at twenty-seven Sigrid felt she was far too old to start a new life.

Even if I wanted to start over, she chided herself, what would I do? Who would have me, an old spinster with nothing to offer?

She looked around the circle of mourners to find friends and family whom she cherished dearly. She was alone. They had each other. They were husbands and wives and children, and together they made up families. Her family had started out to include a mother, father, sister and brother, but now they were gone. Father had died fifteen years ago in a railroad accident, and with that one stroke of fate, her life had changed. At twelve she had been forced into adulthood in many ways.

"Let us close by singing together," the pastor stated, then boomed out the words of a well-known hymn in a deep heavy bass.

Sigrid mouthed the words, uncertain that she could actually sing. *How can you sing when your heart is so heavy?* She glanced up to find Erik Lindquist staring at her with a sympathetic, yet otherwise unreadable expression. His blue eyes were the same shade as her own, a rather pale, icy blue. His blond hair, straight as string as her mother would have said, was parted down the middle and slicked back on either side. He looked most uncomfortable in his "Sunday-go-to-meeting" clothes and Sigrid would have laughed had the circumstance not weighed so heavy on her heart.

Erik had been her mother's hired man for the last twelve years. He owned the property next to theirs and when he learned of the Larsson women's struggles to survive and keep the farmstead running, he had gone to Bothilda Larsson, or Tilly, as most folks called her, and struck a deal. He would farm their land, as well as his own, and split the profits down the middle. Bothilda and Sigrid would care for the dairy cows, pigs and chickens as was in keeping with Swedish traditions. American men might take the reins of caring for the animals, but Tilly thought it funny to see a Swedish man trying to milk a cow.

The arrangement worked well for everyone, including Sigrid's brother, Sven, who had a new family and land of his own to worry about. He seemed more than happy to turn over the responsibilities of his parents' homestead to Erik. Sigrid had been the one to protest, but she knew it was of little use to argue. She couldn't very well farm the land herself, yet she had resented the interference of an outsider. Even if that outsider was a rather nice-looking, young Swedish man.

The singing had concluded and people were coming up to offer her their condolences.

"Tilly will be missed for sure," Mr. Anderson told her.

"Ja, t'ings won't be the same without her," another

man assured Sigrid.

Mrs. Swanson and Mrs. Moberg both took hold of her hands at the same time and tearfully lamented the loss of their dear friend. Sigrid tried not to notice that her mother's casket was slowly being lowered into the ground.

"Come along," yet another of her mother's friends announced, "we've laid food at your house, Sigrid."

Sigrid nodded and allowed the women to herd her along to the awaiting carriage. She thought it funny that she should ride when so often she had walked the distance from church to home. But the women insisted she ride, in spite of her own longing to be left alone. Grief and mourning make folks do strange things to offer comfort, she thought.

The Larsson farmstead was situated on the east side of Lindsborg, just far enough away to make a walk into town a good stretch of the limbs. Her father had managed to secure a prime tract of land when they'd first come to the area in 1869, and in her entire life, Sigrid had never ventured any further than a ten-mile radius from the tiny town.

She loved her home, and her heart swelled with pride as they approached the narrow drive that marked the property. Sigrid stared at the white clapboard house and felt a real sense of peace. Her mother might be gone from her in a physical sense, but she would live on in this house and in the things that surrounded Sigrid. She would simply remain here the rest of her days, living as best she could, and always she would remember the good times she'd known when her family had all been together.

The carriage came to a halt and before she actually realized what was happening, Erik Lindquist had appeared to help her down. She felt small beside his six-foot-two frame. He towered over her by nearly a foot and his big, callused hands betrayed signs of hard work. Farming in Kansas was at worst a practice in futility, and at best a labor of love. Her mother used to say that Job's patience had never been tested to the extent of trying to grow crops in Kansas. Sigrid smiled at the thought and Erik seemed taken aback.

"Someone tell a joke?" he asked, leaning down to whisper in her ear.

She startled at the warmth of his breath on her neck. "No, I was just remembering something Moder used to say."

"If you were remembering Tilly's words then I'm sure I understand."

He offered her a gentle smile and stepped away just as Sven approached.

"Sigrid, Ina and I want to talk to you."

Sigrid sighed and nodded. She could well imagine that neither her brother nor sister wanted to worry about her grieving on her own. They were no doubt going to suggest she come spend a few months living with one or the other of them. And, frankly, most folks would expect her to do something just like that. But Sigrid didn't want to leave the house. She wanted to stay on and think about her life. She wanted to watch another spring blend into summer and then autumn.

She followed her stocky, blond brother into the house

and was surprised to find Ina standing alone while her husband, Clarence, herded their five children outside.

The sisters embraced and nodded at each other with stoic expressions securely fixed in place. Their family had never been given to public spectacles of grief and as was true of many of their Swedish friends and extended family, they weren't ones for showing much emotion.

"So, what is it you wanted to talk about?" Sigrid asked, looking from Ina to Sven and back again. In the background, the clatter of dishes and women's chatter caused Sven to motion the sisters to one of the side bedrooms off of the main living area.

"Ina and I have discussed it and we both agree that the house should be sold immediately," Sven said, as though the matter was settled. "I've talked to Olga and she said it would a great help to have you around the place."

"You want to sell *Fader* and *Moder*'s house?" she asked in disbelief.

It was as if no one had heard her, however, as her sister picked up the matter. "I'm happy for you to come and stay with us part of the time, as well. You could sleep with Bridgett in the loft bedroom. You know how she adores you."

Sigrid stared at them both as though the meaning of their words had eluded her. "I don't know what to think."

"That's why I figured on taking care of the matter for you," Sven said, with the authoritative air of an older brother. "I'll put up a notice and—"

"No!" Sigrid said, suddenly finding her voice. "I don't want to sell."

Ina looked at her with wide blue eyes. "What do you mean? Surely you don't want to stay on here alone. Moder wouldn't want you to be here alone."

"Of course, she can't stay here," Sven said, quite seriously.

"I'm a grown woman, Sven. There is no reason why I can't stay here. I'm fully capable of doing what work needs to be done. Erik is taking care of the farming, and the rest of the work was pretty much my responsibility anyway." She paused to settle her nerves. With only the tiniest hint of emotion in her voice, she continued. "Erik already has the ground turned and the planting will be finished within the week. I've got peas and potatoes planted and you can't expect me to just up and let someone else reap the benefits of my labors."

"I've got plenty of peas and potatoes at my place," Sven countered. "Be reasonable, Sigrid. Ina and Clarence need the money and so do I. Last year's crops weren't that good and—"

"I don't want to move. This is my home. I stayed behind while you both married and went your ways," Sigrid protested in uncharacteristic anger. "I think I deserve to live out my days here."

"You could marry," Ina suggested. "You aren't so very old that a bachelor or widower wouldn't see the use in having you around."

Sigrid felt as though her sister had somehow just insulted her. It wasn't that she didn't know the odds were against her finding a love match and marrying. It wasn't even that her sister spoke aloud the sentiments that Sigrid had already considered many times. It was. . .

well. . .it was just more than she wanted to have to deal with at that precise moment.

"We can talk about this tomorrow," Sven said, opening the bedroom door. He looked out into the living room as if seeking someone. "Olga's going to wonder what's keeping me."

"Come stay with us tonight," Ina said, softly as she turned to follow Sven.

"No," Sigrid stated firmly. "I'm not going anywhere."

Ina shrugged, while Sven rolled his eyes and grunted something unintelligible before leaving the room. Sigrid closed the door behind her sister and leaned back against it to calm herself. *How dare they try to force me from the only home I've ever known!* She felt somehow betrayed and the only thing she wanted to do was hide away in this room until everyone else went home.

She glanced around and sighed. *Am I being foolish? Is it completely unreasonable to want to stay here, even if it means staying alone?*

A light rap sounded on the door. Sigrid bolstered her courage and turned to open it. Ella Swanson, Sigrid's lifelong friend, stood holding a bowl of *ostkaka* and lingonberries.

"I thought your favorite dessert might help," Ella offered.

Sigrid smiled and nodded. "You always know just how to cheer me up." The ostkaka looked most appealing and Sigrid realized she was quite hungry. "Thank you, Ella."

"Ja, sure. You'd do the same for me."

Sigrid's smile faded. "This day has been so hard."

Ella's countenance mirrored the way Sigrid felt inside. It was a blend of confusion and sorrow. "Ja," Ella whispered. "Your moder was a good woman. I miss her too."

Sigrid thought how strange she should have to struggle with such a riot of emotions in one single day. The sorrow over losing her mother was enough to keep her drawn within herself, but her anger at Sven's insensitivity to her needs threatened to burst forth without warning.

"Everything okay?" a masculine voice questioned from behind Ella. It was Erik.

Sigrid shook her head. "No. I don't think anything will ever be okay again."

"What's the matter?" he asked. Ella seemed eager to know the problem as well, but just then her mother called her away leaving Sigrid to awkwardly face Erik alone.

"Sven wants to put the property up for sale right away," she finally managed to say. She refused to say anything else as she was desperately close to tears. Cradling the bowl in her hands, Sigrid tried to focus on the pudding and berries instead.

"I hope you won't sell it off without giving me first chance to buy it," Erik said.

Sigrid's head snapped up and she knew without needing to see for herself that her face clearly registered her anger. "Erik Lindquist, I have no thought to see this place sold to anyone. This is my home. I have nothing else now, and I'm tired of people trying to separate me from the only thing left me."

Erik seemed notably surprised by her outburst. Unable to bear up under his scrutiny, Sigrid pushed him aside and made her way into the living room. *I'm not going to deal with this today,* she thought, lifting a spoonful of ostkaka to her lips. The dessert seemed flavorless to her, and what would normally have been a rare treat was now souring on her stomach. Would this day never end?

Chapter 2

Skorpor
(Swedish Rusks)

1 cup sugar
½ cup shortening
1 egg
1 cup sour cream
½ tsp. soda
½ tsp. salt
1 tsp. baking powder
1 cup nuts
3–4 cups flour (enough to make dough stiff)
Oven at 325°F

Mix all ingredients together and pour onto a long sheet pan. Bake 1 hour at 325°F. Take out of oven and turn oven to 200°F. Then cut *skorpor* into strips about 1 x 4" while still in the pan and put back in the oven to dry until hard and light brown (about 1 hour). These make great dunkers for coffee.

Sigrid's week went from bad to unbearable. Sigrid remained firm as Sven continued to nag about selling the property, but when a town meeting was called to discuss the railroad moving into the area, she had second thoughts about maintaining her life in the quiet town of Lindsborg. Building the railroad had brought her parents from Illinois to Kansas in the first place, but the railroad had also cost her father his life.

"The railroad is bringing new life to your community," an older man in a black suit assured the crowd. "The railroad will bring new people to settle the area and with them will come new industry and growth. A community like Lindsborg needs the railroad and," he paused to play up to the crowd, "the railroad needs Lindsborg."

The townsfolk murmured amongst themselves while Sigrid found an inconspicuous place for herself at the back of the meeting hall.

"Excuse me," a soft masculine voice whispered over her shoulder. "You aren't leaving, are you?"

Sigrid turned to find a handsome, dark-haired stranger eyeing her with consuming interest. "I'm not very interested in the topic," she managed to reply.

"Oh, but you should be." The man's brown eyes seemed to twinkle and a broad grin was revealed beneath his thick, handle-bar mustache. "I'm Ruben Carter. I work with this railroad." He said the words as though she should be impressed with such an announcement.

Instead, Sigrid dismissed herself and went outside to wait for Sven and Erik. Both were enthusiastic, or so it seemed, to at least hear what the railroad was offering the community.

"Wait, Miss. . ." Carter called, following her.

"I'm sorry, Mr. Carter," Sigrid said, rather stiffly. "The rail holds nothing but bad memories for me. My father was killed in a railroading accident near Salina."

"I'm sorry to hear that, Miss. . ." again he paused, waiting for her name.

"Larsson," she replied flatly.

He gave her a sweeping bow and pulled up with a grin. "Miss Larsson, it is a pleasure to make your acquaintance."

Sigrid smiled in spite of herself. "Thank you, Mr. Carter. Now, if you'll excuse me—"

"But we've only just met," he interjected. "You can't go now. Why don't you tell me what happened to your father?"

Sigrid smoothed the dusty folds of her dove gray skirt. "He was pinned between two cars. He died soon after they were able to free him."

"I'm sorry. But you know, that doesn't make the railroad evil."

"No, I suppose it doesn't," Sigrid admitted. "But it does make me wary of having it in my town."

"Where do you live? Perhaps the railroad will be far removed from your daily routine."

Sigrid shook her head. "No such luck. We've already received a notice saying that the railroad will pass over a corner of our property. No one asked me if I wanted it there. We were simply told that it will be placed there and we will be given a modest amount of money to compensate the taking of that which never belonged to the railroad in the first place." Her words were delivered in a stern, unemotional manner.

Ruben nodded sympathetically. "I can understand, but you mustn't fret so over it."

"I believe we've adequately discussed this issue," Sigrid said and turned to go. She was barely halfway down the street when Ruben caught up with her.

"At least allow me to make a suggestion," he offered. "We will be looking for ways to feed our workers. Perhaps you would care to assist us by cooking for the railroad?"

Sigrid shook her head and continued walking. She had absolutely no desire to be responsible for aiding the railroad's entry into Lindsborg. She might not be able to stop its arrival, but she certainly didn't have to assist it.

"Wait, Miss Larsson," Ruben called out again, then joined her matching her stride.

Sigrid said nothing for several moments. She wondered who this man really was and what his part was with the railroad. Perhaps he had a great deal of money tied up in the development of Lindsborg, and maybe all of that hinged on the successful presentation of the railroad to the citizens of the small town. But most folks were quite excited about the railroad, so surely talking her into a favorable response wasn't all that important.

"Please just hear me out. If nothing else, do it for the sake of Christian charity," Carter said with a pleading expression.

Sigrid felt helpless to argue with the man. Moder had always said that God expected folks to treat one another as they would if Jesus himself was standing in their place. "All right," she replied, looking Ruben Carter full in the face. "I'm listening."

Ruben smiled. "Would it be possible for you to have me to coffee?"

"Swedes are famous for always having a pot on the stove," Sigrid said, warming to his smile. He seemed like such a gentle-natured man and his soft-spoken words were methodically relaxing her prejudices. "I suppose the men will be along directly," she said glancing back at the main street of town.

"Yes, they were very near to concluding their discussion," Ruben agreed.

"All right, Mr. Carter, I will give you coffee and hear you out," Sigrid said.

❧

"So you see," Ruben told her as she poured steaming black coffee into his cup, "the railroad likes to work with the folks of the community. We have a great many workers who set the rails in place and bring in supplies. We rely upon good folks like you to help us with the feeding and sometimes the housing of our workers." He took a drink of the coffee and nodded approvingly. "This is very good."

Sigrid smiled and brought a plateful of skorpor to the table. "These are for dunking in the coffee," she paused as his gaze seemed to roam the full length of her body before resting on her face.

"I think I've died and gone to heaven," he said, taking one of the skorpor.

Sigrid, not used to open flirting, felt her face grow flushed. As she turned quickly away, she saw out the open kitchen window that Erik and Sven were coming up the lane. Their heated discussion seemed to indicate a problem and Sigrid could only wonder if they were discussing the sale of her home.

"So now that I know exactly where you're situated," Ruben began again, "and I know you can cook, what say you to the possibility of hiring on to fix my men breakfast each day? You'd be well paid."

Sigrid immediately thought of her brother's need for money. *What if I were to find enough or make enough money to buy out Sven and Ina's shares of the property? Would that satisfy them?*

"How much would I be paid?"

"Oh, it depends," Ruben said, looking up to the ceiling as though to mentally calculate the matter. "If you were to provide a full breakfast, and remember those are hardworking men with hearty appetites, it could be a very satisfactory sum."

"I assure you, Mr. Carter, farmers are hardworking men with hearty appetites as well. I've fed plenty of farmhands and I know how men can eat. What I don't know is what the railroad considers satisfactory."

"Enough to cover your expenses and then some," Ruben replied. "Look, if you'll consider this, I promise to make it well worth your time and trouble. The men need to be fed before first light every morning so that they can be to work by sunup. There will probably be about twenty or so in number, and you only have to worry about the morning meal. I'll arrange other plans for the noon and supper meals."

Sigrid finally felt intrigued by the idea. She could easily feed twenty men, and making money from the railroad seemed a promising way to keep Sven from forcing her to sell the homestead. "How long will you need to keep this arrangement?" she asked, glancing back out the window to find Sven and Erik stopped at the gatepost. They appeared to be in no hurry to come inside.

"Probably six or seven months, maybe less," Ruben replied.

Sigrid turned back to find him dunking yet another skorpor into his coffee. "All right," she said, taking the chair opposite him at the table. "I will consider doing this thing, but only if you put all the details in writing. I don't want the railroad cheating me for my efforts."

"You certainly have a low opinion of us, don't you," he more stated than questioned.

"You would too, if you'd lost your father and found your family forgotten and destitute by the very organization that took his life." She knew her words sounded pain filled, yet Sigrid couldn't stop herself from continuing. "Frankly, I'm grateful that my mother won't have to see the railroad come to this town. It would break her heart and make it seem like losing my Fader all over again."

"I'm truly sorry for your loss, Miss Larsson. My own parents are still alive, so I cannot possibly know your pain. Please believe me when I say the railroad will be honor-bound in their arrangements with you. You need not fear that you will be cheated in any way."

For a moment, Sigrid lost herself in his compassionate expression. His brown eyes seemed to reach inside her with a comforting assurance that every word he spoke was true. She wanted to do nothing more than listen to his promises and know that she wouldn't have to leave her home, but the slamming of the back porch screen door brought her out of her reverie.

Sigrid jumped to her feet to get two more coffee mugs.

With emotions fading and senses returning, she called over her shoulder, “I’ll do the job, but I still want it in writing.”

RAGMUNKAR

(Swedish Potato Pancakes)

3 cups grated raw potatoes
½ cup milk
1 egg, slightly beaten
2 T. flour
1 ½ tsp. salt
1 T. onion, finely chopped

Beat egg into the milk and immediately add potatoes. Sprinkle in flour, mixing well and add salt and onion. Fry in greased skillet, as you would regular pancakes, until golden brown.

Sigrid went to work immediately to prepare her house for the railroad workers. She cleared the living room of its normal furniture, with exception of the piano and wood stove, and brought in tables and chairs from every other corner of the house. Ella had even managed to loan her an extra table, and with that, Sigrid was able to put five men to a table with enough space to accommodate them all comfortably.

She rose every morning at three-thirty in order to have the stove hot and the food ready for the workers. It caused some havoc with her normal routine, but after a week or two Sigrid had worked through all the minor problems. Her supplies had used a fair sum of her funds, but she was already turning a profit. Not to mention that her jelly jar was now rapidly being filled with money. Not only was the railroad paying her to feed the men, but some of the men paid extra for things like cookies, pies and biscuits. Sigrid was finally seeing a way to satisfy Sven, although he'd been none too impressed with her method of earning the money.

Erik was even less impressed.

As a hired hand, Erik had made a routine of sharing the morning and sometimes the evening meal, with Tilly and Sigrid. He seemed to resent having to share his sanctuary with fifteen to twenty rowdies every morning. Sigrid ignored his scowls and comments that the men would just tear up the place. She was happy to have something to focus on other than her mother's death and her brother's insistence that she move. She'd even managed to make a small peace with the railroad. She would never embrace this mode of transportation as being of particular importance in her life, but she could overlook their intrusion so long as it meant she could keep her parents' home intact.

"My, my, but aren't you the sun in the sky," Ruben said, as he joined the men who were filing into the living room for breakfast.

Sigrid said nothing, but glanced down at the yellow calico gown. It was worn, yet serviceable, and she'd put it on with the intention of brightening her own day. She was tired of the dark woolens she'd worn all winter and tired of feeling a sense of loss for her mother every time she reached for something black. Spring was a time of colors and Sigrid wanted to bring such color back into her life.

"Smells mighty good in here, ma'am," a burly man with a matted black beard announced. "Hope you're servin' them thar Swedish pancakes again."

Sigrid smiled. "There are whole plates of them already on the tables, and I'll be in directly with ham and eggs."

Ruben followed her into the kitchen and reached out to touch her arm. "I meant what I said. You are about as pretty as a picture today. I like what you've done with your hair, too."

Sigrid reached a hand up to the carefully pinned blond bun. She usually just braided her hair and pinned it up at the nape of her neck, but today she'd felt like something different. With a surprising flair of artistry, Sigrid had woven her hair atop her head, leaving wisps to fall around her face. In a moment of pure vanity, she'd even taken a fork and heated the tongs to carefully curl each wisp until it conformed to her desired style.

"It really makes you look much prettier," Ruben said. "Not that you weren't already quite pretty to start with."

Sigrid felt her cheeks grow flushed and turned in a panic to check on the biscuits. Bent over the open oven door, she hoped that the redness of her cheeks would be explained away by the heat.

"You shouldn't find my praise so embarrassing," Ruben whispered as she straightened up. "I'm quite sure any of these men would agree with me."

"You do go on, don't you?" Sigrid said, busying her hands with slicing additional pieces of ham. "You'll have to excuse me, I need to get these on the table." She lifted two large platters of ham and eggs, but Ruben took them from her and leaned close to her ear.

"Perhaps you would honor me with a walk later?"

Sigrid jumped back, startled at the way his hot breath made her skin tingle. "I. . .ah. . .I have too much work to do."

"It can wait," Ruben said with a roguish smile. "But I can't."

He left her standing there cheeks flushed and heart racing, to stare after him. Sigrid had no idea how to deal with his attention. She'd never allowed herself to enjoy the attentions of any man, and now Ruben Carter was putting her resolve to the ultimate test.

But why not enjoy it? she thought. *I'm twenty-seven years old. It's not like men are beating down the door to court me.*

Erik watched from the doorway as Ruben wooed Sigrid with his smiles and words. A pang of bitter jealousy coursed through him, and he didn't like it at all. He'd known Sigrid for what seemed an eternity, but more than this, he'd loved her for nearly as long. And, he'd come to think of her as belonging to him.

He remembered the first time he'd seen her at a church youth function. At least, it was the first time he'd seen her as anything other than a child. She was fifteen and the new pink gingham dress that she wore more than showed off her womanly charms. She had just started to pin her hair up and looked so very grown up that, for a moment, Erik had wondered who she was. It wasn't long until he realized that this was the little Larsson girl. And, she wasn't so little anymore.

As Ruben passed by with the ham and eggs he gave Erik a sideways glance. Erik, feeling rather embarrassed, realized that he was scowling. He was even more embarrassed when he found Sigrid staring at him with a questioning look.

"Something wrong, Erik?" she asked, before turning to pull biscuits from the oven.

Erik crossed the small kitchen amidst the noise of the railroad workers hearty approvals. "This is wrong, Sigrid," he said flatly. "You have a house full of rowdy men and no chaperone to keep you from their attention should somebody get out of hand. You know what they're saying in town, don't you?"

She straightened and put the pan of biscuits on the counter. "No, I'm sure I don't. I scarcely have time to lounge around town listening to gossip."

Erik's conscience smarted, but not enough to leave the thing alone. "You're risking your reputation here, and I think that Carter fellow is way too familiar with you if you ask me."

"Well, I didn't. Stop playing big brother to me and stay out of it."

Erik wanted to pull her into his arms and tell her that being a big brother was the furthest thing from his mind, but instead he crossed his arms against his chest. "So you don't care what people think?"

"Not when they are misjudging me without bothering

to learn the truth," she said rather defiantly.

Erik wondered if he was included in that group. Had he misjudged the situation? Was it mere jealousy that fanned his concern? He waited while Sigrid took out biscuits and coffee and tried to think of what he would say next.

When she came back into the kitchen, she looked up at him for only a moment before heading to the back door.

"Where are you going?"

"I need more wood," she said, motioning to the empty bin beside the stove.

"Let me get it," he offered.

She looked at him hard for a moment, then nodded. "All right, but you must promise no more lectures."

He smiled. "I have to promise good behavior in order to haul wood?"

He watched her fight back a smile before rolling her eyes. "No, but if you want breakfast then you must mind your manners."

He went outside into the darkness of the morning and noted that the faintest light was now touching the eastern horizon. They followed the well-worn path around the side of the house and Sigrid began picking up logs.

"Here," Erik suggested holding out his muscular arms, "just load me up." Sigrid did as he told her and they worked silently for the remaining time.

After making three more trips, the bin was full and the coffee perked cheerily atop the stove. The day was dawning, and with it, the railroad workers were taking their leave. One by one they filed out the front door, stopping only long enough to leave bits of change in the jar by the door. Ruben seemed reluctant to leave, but Erik made it clear that he was staying on and in no hurry to go about the farm's daily chores. Returning Erik's look of unspoken challenge, Ruben finally donned his hat and bid a busy Sigrid good day.

"I'll stop by later," Ruben assured her, "with a railroad check. Maybe you won't be too busy to take that walk then?"

"Thank you, Mr. Carter, and we shall see," she called over her shoulder, her arms filled with empty plates.

When Carter had let the screen door slam behind him, Erik picked up a stack of plates and followed Sigrid into the kitchen. He wanted to question her about Carter's mention of a walk, but he knew she'd only take offense.

"You really shouldn't wear yourself out doing this," Erik began. He wanted to plead a case that would appear entirely sympathetic to her own condition. "Getting up at three-thirty and adding this to your other chores is taking on way too much."

Sigrid laughed at his concern. "Erik, I need the money, and you know as well as anyone that a little hard work never hurt a body."

She was plunging the greasy plates into soapy water, but Erik took hold of her arm anyway and pulled her with him to sit at one of the empty tables. "I want to talk to you about all of this."

She wiped soap suds onto her apron and shook her head. "There's nothing more to be said. You heard Sven.

He wants this place sold or he wants the money entitled him. I can work hard and give him the latter, but I can't lose this place. Not yet." Her expression softened and her gaze traveled the interior of the room. "I'm not ready to say good-bye yet. I know it might sound foolish, but that's just the way I feel."

"I'm not asking you to say good-bye, nor to sell the house, unless of course you want to include me in on the deal." He held up his hand as she started to protest. "You've got to understand, in many ways, I'm just as tied to the place as you are. After all, I've been helping to farm it for almost thirteen years."

"I know all of that," she said, her voice edged with irritation. "That's why you should understand how I feel."

"But I do," he softly replied. He studied her confused expression. Her blue eyes seemed to search him for answers, and he wondered if he could go through with what he planned to do.

"Then why can't you understand my feeding the workers?" she asked flatly. "Why can't you see that by the end of autumn the railroad will be finished, and I'll have saved enough money to buy out Sven and Ina. It's the only way."

"No. It's not the. . .only way," Erik said, hesitantly.

"Then what do you suggest?"

"You could marry me. I'd be happy to pay Sven and Ina whatever they thought fair."

Sigrid's mouth dropped open. She stared at Erik with such a look of alarm that he wondered if he'd actually offended her.

"Marry you? You must want this land bad to offer me

marriage." She got up from the table and Erik could read the anger in her eyes. "You've treated me like an unwanted little sister all of my life. When you ran around with my brother you ignored me or else teased me unmercifully and when it was just Moder and me you. . .well you—" She stopped mid-sentence, her face reddened from the tirade, eyes blazing in accusation. *"Uff da!"* she exclaimed in exasperation. "Why does everyone suddenly seem intent on putting me out of my home?"

She ran from the room before Erik could offer a single word of explanation. Not that he was entirely certain that he would have even tried to speak. She was more angry than he'd ever seen her, and yet he couldn't help but smile. *Little sister, indeed,* he thought. *I've seen you as something more than a little sister for a great long while.* But this thought only frustrated him more as he remembered that Ruben Carter obviously looked upon her in other than brotherly fashion.

Leaning back in exasperation, Erik ran a hand through his hair and contemplated the situation. *How can I convince her that it isn't her land I love?*

Chapter 4

Swedish Rye Bread

1 cup potato water
  (water from a boiled potato)
½ cup all-purpose flour
1 potato
  (boiled and mashed)
2 cups rye flour
1 T. salt
1 package of yeast
2 cups water
  (or buttermilk)

Mix and leave to rise until double in size.

Boil together:
½ cup sugar
¼ cup shortening
½ cup molasses
¼ cup orange peel, finely grated

Oven at 375°F

Cool and put into doubled bread mixture. Work this well with 5-6 cups of flour to make a dough that doesn't stick to the board. Form into 2 or 3 medium-size loaves and let rise until double. Bake at 375°F for 1 hour.

A week later, Sigrid found that there were still no easy answers to the questions that plagued her mind. Erik made himself her constant companion so long as the railroad men were in the house.

He was also more than attentive when Ruben Carter chose to spend time with her, and Sigrid felt great frustration with his interference.

Even now, as she pounded out those frustrations on the bread dough she was working, Sigrid found Erik staring at her from over the rim of his coffee cup. He went later and later into the fields these days, and Sigrid knew that it was because of Ruben's attentions. *He's appointed himself my guardian,* she decided, and the thought of answering to yet another "brother" left a completely sour taste in her mouth.

"Aren't you worried about rain?" she asked, patting the dough into a ball.

Erik glanced at the window, as if contemplating her question, then shook his head. "It won't rain today. Maybe tomorrow. I've got time."

"Well if you've so much time on your hands you could fix that section of fence my cows keep escaping through. I did my best, but it won't do much to keep them in if they get very determined to seek greener pastures."

"You want me out of here for a reason?" Erik asked, eyeing her seriously.

She looked at him for a moment, thought of an angry retort, then bit it back and turned away. She couldn't very well tell him that he made her uncomfortable. Everyone made her uncomfortable these days. She couldn't even go to church without getting an earful of how scandalously she was behaving. It didn't matter that she was working herself to death in order to save her home from being sold.

"Well? Is that the reason? Is Mr. Carter headed back

to fill your head with more nonsense?"

Erik was referring to a conversation he'd come in on earlier that morning. Ruben had been telling her about his home in Kansas City. Well, *home* seemed a paltry description, compared to the glorious details Ruben had offered. *Anyway, it wasn't any of Erik's business,* she reminded herself.

"Sit here all day, if that's what you want," she snapped and glanced out the window in time to see her brother coming up the walkway. "Oh, great. Now I'll have two of you to deal with."

"What?" Erik said, getting to his feet. "Carter is back, isn't he?"

Sigrid turned angrily. "It's Sven, if you must know. Now sit down and finish your breakfast. You might as well talk with Sven, because I have nothing more to say to either of you."

She covered the rye dough with a clean towel and went into the living room to pick up the last of the dishes. Sigrid could hear Erik greet her brother with an offering of coffee. She felt herself tense, wondering why she couldn't understand Erik's protective nature. He'd never been one to watch over her like this. Then again, Moder had always been alive to keep watch over her. *But I'm twenty-seven,* she thought with a sigh of exasperation. I don't need *someone to look after me.* Then she thought of a prayer she'd been taught by her mother.

Gud som haver barnen kar, Se till mig som liten ar.

"God who holds the children dear, Look after me so little here," she whispered.

Tears came to her eyes. "Oh, Moder," she whispered. "I miss you so. I do need God to look after me. I know that. But I don't need—"

"Well, Erik said you were hard at work," Sven boomed, coming into the living room. "I don't suppose you're ready to put an end to this foolishness?" He didn't bother to wait for her to answer. "I'm tired of hearing the talk about you in town."

Sigrid gave him a casual glance of indifference. "But I suppose you aren't too tired of it to repeat what you've been bothered by."

Sven's broad face tightened at the jaw, but otherwise he showed no other expression of emotion. "Those men seem to have a right good time taking their breakfast here."

"Good," Sigrid replied and went back to wiping down the table.

Erik had joined Sven by now and added his own thoughts on the matter. "I heard your name bandied about by that Carter fellow. He's taking an awful liberty if you ask me—"

"Well, I didn't," Sigrid replied and gathering up her things, whipped past both men before either one could respond.

Sven was first to follow, and when he caught up with her he took her by the arm and made her come to sit at the table.

"You're going to talk about selling the land," he said. "I know several people who are interested in buying—"

"No!" Sigrid interjected. She crossed her arms and glared at both Sven and Erik. The men took seats opposite her and waited for her to calm.

"Sigrid," her brother began.

"No, Sven. I don't want to leave. Maybe next year. But not now. I need this house. I need to feel Moder's presence. It gives my heart peace. I need to think about what I want to do. Where I want to go. Is that so hard to understand?"

"No, but as I've already said, Ina and I could use the extra money."

"I'm planning to buy you both out," Sigrid announced, surprising her brother. "That's why I took on the job of feeding the railroad workers. Ruben, that is, Mister Carter," she added after noting the look on Erik's face, "has seen to it that I'm amply paid."

"You think you can make enough to buy us out?" Sven asked with a look of disbelief.

"How much are you expecting to make?" she asked, happy to at least have his attention turned in a direction she could deal with.

"Well, I figured there would be at least fifty dollars for each of us. Tom Anderson said the place is worth at least one hundred fifty dollars, maybe more."

"I know I'd pay you that," Erik threw out quite casually.

"Fifty?" she asked, her voice faltering. "Each?"

"Ja, that seems more than fair."

Fifty to each, she thought. That was one hundred dollars, not counting her own share. It might as well be a million for all the good it would do. She did a quick mental calculation and realized that if the railroad stayed in the area until November, she could amass the money needed. Maybe even by then, she could sell extra vegetables from her garden, as well.

"Give me until Christmas," she finally said.

Sven rubbed his chin and exchanged a glance with Erik. "It would be mighty hard to wait."

"Well, I can give you part of your share now, and if Ina can wait, I'll have the rest by then."

"How much are you talking about?" Sven questioned.

Sigrid could see that she had his interest. "Twenty dollars."

"Twenty?" He perked up at this and rubbed his chin again. "I suppose I could wait until Christmas."

"Good," Sigrid said, jumping to her feet. She rushed to her room and took out twenty dollars from the money she'd saved back. It didn't leave her much, but in a few weeks she would make it all up. Hurrying back, she thrust the money into Sven's hands before he could change his mind. "Now, I have work to do."

Going back to the sink, she ignored the hushed talk between her brother and Erik. *Please God, let it be enough to make Sven go in peace,* she prayed. She understood her brother's need for cash, but it hurt her that he couldn't understand her reluctance to leave the home of her birth.

"Well, I'll go then. Olga will wonder why I've been so long to town."

"Don't lose your money," Sigrid called out, turning to watch him go.

When Sven had gone, she could see that Erik had more to say. Wiping her hands on her apron, Sigrid came to sit down once again and folded her arms. "All right, speak Mr. Lindquist, and tell me what I've done to offend you now."

Erik shook his head. "You haven't offended me. I just wish I could explain some things to you. I wish you'd let me help."

"Help do what? Buy the farm?"

"I could help you in that way. You know I wouldn't expect you to move. Letting me help you would be a whole sight easier than working yourself into an early grave."

Sigrid could see that he was genuinely concerned and that his words were given in an attitude of sincerity. She felt her resolve crumble. He had been good to her and Moder, and to turn her back on him now would be cruel.

"Erik, you are kind to offer, but I don't think I could live here with you owning the land. I could never afford to pay for my keep and it wouldn't be right to expect you to let me live here for free."

Erik smiled. "Like I said before, we could get married. I'd be happy to pay Sven and Ina their fifty dollars, and we could even live on here if you wanted to."

Sigrid was touched more deeply than she could express. That Erik would offer himself up in that manner seemed to say that her welfare was of more importance to him than his own. "That's very kind, Erik," she murmured. "Kind, but not very practical for you."

"I don't want you thinking that it would just be an act of kindness," Erik said, seeming to struggle for words. "I mean. . .well—"

"You don't need to explain," Sigrid interrupted. "I know how you cared about Moder and you probably feel obligated to see me cared for, for her sake. I think, too, that you understand why I want to stay on. But, I'd like to accomplish this myself. I don't want anyone marrying me out of pity, all so that I can keep a parcel of land and a run down house."

"Sigrid—"

"No, hear me out, Erik. It's important to me that you know how much I appreciate your offer. It shows what a good friend you really are. I'm sorry I got so mad at you earlier, but you have to understand I'm a grown woman. I can't have you telling me who I can and can't talk to, and I don't want you worrying about the men coming here to eat. God watches over me, and He knows my heart in this matter."

Erik's expression seemed almost pained. Sigrid thought it would be better to put the matter behind them. "I've got to get to work, whether you do or not," she said, trying to sound lighthearted. She got to her feet and went back to the sink. "God will work out the details."

Erik left the Larsson house feeling more frustrated than ever. God might know Sigrid's heart, but he sure couldn't figure it out. Had she fallen in love with that Carter fellow? Why couldn't she see the trouble Carter could be? She was too naive, too sheltered. He wanted to explain all of those things to her, but she'd only see it as interference.

Kicking at a rock, Erik looked up at the sky. Wisps of lacy white clouds were strung out against the brilliant blue. It would rain tomorrow or the next day for sure, and he still had work to do in the fields. Maybe he would give Sigrid another day to think about things and then he would bring up the subject again. *Only this time,* he thought, *I'll find a way to tell her how I feel about her.* Surely that would make a difference.

Chapter 5

SMORBAKELSER
(Swedish Butter Cookies)

1 cup butter
2 egg yolks
½ cup sugar
Oven at 400°F

2 cups flour
1 tsp. almond extract
1 tsp. vanilla extract

Cream butter, egg yolks, sugar and extracts together until light and fluffy. Add flour and mix well. Dough will be soft, but not sticky. Roll out (don't overflour) and cut with cookie cutter or use in cookie press. Bake at 400°F for 8–10 minutes. They burn easily, so be careful.

The September wedding of her widowed friend Ella Swanson gave Sigrid something else to focus on other than work. Ella, with her three fatherless boys, was quite happy to accept an offer of marriage from Per Anderson. The thirty-five year-old bachelor seemed overly quiet and reserved for Ella's rambunctious bunch, but Sigrid could see that the boys adored the man. And, Ella seemed quite satisfied with the match.

With the weather cooperating perfectly, the wedding

supper was held outside in picnic fashion on the church lawn. Sigrid had baked several dishes to bring to the supper, including one of Ella's favorites, *smorbakelser,* little butter cookies so light and rich, that they instantly melted in the mouth. *They appear,* Sigrid thought with a smile, t*o be one of Erik's favorites as well.* Seeing him make yet another trip to the dessert table, she watched him grab up a handful of the cookies and plop them down on his plate in a rather possessive manner.

"Oh, there you are," Mrs. Moberg said, coming up from behind Sigrid. "I hoped to talk to you. I heard it said that the railroad is planning to buy your land for a depot. Is that true? What will you do then? Are you going to live with Sven and Olga?"

Taken aback by the rapid interrogation, Sigrid shook her head. "I don't know anything about a depot, but I don't plan to sell the farmstead to the railroad. Where did you get such an idea?"

The robust woman jutted her chin in the air. "Mr. Moberg told me, and where he heard it from, I can't say."

"Well someone obviously has their facts wrong."

"Wrong about what?" Mrs. Swanson questioned and before waiting for an answer, added, "Don't Ella look nice?"

They all agreed that Ella made a radiant bride before Mrs. Moberg relayed her information on the railroad.

"Ja, I heard there was talk of a depot and roundhouse for the engines. Your farmstead is a good place for these things."

"That's not my opinion," Sigrid said. "I intend to get

down to the bottom of this gossip right away." Leaving the two old women to stare after her in stunned silence, Sigrid went in search of Ruben.

Weaving her way through the crowd, Sigrid felt disheartened at not being able to immediately locate Ruben. She knew he'd been invited to the celebration, and she had counted on seeing him here. It was funny the way he made her feel. Sometimes she welcomed his visits and other times he made her feel like a creature misplaced in time. He laughed at her crude lifestyle and told her that with the coming of the new century, her way of life would rapidly become obsolete. Still, he made her feel like a woman, all feminine and girlish. She found herself wanting to impress him, and she wanted him to take notice.

Spying him watching a game of horseshoes, Sigrid slipped up from behind and pulled on his coat sleeve. "Can we talk for a moment?"

He flashed her a grin that suggested she'd just made his day, and with a hand to the small of her back, he led her away from the crowd to a near by stand of trees.

"What would you like to talk about?" he asked, rubbing one of the handlebars of his mustache between his thumb and finger. "I've known weddings to bring even the shyest girl out of her shell."

Sigrid felt her cheeks grow hot. Ruben seemed to imply that she was interested in some kind of romantic tryst, and while she could easily see herself in the role, she had to know the truth about her property.

"I've been told by some of my friends that the railroad intends to try to build a depot on my land. Maybe even take the entire farmstead for a roundhouse and such. Is this true, Ruben?" She searched his face, particularly his dark eyes, and waited for some sign that would reassure her.

Ruben took hold of her hand and kissed it lightly. Sigrid found herself trembling from the action and quickly pulled her hand away. "Is it true?" she pressed the question again.

"I have no knowledge of it, if it is," he admitted. "I would have been told if that were the plan, and I know nothing of it."

Sigrid relaxed a bit and sighed. "I hate gossip. It's always getting a person worked up for no reason at all." She felt him move closer to her and thought of moving away. But the thought quickly passed from her mind.

"Sigrid, you are so beautiful. I don't know why you let yourself worry about things. Trust me, I'll find out if there is any truth to the rumors. In the meantime, why don't we spend some time together? We could walk down by the creek and leave the others to their celebration while we have our own private party."

Sigrid stammered at his passionate expression. "I. . . ah. . .I don't think. . ." Before she could finish her words, Ruben pulled her into his arms.

"I don't want you to think about anything but me," he said and kissed her quite soundly on the mouth.

Sigrid stood absolutely rigid as he let her go. She had to remain fixed that way, because she was certain if she so much as took a single step, her knees would buckle from beneath her.

He gently touched the curl of hair that fell over one ear. "You are a magnificent woman, Sigrid. I think I'm losing my heart to you."

Sigrid couldn't look him the eye. The whole idea of being courted was so foreign to her. For so many years she'd kept her heart completely boxed off, knowing that as the youngest daughter she was required to care for her mother until the time of her death.

"Don't be afraid to trust your heart," Ruben said, softly. "Come with me."

Sigrid knew it would be impossible to go with him down to the creek. What little reputation she might have managed to keep intact would be ruined for certain if they were to slip away.

"I. . .I need to go," she finally said, and turned to walk briskly away.

Ruben did nothing to stop her, and a part of her was hurt by this. If he cared so much about keeping her company, why didn't he at least call after her? But another part of her was just as grateful that he didn't. She'd never been kissed on the mouth before, and it seemed such a glorious and wondrous experience that Sigrid wanted to find a way to go off by herself and contemplate what had just happened.

"I just saw him kiss her," Mrs. Moberg was saying to a collected gathering of older women. "I think that more than suggests what I said was true."

Erik came upon this conversation as he made his fourth trip to the supper tables. His agitation at not being able to spend time alone with Sigrid had made him poor company for everyone else. She was ignoring him, and in the months that had passed since his offer to marry her, Sigrid had never allowed him to speak on the matter again. He'd hoped the atmosphere of a wedding might give him the forum to declare his love, but so far Sigrid had remained completely out of his company.

"You know I heard they were close to an understanding," one of the women continued the conversation.

"Bah!" exclaimed Mrs. Moberg, "I've heard it said that Sigrid has already accepted his proposal. Think on that, our Sigrid married to Ruben Carter. Why I don't imagine she would stay in Lindsborg long after that."

"No, indeed," a third woman countered. "I heard he is rich. Lives in a fancy mansion in Kansas City. No doubt she'd prefer spending the winter in luxury rather than on the prairie."

Erik's chest tightened as the words of the conversation permeated his brain. Sigrid and Carter were engaged? When had this happened?

"Well, from the looks of the way he was kissing her just now, I'd say they'd better do something in a hurry," Mrs. Moberg added in a rather haughty tone.

Erik left his plate at the table and walked away in a daze. Carter had kissed Sigrid? And she'd let him? Anger slowly welled inside. It seemed to pulsate to life from every part of his body, until there was a hard, black ball knotting up in his stomach. She couldn't be in love with that two-faced, no-good.

"Erik, have you seen my sister?"

Erik glanced up to find Sven coming towards him. "No, but apparently a good many other people have."

Sven stared at him with an expression of confusion. "What do you mean by that?"

Erik started to explain, then bit back the retort and shrugged. "I can't seem to locate her, but I've heard others mention having seen her. She must be around here somewhere."

"Ja, I suppose she's found some way to keep busy."

Erik grimaced. "Yes, I suppose she has."

He walked away quickly, lest he should open his mouth and let pour the anger inside. Hurrying away from the party, Erik found himself taking the long way back to his house. He realized that he wanted nothing more than to find Sigrid and force some sense into her head. And then, he wanted nothing more than to kiss her himself and show her that he meant business.

"I'm powerful angry, Lord," he said, looking skyward. "I don't mean to be, but I am and there's no use denying it. I've tried to be reasonable about things. I've tried to keep my hands and mind busy so that she'd have time to consider my proposal, but it isn't my proposal she's considering."

He slowed his stride as his anger spent itself in prayer. "I don't want to lose her, but how can I convince her that I love her?"

Just tell her, a voice seemed to say.

Erik stopped in his tracks and glanced around him. Nothing but a few buildings and cornfields greeted his gaze. Maybe God was trying to speak to his heart. Maybe he had relied too long on his own understanding, and now it was time to face doing things another way.

"Have I ignored You, God?" he asked suddenly. Shoving his hands in his pockets, Erik moved on down the lane. He tried to imagine what God would have him do.

"Tell her? But she already knows how I feel about her. After all, I asked her to marry me."

You asked her to marry you so that you could keep her on her land, his heart reminded him. *You said nothing of love.*

"Well, maybe it's time I did," Erik declared, suddenly feeling a bit of his self-confidence return. "After all, they aren't married yet."

Chapter 6

Egg Gravy

2 T. bacon or sausage drippings
4 cups milk — 2 egg yolks
2 T. flour — ½ tsp. salt

Put meat drippings into a skillet over medium heat. Add flour as you would for gravy. Blend and leave to brown a bit. Mix milk, egg yolks (slightly beaten) and salt, and add to flour and grease. Mix this until thick, but don't allow it to curdle. Add more milk if you like thinner gravy. When mixture is the right consistency for you, remove from heat and serve over Swedish rye bread.

Harvest was a busy time of year for all of Lindsborg, but Sigrid found it especially trying. It was easy to see now how hard her mother had worked. Even though Tilly was unable to do much of the heavy work, she had prepared the vegetables for canning and helped with the livestock. Now that all of this fell to Sigrid's shoulders, her only saving grace was that the railroad had completed its line and she was no longer needed to feed the workers.

Still, she'd been up by four that morning to do her own chores, and throughout the course of the day, there'd been little opportunity to even pause for the briefest rest. Most of the morning had been spent in cleaning vegetables and the afternoon would be devoted to canning them.

Glancing at the clock, Sigrid was startled to find it was nearly one-thirty, and she hadn't fixed anything for lunch. During harvest time, Erik usually made his way to her house for the noon meal. Since she was already spending most of her time in the kitchen canning, making lunch for the both of them made sense. What didn't make sense was sending Erik back to his own place or even into town for a bite to eat. But now, she'd let it slip her mind completely and she feared he would show up starving, and she'd not have a single morsel prepared.

Staring at the cupboards trying to decide what would be quickest, Sigrid finally decided egg gravy would be the best solution. Her mother said there was always a meal to be had in egg gravy and rye bread. Sigrid hoped it would be filling enough to meet with Erik's hearty appetite. She fried up a panful of bacon to go along with it, then used the drippings for the base of her gravy. She had just finished adding the final ingredients when she heard a knock on the back door.

"Come on in, lunch is nearly ready," she called and hurried to slice tomatoes and rye bread.

"Well, I didn't know you were fixing lunch for me," Sven said, lumbering into the kitchen.

"What are you doing here?" she asked in surprise. "I figured you'd be cutting broomcorn."

"Ja, we've been hard to work on it, but something else came up."

Her brother's expression appeared a cross between anxious and hesitant. "So what is it that brings you here?"

"I want to talk to you about our agreement."

"You mean regarding the property?" she asked, turning back to give the gravy a quick stir before removing it from the stove.

"I know I told you that you could have until Christmas, but—" he fell silent as though trying to figure out how best to explain..

"Sven, what are you up to?" she asked flatly. "If it's the money, I can pay you now. I have enough put together to pay both you and Ina. So if that's what you're here for, I can accommodate you."

"No, Sigrid. Sit down."

She sat obediently as a sense of fear ran down her spine. Something had changed his mind. He's come to break our deal.

"The railroad has offered to pay double what we talked about," Sven announced. "They are willing to give us three hundred dollars for the farm."

"So they are trying to get this land for a depot and roundhouse. Is that it?" Sigrid asked. Why hadn't Ruben known about this yesterday when she'd asked him?

"I guess that's the idea," Sven replied. "I can't say for sure. Maybe they just want the extra space for a spur line to work on the cars."

"Well, they can't have it!" she declared firmly. "Sven, you've been taught to be a man of honor. Moder would expect you to keep your word, and so do I."

"Be reasonable, Sigrid. That's a hundred dollars a piece. I could use that money and so could Ina, especially now that the new baby is nearly here. She and Clarence barely have room as it is and a hundred dollars would go a long way to help them build onto the house and get some of the things they need. And, if you're still determined to live alone, a hundred dollars could buy you a little place in town. You wouldn't have to work nearly so hard. You could probably live off that money for a good long time."

"I don't want a place in town, Sven. I want this place. This is my home. Or at least I always thought it was. I love this place. It's a part of Moder and Fader, and I don't want to let that go."

"I'm your brother, and I'm the head of the family now. I'm sorry, Sigrid, but I'm going to talk to Ina about this. I'm sure she'll feel the same way I do." He got to his feet and walked to the back door.

Sigrid had no other choice but to follow after him. "You can't do this. If you love me, you won't do this." She knew the words cut him like a knife. She could see even with his back turned to her, that his shoulders slumped a little lower.

"I'm sorry," was all he could say.

Sigrid's vision blurred with tears. She watched Sven walk away and wished she could think of something to say in order to change his mind. She could never pay him and Ina both one hundred dollars. She barely had enough to pay them the fifty each.

"What did Sven want?" Erik asked, coming from around

the corner of the house. His face and arms were still wet from having washed up at the pump.

"To ruin my life," Sigrid barely managed to whisper before fleeing into the house.

She wiped her eyes with the apron, not wanting Erik to see her cry, but he had followed on her heels and knew exactly what was happening.

"What is it? What did he do that would make you cry?"

Sigrid swallowed down a lump in her throat. "He plans to sell the farm to the railroad."

"He can't do that," Erik said, and his expression told Sigrid that he was every bit as upset at the prospect as she was.

"That's what I told him, but he doesn't care. They are offering him three hundred dollars, and I can't possibly match that." She sat down hard on the chair. A thought came to her, but she quickly pushed it aside. If she married Erik then perhaps they could combine their money and pay Sven and Ina. But no! That was no reason to marry. Besides, the haunting reminder of Ruben's kiss stood between her and Erik now.

"Ruben said he knew nothing about this," she said, mindless of the effect on Erik.

"Apparently he had other things on his mind," Erik said, not even attempting to hide his bitterness.

"What is that supposed to mean?" Sigrid asked.

"There's rumors about you two. I guess you made quite a spectacle of yourself yesterday." He looked at her seeming to dare her to deny his words.

"It's none of your business," she snapped and got up

to bring the food to the table. "You'd better eat before this gets cold."

Erik surprised her by taking hold of her arm and forcing her to face him. "You can't trust Carter. He isn't one of us. He isn't from around here. He doesn't know the first thing about farming and you can bet your pretty little head, he doesn't intend to stay in Lindsborg for long."

"Stop it!" Sigrid said, pulling away. "You don't know anything about him. You're just mad because I won't sell you the farm."

"What do you know about how I feel? You haven't bothered to give me so much as two words at one sitting. I come here, you throw food at me, and then I leave to go tend the livestock or garden, or go to town. I know you're hurting over this, but you aren't hearing me."

"I've heard enough!"

"Then you don't care that people think you are playing fast and loose with Ruben Carter? You don't care that folks did more talking about you and Carter kissing yesterday than they did discussing Ella's wedding?"

Sigrid felt the heat rise from her collar. She couldn't deny what he was accusing her of, and for reasons she couldn't understand, this only made her more angry. Jerking away, she waved to the food on the counter. "Eat or not, but I refuse to talk to someone who only wants to yell at me!"

She stormed off to her bedroom and slammed the door as loudly as she could to make her point. Turning the key in the lock, she hoped it made enough noise to leave Erik without a doubt as to how she felt about him at that moment.

Throwing herself across the bed, Sigrid began to cry in earnest because she really didn't know how she felt about anything. Especially Erik. Why did this have to be so difficult? She cared a great deal about Erik, but Ruben made her feel so excited and alive. Ruben had only to look at her a certain way, and she trembled from head to foot. Erik certainly never did that for her.

Or had he? She thought back on times when she'd caught him smiling at her a certain way. Her stomach had always seemed to do flip-flops when that happened, but she had always ignored it. *But he doesn't think of me the same way Ruben does,* she thought, and hot tears fell from her eyes. *Ruben desires me as a woman. Erik just thinks of me as a child. He only wants me for the land.*

Beating her hands against the pillow, Sigrid cried until there were no tears left to cry. It was only when she'd dried her eyes and rolled over on her back that she thought to pray.

"Oh, God," she mournfully whispered, "I'm so confused. I don't know what to do. I don't want to leave my home, but it seems that Sven has made up his mind. I have no choice but to do as others direct me to do. But I want You to show me what to do. I want You to guide and direct me. Please help me to know what's right in Your sight, and give me the strength to deal with this matter."

She sighed, feeling only marginally better. There was a kitchen full of work awaiting her attention, and yet all she really wanted to do was sleep. Just sleep and forget the rest of the world and all the problems that went along with it. The coming months would forever see her life changed, and Sigrid wanted to keep things still, if only for a little while.

Giving into her desires, she closed her eyes and fell asleep. Somehow, God would surely find a way to make it all work out.

Chapter 7

POTATISKORV
(Potato Sausage)

6 large raw potatoes (peeled and ground)
1 tsp. pepper
2 tsp. salt
1 tsp. allspice
1 cup milk
1½ lbs. ground beef
2½ lbs. ground pork
1 medium onion (ground)

Mix all ingredients together and stuff into sausage casings, being careful not to overfill as they will expand during cooking. Prick casing several times with a needle before cooking. Put into a pot of hot water and boil over medium heat for 1 hour. Then brown in a frying pan if desired. Makes six 24-inch sausages.

Cold weather set in, and with it came a frenzy to finish up the harvest chores. Sigrid had scarcely seen anything of Erik or Sven since that dreadful day in the kitchen. She felt relieved to have been left to her own concerns, and yet she rather missed seeing Erik at mealtime. With the heavy work of harvest, Sigrid was used to Erik sharing all of her meals, but after that day, he had simply stopped coming.

Her conscience bothered her when she thought about having hurt his feelings. She didn't know where to fit Erik into her life. She knew she had feelings for him, but they certainly weren't the same kind of physical feelings she had for Ruben. On the other hand, she shared very little of common interest with Ruben. They talked on several occasions since he'd stolen the kiss at Ella's wedding, and each time Sigrid tried to imagine herself spending the rest of her life with him.

These thoughts continued to haunt her as she worked to stuff sausage casings with *potatiskorv*. The potato sausage would be a nice delicacy to have for the holidays, and Sigrid could remember what a favorite it was of her mother's.

"Oh, Moder," she whispered, "I miss you so. Nothing seems right with you gone. I've made such a mess of things."

The sound of the back door opening gave her start. Had her brother come to torment her with the signing over of her home? Or had Erik returned to confront her with her behavior?

"Sigrid?"

It was Ruben.

Sigrid was surprised and more than a little bit embarrassed to have Ruben find her in such a state of disarray. Wiping the sausage from her hands, she put a hand up to her hair, hoping desperately that she wouldn't appear too much of a mess.

"I wasn't expecting you," she murmured, trying hard to steady her nerves.

He glanced around and smiled. "I hope I'm not interrupting.

"Only in a pleasant way," she said, beginning to relax. "I've been making sausages all morning and in truth, I could use a rest." She turned back to put a towel over the entire affair and felt a charge of electricity shoot through her when Ruben came to stand directly behind her.

His warm breath on her bare neck caused Sigrid to tremble. Ruben turned her gently and took hold of her shoulders. "I haven't been able to get you out of my mind. I miss coming here on a daily basis." He tilted her face up and studied her for a moment as though inspecting a rare flower. "I can't get this face out of my mind. When I sleep, I dream about you, and when I awaken, I long to see you and to hold you."

Sigrid felt her breath quicken. My, but this man could bring her blood to a boil quicker than anyone she'd ever known.

Ruben took her tenderly into his arms. "I want to kiss you again. May I?"

She was touched that he should ask. "I suppose so."

He lost little time. Lowering his mouth to hers, Ruben pulled her tightly against him. He kissed her with more passion than she'd ever imagined, and it so frightened her that she pulled away panting. Stepping away from him, she stared back, trying to reason inside her what it was that had caused her reaction.

"I'm sorry," he said, softly. "I didn't mean to frighten you. It's just that I can no longer fight the feelings I have for you. There's something I want to say, and hope you won't think me too forward." His words were methodically delivered and Sigrid found herself very nearly mesmerized by them.

"What. . .what. . .is it?" she barely managed to croak out.

"I want you to marry me."

She gasped. "What?"

His expression suggested he enjoyed the control he held over her. With a smug grin he repeated the proposal. "I said that I want you to marry me."

Sigrid couldn't believe that he'd actually just proposed. She felt the warmth of his passionate gaze pierce her facade of indifference. He wanted to marry her!

"Just like that?" she questioned, forcing her wits to resurface.

"Well, of course. I want us to marry right away. We can take a wedding trip to Kansas City and stay in my parents' home. The place is massive and we won't be cramped for room."

"But Lindsborg is my home," she interjected.

"Lindsborg has been your home, but it doesn't have to stay that way."

Sigrid shook her head. "I must say, this comes at a great surprise. We scarcely know each other."

"We know each other better than most folks," he assured her. "Come sit with me and we can talk about all the things that are worrying you." He reached out for her arm, but Sigrid was unsure that she wanted him to touch her. Strange things happened to her mind when he touched her. Seeing her hesitation, Ruben held up his hands and backed away. "Please. Just come sit with me for a time."

Sigrid took a seat and stared at the wall over his head. "All of my family live in Lindsborg. My friends are here. My life is here. I don't want to live in the city. At least I don't think I do."

"But my dear, you've never seen the city. You've never been outside this tiny town in all of your life. You told me so, remember?" She nodded and he continued. "You have no idea what lies in wait for you out there. The opportunities are too numerous and too wondrous to even imagine. You can never grow bored there."

"I don't grow bored here," she countered.

Looking at Ruben with a new heart, Sigrid tried to honestly see herself in the role of his wife. He dressed immaculately in fine suits, and always looked the epitome of style and fashion. His hands were soft and clean, with perfectly trimmed nails and no calluses to mar their appearance. He would no doubt expect just such perfection from a wife.

"Family is very important to me, Ruben. The man I marry will have to understand that, and he will have to honor God, as well. God is the foundation for all I hold true and dear."

"I understand and completely agree with you." The words came without any appearance of discomfort.

She got up without warning and walked to the kitchen window. "I've grown to love this house and this land. My parents worked hard to make this a home, and now your railroad wants to destroy all of that and put in their depot and their roundhouse."

"So don't sell it to them."

His words were so matter-of-fact that Sigrid couldn't

help but turn to look at him. "Just like that?"

He smiled. "Just like that. Don't sell it and they'll build elsewhere."

"But I thought this location was perfect."

Ruben rubbed his mustache. "It is, and it would make things go a whole lot better for all the people in this town. The railroad doesn't choose a site without weighing heavily the impact it will have on the townspeople. If the people aren't happy, the railroad is doomed to certain failure."

"I hadn't thought about making it easier for everyone else." Suddenly she felt very selfish. "I have to admit, I've only thought of my own pain. My own needs."

Ruben rose to his feet and slowly crossed the room. "As my wife, you need never worry about pain or comfort again. I can give you everything."

"But I have everything I want here."

He smiled tolerantly. "But there's so much more I want to give you. I want to show you the world, and I want to show you to the world. Will you at least think about my proposal?"

Sigrid swallowed hard and nodded. "All right. I'll think about it."

"Good. I'll expect you give me an answer as soon as possible. After all, the holidays are nearly upon us and I know you'll be far too busy to give much thought over to a wedding then."

Sigrid nodded, but said nothing. Her mind was consumed with the weight of Ruben's proposal and all that it might mean to her.

He left without any further attempt to kiss her, even

though for a moment Sigrid had feared that had been his definite intent. She turned back to the kitchen counter and sighed. How could she possibly keep her mind on work now?

She finished her tasks just before the last light of day faded into twilight. Lighting the lamps, Sigrid took down her mother's Bible and sat down to read. There had to be answers for the questions in her heart.

Her hand immediately opened to the tenth chapter of Matthew. Scanning down, she came upon verse sixteen which admonished, "Behold, I send you forth as sheep in the midst of wolves: be ye therefore wise as serpents, and harmless as doves."

Moder had often spoken of Satan's deception in appearing as one of the sheep in order to work his way into the flock.

"If you saw a wolf coming, you would shoot him, ja?" she could hear her mother question. "But when a stray sheep joins in, you think not so very much about it. You figure you will find the owner and return him, but he'll do no harm to graze with your own flock until that time. After all, he's just a sheep."

Erik had warned her that Ruben wasn't all that he appeared—that he wasn't one of them. He told her to mind herself around him, and his brotherly advice bothered her greatly.

Lord, I want to do the right thing. Selling the farm would help Ina and Sven in ways that I can't hope to help them. Giving this land up would benefit the town, and all of my friends and family would have a better life because of my sacrifice. She closed the Bible and laid her head atop it. *I don't mean to put a thing or place above the comfort and need of my loved ones. I guess I'm ready to let go, if that's what You want me to do. It doesn't feel good, or right, but if You want me to do this thing then please mark out the path.*

And as for Ruben and his proposal. She paused, trying to figure out what she should pray. *You know what he's asked of me, and You alone know if he's the one for me. I just feel so confused. There's Ruben, and then there's Erik. Ruben has asked me to marry him, and he seems to genuinely love me. Erik has asked me to marry him, and he seems to genuinely care about me, but I'm not so sure he loves me.*

And whom do you love? her heart seemed to ask.

"I wish I knew," she answered aloud.

JAST KRANS
(Yeast Wreath)

1 package yeast
3 T. sugar
3 egg yolks
1 cup warm milk
4 cups flour
1 tsp. salt
1 cup butter

Dissolve together yeast, sugar and ½ cup warm milk, set aside. Next, beat together egg yolks and ½ cup warm milk, set aside. Mix together flour, salt, and butter (this will be like pie crust). Add the yeast and egg yolk mixtures and mix well. Set in a cool place overnight.

3 egg whites
1 tsp. cinnamon
½ cup sugar
Handful of nuts, dates, or raisins, if desired
Oven at 350°F

In the morning, divide into two portions and roll out thin. Mix 3 stiffly beaten egg whites with sugar and cinnamon and spread this on top of the dough. Sprinkle with nuts, dates or raisins. Roll lengthwise and shape in a ring. Let rise 1 hour or until doubled. Bake at 350°F for

20 minutes. Frost with ¾ cup powdered sugar blended with cream.

Erik sat in the cafe nursing his third cup of coffee. For longer than he cared to remember, he'd been coming here for meals instead of going to the Larsson house. He felt it was only fair to give Sigrid her head. She was going to have to decide for herself if he meant anything to her—anything more than friends and workers of the same ground.

Putting the cup down, Erik decided it was time to return to the fields. But just as he reached for his hat, the unmistakable voice of Ruben Carter sounded from the now open cafe door.

"Come on Hank, I'll treat you to lunch and tell you where things stand."

Erik froze in place, wondering if he should confront Ruben with his concern for Sigrid. He wanted badly to warn the man to leave her alone, but it wasn't his place and so he held himself in check.

Ruben, clearly oblivious to anyone else in the cafe, took the booth directly behind Erik and continued his conversation. Never one to set out to eavesdrop, Erik couldn't help himself when Ruben brought up the subject of Sigrid and the farmstead.

"I figure if I can get her to marry me before Christmas," Ruben told his companion, "I can get her to sign over without too much difficulty."

"You mean you'll keep her so otherwise occupied she won't have time to worry about land, don't ya?" the man said with a dirty laugh.

Ruben chuckled. "Well, that will be one of the benefits of this whole scheme. She's not that bad to look at, although she's the same as the rest of these dirt-dumb farmers. She's actually happy to live here and wants to stay in Lindsborg."

"Maybe that'll change after you propose."

"I proposed yesterday," Ruben admitted.

Erik hadn't realized how hard he was gripping the coffee mug until his hand started to ache. He put the cup down and tried to refrain from jumping to his feet. He couldn't confront Ruben here. Not this way. Not now.

"Did she say yes?" the other man was now questioning.

"Not exactly, but I did my best to persuade her. If you know what I mean."

They laughed in a way that left Erik little doubt that Ruben had probably handled the matter in a most inappropriate way. But he knew Sigrid, and he felt confident that she had probably put Ruben in his place in spite of what the man said to his friend.

"Sigrid will come around, and when she does," Ruben continued, "the land will be ours."

"I thought you had a deal with that brother of hers. Seems a sorry state of affairs that you should have to hitch yourself up with her in order to get the land."

"Her brother's willing to sell me the place, but he hates hurting Sigrid. I tried to play it smooth, let him think I understood his compassion. I let it drop and figured I'd work on Sigrid. If I can talk her into marriage, I shouldn't have any trouble getting her to give up the farm. After all, I made it clear that Kansas City could offer us both a great deal in the way of comfort and charm. After a couple of months there, I'll send her home to her brother. Then she can have her farm town and the railroad can have their depot and roundhouse."

"You mean divorce her?"

"Of course. I don't intend to stay married to someone like her," Ruben said in a voice that suggested how unthinkable such a matter could be. "Imagine trying to take her to New York. She could never hope to fit into my social circle. No, I've spent enough time listening to her stories of Swedish traditions and love of the land. I'll be glad to knock the dust of this town off my feet once and for all."

"But you'll have a good time with her first, I hope," the man said in a much lowered voice.

Ruben laughed. "Of course. I don't mind sampling country cooking, I just don't want it for the rest of my life."

The men laughed while Erik seethed. He wanted to punch Carter square in the nose, but more than that, he wanted to run to Sigrid and hide her away like a precious gem. How dare Carter talk of using her and then divorcing her! How would Sigrid ever live with the shame of such a thing?

The waitress came to serve the two men, and with her keeping them both completely occupied, Erik slipped out the back door of the cafe. He struggled to know what he should do. On one hand, if he went to Sigrid and told her the truth, she might not believe him. She might think that he was only speaking out of a jealous heart or worse yet, that he only wanted to keep her from giving Ruben the land.

"Lord," he whispered, stepping into the dusty alley, "this isn't an easy situation to be in. I don't know what to do to protect Sigrid." He paused and glanced heavenward with a smile. "But then again, I don't need to protect her when You're already on the job."

He walked down the alley and around the building, continuing to pray. *She needs to be kept safe, Lord. I don't know if I should tell her what I overheard or leave it be. You know the answers, and You have a better picture of the truth than I do. What should I do?*

Erik paused beside the general store and looked down Main Street at their little town. He loved it here and he knew Sigrid loved it as well. The land and the community was as much a part of him as anything could possibly be, and he couldn't imagine his life in any way that didn't include living in Lindsborg.

Feeling his turmoil only moderately relieved, Erik sighed and made his decision. *If she asks me straight forward for the truth, I'll tell her. Otherwise, I won't volunteer anything.*

Moving down the street, another even more compelling thought came to mind. *What I need to do is ensure that she doesn't marry Ruben Carter.* He smiled to himself. *I just need to convince her that she should marry me instead of him.* Then his smile faded. Never having been one for romancing and courting women, especially given the fact that his eye had been on Sigrid for more than a decade, Erik wondered exactly how he should go about it.

As if on cue, Sigrid appeared—basket in hand—heading toward the general store. Erik swallowed hard.

She looked wonderful. Her cheeks were rosy from the chill in the air and her eyes were bright and searching. He stepped out of the shadows and smiled, hoping she would smile in return—praying she wouldn't give him a cold shoulder.

"Erik!" she exclaimed, seeming surprised, but genuinely happy to see him. "I haven't seen you in forever."

The ease in which she spoke put Erik's pounding heart at rest. "I went to help Sven with the broomcorn."

"Oh," she said, nodding as if understanding some great mystery. "Have you finished?"

"Yes."

The silence hung between them for several moments. "Have you come to town for something in particular?" Erik finally asked.

"Oh, you know, the usual holiday things. With Advent, St. Lucia's Day and all that goes with Christmas, I don't dare run out of sugar and flour. Not with all of my nieces and nephews to bake for. Oh, and I need some almonds. At least one almond," she said as if trying to burn it into memory.

Erik smiled. "Ah, making *risgrynsgrot*?" He spoke of the favorite rice pudding that was always found at any Swedish Christmas celebration. The trick was to mix in one whole almond and whoever found it in their portion of pudding was said to be the next one to marry or have good fortune.

"Yes, that and about a hundred other things." She smiled and her blue eyes lit up as an idea appeared to come to her. "Say, if you aren't busy, why don't you come for dinner tonight? I'm trying out a new recipe for *jast krans* and I'd love for you to tell me what you think of it."

Erik felt his breathing quicken. It was as if their last meeting had never happened. She beamed her smile and talked as friendly and openly as she'd ever talked to him before. She was beautiful and charming and everything he longed for. Why couldn't she see that his love for her was sincere? "I'd like to come for dinner," he finally answered in a low, steady voice.

"Good. I'll see you at the usual time then." She turned to go into the general store, but Erik reached out to touch her arm.

"I. . .uh. . ."

"Yes?" she looked up at him, her eyes widening.

Erik felt unsure of himself. "It's just that, well. . ." What could he say? What should he say—that he missed her? That a moment didn't pass by during the day that he wasn't thinking of her? "Thanks for the invitation."

She nodded, and for a moment Erik almost thought he read disappointment in her eyes. Had she expected him to say something more?

He let her go and stared at the door to the general store for several minutes before ambling down the street. *Where do I go from here?* he wondered. He wondered, too, at her good mood and her pleasantries. Then a thought came unbidden to his mind. Maybe Carter's proposal had brought this about. Maybe her joy centered around contemplating a lifetime as the wife to Ruben Carter.

Erik frowned and his optimism faded. Maybe her invitation for dinner had been given in order to break the news to him. What if she announced that she planned to accept Carter's proposal? Erik felt his stomach tighten and begin to churn. There had to be some way to convince her that he loved her.

Tell her that you love her, his heart told him. Sit her down and tell her the truth? It was almost too much to think about, and Erik did the only thing that felt right and comfortable. He found his horse and went back to work.

Later that night, after a quiet dinner with Sigrid, Erik found himself no closer to revealing the truth of his heart to Sigrid. She had presented him with a wonderful meal but had gone to no special lengths to entertain him. She talked of her sister Ina and the baby that was on the way. She asked him if he would keep an eye on the house for her as she planned to spend the next few weeks with her sister.

"With the baby due," she had told Erik, "Ina isn't up to the usual holiday cooking. I promised I'd come lend a hand, and since she is on the other side of town, I thought I'd just as well stay on at her place."

Before he knew it, Erik had agreed to care for her livestock and watch over the house, but he hadn't found the right opportunity in which to share his heart. Kneeling beside his bed in prayer, Erik found a restlessness inside that would not be ignored.

"Father, help me," he murmured. "Help me to win her heart."

Chapter 9

LUSSEKATTER
(St. Lucia Buns)

2 pkgs. active dry yeast
¾ cup sugar
½ cup softened butter
1 tsp. salt
½ tsp. powdered saffron
(dissolved in 2 tsp. of milk)
½ cup dark raisins
(optional)
Oven at 350°F

1 cup milk, scalded
6 cups flour
2 eggs
1 tsp. ground cardamom
½ cup blanched almonds
(ground)
¾ cup lukewarm water

Soften yeast in lukewarm water. Dissolve thoroughly and add milk and sugar. Beat in 2 cups of the flour until mixture is smooth. Add butter, eggs, salt, raisins, almonds, cardamom, and saffron. Mix well. Add remaining flour and knead until dough is smooth and elastic.

Place dough in greased bowl, cover and let rise approximately 1½ hours. Punch down and let rise again for 30–40 minutes. Shape into various Lucia bun forms (description contained in chapter) and let rise for another 15–20 minutes. Bake at 350°F for 10–12 minutes. Makes 30–40 buns.

It was already December 12th, and with the celebration honoring St. Lucia being tomorrow, Sigrid would need to hurry to have the St. Lucia buns ready for the holiday. Pulling the dough from where it had risen, Sigrid began to form the buns into a variety of shapes.

First she made the priest locks, or *judge's wigs,* as some called them. These were long thing strips, rolled by hand and shaped on top of each other until it resembled the old powdered wigs that magistrates wore in court. Each strip was curled up at the end to touch the curl above it. Next, Sigrid formed Christian crosses and Bethlehem stars. Then, just to keep with Swedish tradition, she made a great many buns in the shape of the Julbock, the Christmas Goat. Legend claimed that the goat would bring Christmas toys to good Swedish children. Straw replicas of the Julbock could be found in most of the Lindsborg homes during the Christmas season, and the children expected to find them on the Lucia platter.

The knock at Ina's kitchen door startled Sigrid for only a moment. Clarence was gone to town with the children in hopes of purchasing a Christmas gift for Ina. And, since Ina was sleeping, Sigrid had no other choice but to answer the door herself.

There stood Erik, with a light dusting of snow on his shoulders and head, his cheeks reddened from the wind and cold.

"What are you doing here?" she asked, mindless of her manners.

Erik laughed. "I came to see you."

"Well, you'd best come in then," she said, not understanding why she suddenly felt awkward in his presence.

Sigrid went back to the oven and checked on the buns. "Have a seat and I'll get you some coffee." Her heart skipped a beat and her stomach felt like a swirl of butterflies resided inside.

If it's possible, she thought, *he's more handsome than ever.* Then she pushed aside that line of thinking and tried to steady her nerves. Ever since she'd had him to supper the week before, he'd acted all tongue-tied and strange. She'd wondered what he was thinking, but it seemed rude to press him for an answer.

"Smells mighty good in here," Erik said.

Sigrid straightened and went to the cupboard for a cup. "I'm baking the St. Lucia buns," she told him and poured steaming coffee into the mug. "Ina's not feeling very good. I'm guessing the baby will probably come tonight or tomorrow."

She put the coffee down on the table before realizing that Erik held a wrapped package in his hands.

"This is for you," he said, holding out the gift.

"For me?" She knew her voice registered distress and disbelief. "It's too early for Jul gifts."

"It's not for Jul," he said quite seriously. "I've been doing a lot of thinking and there's some things that need settled between us."

She felt her mouth go down. "There are?"

"Just open the package and I'll explain."

She sat down at the table and pulled at the strings which held the paper in place. The paper fell away and inside she found two artfully carved wooden spoons. Tears came to her eyes.

"You know what these spoons represent," he more stated than questioned. She nodded but said nothing. "I figured it was time to speak my mind, Sigrid. I don't want to lose you to that Carter fellow. He's boasting all over town how he asked you to marry him, and I'm not giving you up without a fight."

Her head snapped up at this. "You want the land that bad?"

Erik slammed his fists down on the table. "It has nothing to do with the land. I want to marry you. I know how you hold to tradition, so I carved the spoons for you and I'm here to ask you to be my wife."

Still she said nothing. She couldn't speak. Between the tears that were overrunning her eyes and the lump in her throat, Sigrid was afraid to even try to talk.

"I know you think this is about the land, but it isn't," he continued. "Seeing that I have competition and that there's a real possibility you might slip away gave me cause to think. I don't want to lose you, Sigrid. I've loved you since you were a little girl."

At this Sigrid couldn't sit and face him any longer. All she'd ever hoped for was that he might actually declare his love for her. Why did he have to wait until now? Now, when Ruben was offering her the world. She walked away from the table, clutching the spoons to her breast. *What do I do?*

"Did you hear me, Sigrid? I love you. I want you to marry me." Erik came to where she stood with her back to him. He gently put his hands on her arms as if to turn her to face him.

This only caused Sigrid to draw her shoulders in tighter. She couldn't face him. She'd been such fool. Tears streamed down her cheeks. *He loves me. He wants to marry me because he loves me.* The wonder of it all was too much.

With a low groan that seemed something between anguish and anger, Erik dropped his hold and walked away. Sigrid thought he was taking his seat at the table until she heard the door open and close. She wanted to run after him, and had actually turned to get her coat when Ina called to her. Erik would have to wait.

Throughout the night, Ina suffered in heavy labor to give birth to her sixth child. Sigrid stayed by her side, wiping her brow and praying. The breech-positioned infant girl was finally delivered by the doctor just after midnight, and Ina immediately bestowed the name of Bothilda upon the child. It was understood that she would be called Tilly, and Clarence thought it extremely good fortune that she had been born on St. Lucia's Day.

Sigrid's head had barely hit the pillow when Bridgett, the eldest daughter of the family, donned her white robe with the red sash. Yawning, Sigrid forced herself to get out of bed.

"I'll help you with the crown," she said, stifling a yawn.

Bridgett, taking her role as the Lucia Bride or *Queen of Lights* very seriously, nodded and positioned the wreath on her head and gingerly made her way down the loft stairs. Sigrid followed, finishing up the buttons of her dress as she went.

Bridgett arranged buns and cups on a tray while Sigrid made coffee.

"I love this day," Bridgett announced. "I always feel so special."

"I envy you," Sigrid said, and yawned once again. "I never got to be the Lucia Bride when I was growing up. In fact, as youngest, I didn't have a lot of privileges."

"Moder says you made a wonderful sacrifice to insure the happiness and well-being of your family."

Sigrid couldn't hide her surprise. "Ina said that?"

"Sure." Bridgett brought out the candles and handed them to Sigrid. "She said you did her a special favor by taking care of Mormor. She was afraid that since she'd just married Fader, she might have to take Mormor to live with them, and," Bridgett giggled for the first time that day, "she wanted to have Fader all to herself."

Sigrid smiled. "I can well imagine." She positioned the candles, thinking of Ina's gratitude and how she'd not only felt those things, but shared them with her daughter as well. It was rather like an honor, and Sigrid suddenly loved Ina more than ever.

Bridgett waited while Sigrid lit the last of the candles. She held the platter proudly and smiled. "Well, here I go." She took a deep breath and began to sing. *"Sankta Lucia, ljusklara hagring, sprid i var vinter natt, glans av den fagring."*

Sigrid smiled and thought of the words. *Santa Lucia, thy light is glowing, through darkest winter night, comfort bestowing.* She thought of their traditions and how they honored this young martyr. Legend in Sweden held that Lucia, a young medieval saint, brought food to the hungry in southern Sweden. But Sigrid also knew the celebration to date back even further. The first Lucia was a young Christian girl who gave her entire bridal dowry away to the poor folk of her village. She was later accused of witchcraft and burned at the stake on December 13, in the year 304 A.D. But no matter which Lucia you considered, Sigrid knew that the celebration was a representation of sending light into the darkness.

"Lucia brings the symbol of the light to come," her moder had told her when she was very young. "Jesus is the light who comes to us and makes our darkest night to shine as day."

Sigrid wrapped her arms around her. She could hear Bridgett singing to her family, and the sound left an aching in her heart. She had no family to celebrate with. As the spinster aunt, she had to borrow upon her sibling's family. A tear slid down on her cheek and the only thing she desired in that moment was to find Erik and tell him that she loved him.

"I love him," she whispered. "How could I have ever doubted it?"

Suddenly, even the thought of kissing Ruben sounded less than appealing. How had she managed to get so completely swept away? Was she so desperate for affection and attention that she couldn't see how Erik's quiet love had been there all along?

Chapter 10

KOTTBULLAR
(Swedish Meat Balls)

½ lbs. ground beef	½ lbs. ground pork
2 eggs (beaten)	½ cup bread crumbs
½ cup cream (heated to a boil)	½ tsp. salt
	⅓ tsp. pepper
¼ tsp. allspice	3 T. onion (finely minced)

Oven at 325°F

Soak bread crumbs in cream and set aside. Blend the remaining ingredients together. Pour cream and softened bread crumbs into meat mixture and mix well. Roll into balls the size of walnuts and fry until outside is browned. Put into a baking dish with 2 T. oil and 1 T. water; cover and bake at 325°F for 1 hour.

Sigrid barely waited until the sun was fully risen before pulling on her coat and boots. With mysterious excuses delivered to Ina and Clarence, she made her way home in the pale pink light of dawn. Grateful that there was only a faint dusting of snow on the ground, Sigrid pressed toward town with only one thought in mind. . .Erik.

She had to find him. She had to tell him how she felt and how she'd ignored those feelings for most of her life. He'd always just been there: comforting, familiar, loving, although she couldn't see it for the nearness of it. Feeling a song in her heart, she hummed Santa Lucia and forced herself not to run.

Chilled to the bone but warm in spirit, Sigrid crossed Lindsborg's Main Street and hurried in the direction of home. She'd just passed from town when Ruben came from seemingly nowhere.

"Sigrid! I was hoping to see you today. I was just on my way to your house."

She stopped and looked at him sternly, wondering what it was about him that had held her captive for so long.

"What?" Ruben questioned. "Isn't my hat on straight?" He reached up as if to adjust it.

"No, it isn't that," she smiled, not realizing how appealing she looked.

Ruben swept her into his arms, mindless of the very public scene they were making. "I've come for an answer to my proposal. You've put me off long enough." He tried to kiss her, but Sigrid turned her face away and pushed at his arms.

"Let me go, Ruben. I can't marry you."

Ruben dropped his hold and stared at her in surprise. "What do you mean, you can't marry me?"

"I don't love you, Ruben. I can't marry you, because I'm in love with someone else. I'm sorry." She didn't wait for his response but instead kept walking toward home. Home and Erik. She knew he'd be close by and whether he was caring for her livestock or working in his own barn, she would find him and declare her love to him.

"You can't be serious," he said, catching up to her.

She picked up speed and nodded. "But I am."

Ruben grabbed her and pulled her away from the road. Pushing her up against the thick trunk of a cottonwood tree, he glared at her. "You can't do this to me. I have plans."

"I'm sorry." His grip tightened. "Let me go, Ruben."

"No. You're being stupid. It isn't like something better is going to come along."

She smiled. "Something better already has come along. I just didn't realize that he'd been there all along."

"You're coming with me. We're getting married."

Sigrid's mouth dropped open as Ruben dragged her along behind him. She began protesting, yelling, almost screaming for him to leave her alone. Then suddenly, without warning, Sigrid felt her free arm being pulled in the opposite direction. Looking back, she found Erik.

"Let her go, Carter. You heard for yourself, she wants nothing to do with you."

Ruben dropped his hold, completely intimidated by the huge Swede. He opened his mouth as if to say something, then growled and took off in the direction of Main Street.

Sigrid looked up at Erik, not knowing what to say. Her heart was full to busting with the love she felt inside. He had come to save her once again.

Erik said nothing but simply took hold of her arm and led her home.

❧

Once inside the warmth of her kitchen, Sigrid felt shy and uncertain. What if she declared her love and Erik no longer wanted her? She swallowed her pride and decided the best thing to do was to be honest.

"I didn't expect to see you today," Erik said softly.

"I know." She tried to think of what to say next. "I had to see you."

"Why?"

She drew a deep breath and faltered. Lowering her gaze, she looked at her hands.

"Why, Sigrid?" Erik repeated.

"Because I love you," she whispered.

"What?"

She looked up and found him smiling. He'd heard all right, but he wanted to hear the words again. "I came home to tell you that I love you, and if you still think you want to marry me, then I'd love nothing more."

Erik laughed. "I suppose I could tolerate the idea."

Sigrid smiled and raised a single brow. "Only tolerate?"

"Well, I guess you've got me there."

He got to his feet and came to take her in his arms. Sigrid melted against him, feeling her heart pounding so hard that she was certain he could hear it. She looked up into his eyes and found all the love she'd hoped to find. "Do I really have you?" she whispered.

Just before his lips touched her in a passionate kiss, Sigrid heard him whisper, "You've always had me."

After the Julotta services at church on Christmas morning, Erik and Sigrid joined the rest of her family at Ina's house. The smorgasbord was laid out with all of the traditional foods of their ancestry. Pickled herring, Swedish meat balls, *lutefisk,* ostkaka and, of course, rice pudding were among the many overflowing platters of goodies.

Sven offered a prayer at Ina's request, and as he finished, Erik requested everyone's attention to announce that he and Sigrid were to be married as soon as the holidays were completed.

"Oh, Sigrid!" Ina squealed in girlish delight. "I'm so happy for you."

Sigrid embraced her sister. "That's not all. Erik and I intend to pay you and Sven the same amount of money that the railroad is offering for the farm. We want to live on the farmstead. I want to raise our children where Moder and Fader worked so hard to make us happy."

Erik lost no time in pulling papers from his pocket. "I know it's Christmas, but this is to show you we mean what we say." He handed the papers to Sven. "I hope you will understand how much this means to both of us."

"Of course we understand," Ina said.

"But I struck an agreement with the railroad," Sven replied rather sheepishly.

"No money changed hands," Ina reminded him. "Besides, I never agreed to it. Erik talked to me some time ago, and I thought his proposal was much better."

Just then a knock sounded on the door and Bridgett went to open it. Ruben Carter didn't wait to be announced but pushed his way past the girl and came to where Sven was still studying the paper Erik had given him.

"I want to finish our agreement," he told Sven.

"Sorry you had to come all this way, Mr. Carter," Ina said, before Sven could reply. "We aren't selling the land to the railroad. Sven had no right to make an agreement without Sigrid's and my approval."

"He's the man of the family, isn't he?" he glared at Sigrid as he asked the question.

"Ja," Ina replied, "but Swedish women are just as tenacious as Swedish men."

"Sorry, Carter," Sven offered apologetically. "I guess I'm outvoted."

"But we had an agreement."

"It wasn't a lawful arrangement, Carter," Erik said, moving in between Ruben and Sven. "But this is." He took the papers from Sven and held them up. "I'm buying the property with my wife."

Ruben threw Sigrid a sneering look of disbelief. "He's only doing this to get your land."

Sigrid didn't want to face him in an argument. "No, he did it because he loves me," she said as she turned and walked from the room to avoid any further confrontation.

Taking herself outside, Sigrid prayed that the matter would be concluded without her. She didn't like the way Ruben looked at her, and she didn't want to listen to his threats or foul-mouthed accusations. Walking the full length of the wraparound porch, Sigrid had just come to the front when an angry Ruben bounded out of the house. He instantly saw her and stopped.

"I never wanted you for my wife. I wanted the land,

just like Lindquist." The words were delivered with all the hate and bitterness that Ruben's face featured. "You aren't worth the trouble, Sigrid." He stormed off down the path and left her to stare after him.

His words should hurt, she thought. But they didn't. She only felt sorry for Ruben, and more sure of Erik. What did hurt was that she had ever believed Ruben's flowery words of love.

Turning away, she found Erik standing at the end of the porch. He'd heard everything Ruben had said, and he seemed to watch her for any sign of regret in her choice. And then, Sigrid saw something more in his expression. He showed no surprise or alarm at the words he'd heard. Only patient compassion as he waited for her reaction. He knew! He knew all along and yet he never told me! Her heart swelled with love for him, and she smiled.

Erik held open his arms and Sigrid eagerly went to him, cherishing the warmth he provided against the cold of winter and Ruben's declaration.

"You knew, did you?" she whispered as he kissed the top of her head.

"Yes."

"And you never told me because you knew I wouldn't have believed you."

"Yes." He kissed her again.

"I was such a fool, Erik."

"Yes." This time he lifted her chin with his warm, callused fingers and kissed her on the forehead.

"Moder always said I could trust you. I should have believed her. . .and you."

"Yes." He kissed her right cheek.

"I guess love was so close I just couldn't see it. Forgive me?"

"Yes." His low, husky voice warmed her as much as the kiss he placed on her left cheek.

Sigrid smiled and pressed herself closer. "Love me?"

"Oh, yes," he half moaned, half whispered, and pressed his lips to hers.

Sigrid sighed and wrapped her arms around his neck. She returned his kiss with matched enthusiasm and felt the heat of passion radiate throughout her body.

He pulled away, and Sigrid opened her eyes to find him grinning as though he'd just won first place in a race. "*God Jul,* darling," he whispered.

"Merry Christmas to you." She strained on tiptoe and pulled his face back to hers. "The first of many." She kissed him gently.

"Kisses or Christmases?" he whispered as their lips parted.

"What?"

"The first of many kisses or Christmases?" he teased.

She didn't hesitate. Kissing him again, she pulled away to whisper in his ear. "Both."

Tracie Peterson

Author of twenty-six inspirational romance books—many with Heartsong Presents—Tracie recently hit the bestseller lists with "Ribbons of Steel," an historical series cowritten with Judith Pella for Bethany House Publishers. Her short story, *King of Hearts*, published within *Summer Dreams* (Barbour Publishing), also made this year's best-seller lists. Tracie makes her home in Topeka, Kansas, with her husband and three children.

Christmas Flower

Colleen L. Reece

Chapter 1

Tattered banners of crimson, green, and violet fluttered in the autumn sky over the tiny village of Tarnigan, like a shattered kaleidoscope spilling broken rainbows. Fantastic patterns painted the white hills and valleys in the shadow of the Endicott Range. The yellow glow from lighted windows paled by comparison, even those shining brightly in Nika Illahee, the Clifton-Anton home. The distant din of war had faded in the mid-1920s. Peace shrouded the top of the world.

High atop a snow-covered slope above the little village, a parka-clad girl with large dark eyes and wild roses in her cheeks caught her breath at the wondrous sight. She laid a mittened hand over her heart. Shoshana Noelle Clifton, "a rose, born on Christmas Day," pride of Tarnigan and all of north central Alaska, wound the fingers of her free hand in her malamute Kobuk's collar. He whined, then stilled beneath her touch.

Did the aurora borealis, she wondered, give her dog the same sense of tension it roused in her? She silently watched the display, held by its splendor, yet unable to shrug off a feeling of apprehension. For twenty years she had marveled at the northern lights. This night felt different, although she could not explain why. The beauty mocked her, bringing pain so exquisite she wondered if she could bear it. The northern lights seemed to whisper a single word to her: good-bye.

Shana flung her head back and cried, "God, what do You want of me?"

Kobuk stirred restlessly and whined again. The heavens glowed with the aurora's mad dance, and Shana stubbornly refused to give way to the growing coldness inside her well-wrapped body. Like snow figures created by laughing children and left to the mercy of the night, she and her now-silent dog remained still. The performance of lights reached its zenith and began to fade. Only then did Shana tear her gaze from the skies and command, "Home, Kobuk."

She turned and started for Tarnigan, spurred by nameless dread. Surely her fancy was running away with her, she told herself, but her momentum increased with every step, as though she could escape that single, whispered word. Soon she was running. With a joyous, "Woof!" Kobuk ran beside the fleet figure, as his father before him had run during Shana's younger years.

Halfway down the slope, a tall figure stepped from behind a cluster of giant spruce trees, halting girl and dog's impetuous rush. Strong, gloved hands grabbed Shana's shoulders and shook her. "You know better than to pelt down that slope," an angry young voice accused.

"Let me go!" Shana jerked free from the gripping fingers. Knowing she was in the wrong added fuel to the fire of her anger. "You aren't my keeper, Wyatt Baldwin. Just because Strongheart called you Little Warrior when you were born—"

"Don't forget Dad and Mom recognized even at that young age how appropriate it was and obligingly gave me my French name because Wyatt means the same," the young man taunted.

Shana knew without seeing that his ocean-blue eyes —so like Arthur and Inga Baldwin's—crinkled with mischief. "When are you going to grow up and treat me as I deserve?" she demanded. "The Bible says to respect your elders."

He shouted with laughter that brought an unwilling smile to her lips. "Never going to let me forget you ar-rived a few weeks before I blessed the world with my coming, are you?" His mirth died. "Right now you deserve to be tied to your bedpost, Shoshana Noelle. Running down the side of a mountain at night is just plain stupid."

Piqued because he was right and they both knew it, Shana brushed aside the comradely hand he held out to her. Not for the world would she tell Wyatt of the need she had felt to get away from the night. "Even if I fell down, which I didn't, it would be like landing on a feather bed," she muttered.

"Sometimes you're a featherhead, pal. Come on. Let's go home."

Shana sedately walked to the foot of the slope. Yet the moment her boots touched even ground, she gathered her muscles and sprang forward with the speed that made her one of the fleetest runners in Tarnigan. Even Wyatt was normally hard put to keep up with her and tonight she had a head start. Down the lane she sped, straight for Nika Illahee, here family's homestead, the name of which meant "my dear homeland in Chinook. Wyatt's snow-muffled steps thudded close behind. A peal of laughter rang out when she reached the steps and burst onto the porch a single step ahead of him.

"You'll never catch me," she taunted between hard breaths.

The light from the windows showed his gleaming white smile. A burnished lock of hair had escaped his parka hood and dangled over his forehead. A curious biding-my-time glint in his blue eyes sent warning chills skittering through Shana's veins. So did his low, "I wouldn't bet on it" and the odd little laugh that followed.

The door swung open. "Are you two being chased by wolves?" Dr. Bern Clifton wanted to know. His dark eyes twinkled. "Daughter, you look more like your mother every day."

"Thanks, Dad." She slipped out of her parka, fashioned from a white wool Hudson's Bay blanket with scarlet trim and warmly lined with fur. Shana grinned at her mother, pretty Sasha Anton Clifton, whose coronet of gleaming dark braids interlaced with crimson ribbons made her look just a few years older than Shana. "That's quite a compliment."

"You're almost as good a nurse, too," Bern told her. He ran one hand through the soot-black hair that gleamed with silver threads. His black eyes twinkled. "Tarnigan's mighty lucky to have us, plus Wyatt's folks."

She fell silent, remembering. First Dr. Bern Clifton, then his best friend Dr. Arthur Baldwin, had come to Alaska by tangled trails. Both had found love and settled in Tarnigan. Shana privately considered her parents' and the Baldwins' love stories even more romantic than Sir Walter Scott's novels. She felt a quick flush rise to her face and ducked her head so it wouldn't show. Would she find love one day? The kind that shone in Inga's eyes for her husband, in Mother's eyes for Dad? If so, when? With whom?

Shana shot a sidewise glance at tall, handsome Wyatt, her best friend since cradle days. Why had he looked at her the way he did in the glow from lighted windows? Surely after all this time he wasn't getting notions about his playmate, was he? *I hope not.* Her mind quickly rejected the idea. *I wouldn't want him to consider marrying me just because I'm the only girl around. Or because he doesn't want me to be an old maid. I'll be twenty-one on Christmas Day, pretty old to be unmarried in the north.*

The sense of standing tiptoe on the very edge of something too fragile to put into words made Shana mentally back away. Wyatt glanced at her, as if the girl's close observance had caught his attention. His eyes widened, but he seemed no different than usual. Shana bit her lip and turned from him, relieved, vaguely disappointed, and disgusted with herself, all at the same time.

"You're different lately," Wyatt remarked to her a few days later. "Something's changed, hasn't it?" He gave her a long, thoughtful look, as though he were searching her thoughts.

Shana flushed and turned her face away. "Leave me alone, Wyatt. Sometimes people just need a little solitude for a change."

His eyes lingered on her face, but then he shrugged

and walked away, leaving her alone as she'd requested. When he did not seek her out the next day or the one after that, she was irrationally peeved, and when she realized an entire week had gone by without Wyatt's presence, a wave of loneliness swept over her.

Still the time alone gave her a chance to finally pinpoint what troubled her. The compelling feeling God was calling her to use her nursing skills—skills the two doctors had taught her from as far back as she could remember—gnawed at her like a mouse nibbling rawhide thongs. With it came fear. What if He asked her to take those skills elsewhere? Away from Tarnigan?

"No!" she protested in a mighty surge of rebellion. "God, You won't make me leave everything I know and love, will You? I'm needed here." Yet was she, really? Both her mother and Inga Baldwin were excellent helpmeets for their doctor husbands. Shana could be spared, should it be God's will.

For days she denied the growing feeling in her heart, scoffing at the idea a person could actually be pulled toward a place she had never been except in stories. She shut her heart against the tales Arthur had told of the time he served in a place thousands of miles away, a place known only to Shana by fingering it on a map of the continental United States. A silly map, that had Alaska shoved off to one side as though it were of little importance.

Time after time, she stood beneath an iceberg-cold moon, the sky again alight with the aurora borealis. The low-hanging stars offered no answer. Neither did the flashing lights with which she had grown up. Yet amidst their magnificence, memories more vivid than the dancing heavens filled her mind. A small girl at her mother's knee, inviting Jesus to be Ruler of her life. A fourteen-year-old kneeling with her friend Wyatt, both promising to go wherever God might choose to lead them.

"Lord, when did my fascination with the valley tucked away in a fold of the Great Smoky Mountains in North Carolina begin to pull me toward 'the Hollow?' " she brokenly prayed. "When did the creeping suspicion I must one day go there take root in my mind? You know how I laughed at first. How ridiculous to believe You would expect such a thing of someone who loves Alaska as passionately as I do."

She shivered. Bern and Sasha had taught her since babyhood that God works in mysterious ways to accomplish His purposes. What if He asked her to leave all, including Wyatt? "Don't be foolish," she told her rapidly beating heart. "Never by word or deed has he spoken of anything except friendship."

Shana continued to struggle, saying nothing to family and friends, but pouring out heart and soul to her heavenly Father. Her mother's dark, troubled eyes, so like her daughter's, showed she realized all was not well. She said nothing and Shana appreciated it. For several years, Sasha Clifton had allowed her daughter to come to her, rather than attempting to discover what troubled her only child.

One night, Shana again climbed to her observation point. Helplessness swept over the girl, alone on a snowy hillside except for her faithful dog. Everything she held dear lay below her. She could not leave it. Yet how could she refuse, should going be God's will? A torrent of tears rushed to her eyes. Her cry echoed in the encroaching night, the cry of every follower who stands at life's crossroads, longing for guidance. "How can I know if it's really what You want?"

Kobuk laid one paw on Shana's sturdy boot. She dropped to the ground and hugged him fiercely. If she were called, he too would be left behind. Face buried in the dog's fur, she whispered her prayer of submission. "God, if it's truly Your will, I'll go. I know we're not supposed to ask for signs, but I feel so torn. Like a wishbone, pulled two ways until it breaks, leaving jagged edges." Her voice trailed off. After a long time Shana slowly stood and started down the slope toward Nika Illahee, one hand resting on Kobuk's proudly lifted head. No running this time. No Wyatt, scolding and exasperating. Just the drained feeling she had done what she must. The outcome was hid in the mighty hand of God.

An uneasy, waiting week passed. Two. Shana regained some of her peace. Perhaps God didn't require such a sacrifice. Perhaps He was merely testing her to see if she were willing. Then, just a few days before Christmas, a letter arrived. It shattered Shana's new-found tranquillity like a thunderbolt from the blue. Dr. Aldrich, the physician who had replaced Arthur at the Hollow wrote:

It breaks my heart to admit it, but soon I won't be able to carry on. I've tried in vain to find someone willing to at least assist. I know from the stories you share in your letters there's no chance you or your friend Dr. Clifton can come. Your people's need is too great. Do you know of anyone with even rudimentary skills who might help me? I have grown to love these people, as you predicted I would. I'll continue until I drop, but I shudder to think what will happen here when I do.

Arthur read the letter to the Cliftons. His handsome face, so like his son's, looked troubled. Regret darkened his blue eyes. "He's right. Neither of us can be spared. We're the only doctors for hundreds of miles. When one of us is away on call, the other is needed here." He spread wide his sensitive surgeon's hands in a gesture of hopelessness. "There's nothing we can do."

Bern sighed. "If we only knew someone, anyone, who would leave all and go serve." His massive shoulders sagged. "Arthur, I am so sorry."

Shana felt her heart skip a beat. Then it began to pound the way it did when she ran long distances. Her mouth dried. Three times she started to speak. Three times words failed her. On the fourth try, her clear, steady voice rose above the hard beating of her wishbone heart. "Father, there is someone. I will go."

Chapter 2

If Shana lived to be older than the Endicott Range, she would never forget the pool of silence that descended following her announcement. She averted her gaze from the battalion of eyes staring at her and focused on the room she loved. Colored by the impending departure, the handcrafted furniture covered with buckskin, the wolf skin rug, even the oversize fireplace with its six-foot lengths of logs that warded off Tarnigan's far-below-freezing winter nights, all looked unfamiliar.

Would she ever see them again? Shana swallowed the obstruction that leaped to her throat at the thought. A minute or an eternity passed. She looked at Bern, jaw ajar in amazement. She had involuntarily called him Father instead of Dad. Had it sprung from the knowledge she must be considered an adult? Otherwise, his beloved daughter could never convince him she must carry out what she now knew beyond the shadow of a doubt was her calling.

Bern shook his head, as if disbelieving what he'd heart. "You?" His voice sounded hoarse, strained. "You want to go to North Carolina?"

"No, but I must!" Shana burst into passionate speech. "It's tearing me apart. I don't know how I can ever leave you and Kobuk and Tarnigan." She looked at her mother appealingly. "I've fought and fought. For a long time, I tried to convince myself it was just hearing Uncle Arthur's stories." Her lips quivered and she clenched her hands into fists. "Deep down, I knew better. Every time I thought of the Hollow, something deep inside me stirred." She paused and licked dry lips. "I can't fight any more. Wyatt and I told God years ago we'd go anywhere He sent us. I just didn't dream it would be so hard."

The dam behind Shana's eyes broke. She ran to her white-faced mother and buried her face in Sasha's lap. Drenching tears poured. The silence continued. At last Shana raised her head and looked around the circle of concerned faces. "I finally told God it—it was all right with me. I had to be sure, so I asked Him to send a sign."

Like puppets released from a spell, the others came to life. Sasha's lovely face twisted with pain. She stroked her daughter's tangled dark hair with the slim and shapely hand that had helped save more than one life. "Dr. Aldrich's letter."

"Yes." Shana glanced around the circle of friends.

A spark flamed in Arthur's eyes. Was he thinking of his own days in the Hollow, of the terrible need, of how he himself had worked with Bern to make Shana an accomplished nurse and helper?

Inga only smiled, but the look in her clear, fjord-blue eyes warmed Shana through and through. Inga understood. Had she not given up life aboard the Flower of Alaska with her ship-captain father to marry Arthur and live in Tarnigan, far inland from the ocean depths she loved?

Shana turned back to her father. Bern Clifton looked ten years older than he had short moments earlier. Yet even as she watched, he raised his head and squared his shoulders. Shana felt a rush of love. No wonder the Indians of Tarnigan called him Hoots-Noo, "heart of a grizzly."

"You are sure." Not a question, but a statement of confirmation.

"I am sure." The words fell from Shana's lips like a sacred vow.

Wyatt said nothing. He stood in a crouch, like a mountain lion waiting to spring. His eyes slitted until only a blue gleam showed between curly golden lashes. Only the whiteness of knuckles strained to the utmost hinted at his agitation. A wellspring of protest raged within, but he dared not utter it in the face of such perfect faith. He felt caught in a whirlpool, tossed to and fro. To deny the white flame of Shana's belief in her call would be an insult. To remain silent was to lose her. *God, how can You allow it?* he silently prayed. *Must I give her up, just when her eyes betray the dawning of a new kind of love?*

Never! He had loved Shoshana Noelle Clifton from the time her mother gently placed the little girl's hand in his and said, "Wyatt, even though you are a few weeks younger, you are larger, stronger. I cannot always be with Shana. When I am not, you must always care for her and keep her from harm."

Clear-eyed, knowing even at that young age his pledge

must not be given lightly, the boy's clear blue eyes manfully gazed into Sasha's dark ones. He squeezed Shana's small fingers with his own slightly grubby ones and said, "I promise. For always."

"Thank you." Sasha's hand rested on the curly blond head like a benediction. It set responsibility burning in the boyish heart. Much later, Wyatt realized the poignant moment also marked the beginning of his journey toward manhood—and the day he would ask Shana to be his wife. No dark-eyed village maiden ever tempted. No laughing trapper's daughter or visiting cousin received more than a polite bow or smile.

With every year, Wyatt's love for Shana grew stronger. He scolded, teased, coerced, and praised. They took turns leading and following. The desire to outstrip Wyatt in canoeing and hiking and running made Shana fiercely competitive. His sunny smile and obvious pride in her accomplishments spurred her on to greater heights. He fought for her when necessary. A certain whey-faced shopkeeper who dared grab Shana with drunken hands when she was sixteen fell victim to Wyatt's clean-limbed rage and magnificent strength. Only the commandment "Thou shalt not kill" saved the man from death. Long before Bern Clifton learned of the insult to his daughter, the man fled in the dark of night again. The wounds inflicted on him by Wyatt's righteous indignation marked the transgressor for the coward and bully he was. He carried scars for months.

Never again did a man or boy lay hands on Shana. At the first sign of any unwelcome attentions by newcomers, someone in Tarnigan quietly took the strangers aside and related the shopkeeper's story. The usual response was a disbelieving, "That good-natured boy? Impossible." To which those who knew reminded through set lips, "Yeah. Cougars look like big pussycats, too, but they ain't!"

Cougars. Bears. Wolverines. Wicked men. Blizzards. Wind and rain and hail. Wyatt felt he could conquer them all. Now, faced with the greatest threat to happiness he had ever known, must he go down in ignominious defeat?

He straightened, a six-foot stripling whose slender build and buckskin suit covered solid muscle. He quickly marshaled the facts. One: He was Wyatt, a warrior. Two: He had promised to take care of Shana. He could not keep his pledge if thousands of weary miles stretched between them. Three: He had also promised to go where sent. He could still feel the solemnity of the moment when he and Shana knelt and dedicated themselves to following Christ wherever their heavenly Father might lead them.

A thrill shot through him. Like a heavy door thrown wide to welcome sunshine, a daring idea poured into him. Never one to waste time on regret, or to turn back once he had set his face forward, Wyatt took a single step toward Shana. Had a second or an hour passed since she had vowed in her solemn voice, "I am sure"? He neither knew nor cared.

Wyatt rose to his toes, then allowed his heels to hit the floor with a little bang of finality. Burning blue gaze fixed on Shana's tear-streaked face, he answered her vow with his own, in a voice that rang in the quiet room. "Mother. Dad. I am going with her."

This second bombshell brought a wave of protest. Wyatt ignored it, intent on watching Shana. Emotions chased over her expressive face like rainbows on a glacier, mingling, ever-changing. Doubt. Delight. Disbelief. They warred for mastery even as she fell back a step and held out one hand, as if to keep Wyatt away. "You?" she said in a strangled voice. "You?"

"Yes."

"Are you going because you also feel a call or because of Shana?" Bern rasped. His eyes glowed like twin coals.

Wyatt met his gaze squarely. His muscles tensed but he didn't flinch. Too proud to deny, too honest to claim divine leading when he wasn't sure about it, he quietly replied, "I don't know. Maybe some of both." He drew in a ragged breath and expelled it. "Sir, it's only a few weeks until Shana and I are twenty-one. I am asking you to release me from my promise."

A curious smile tilted Bern's mouth. "I'm amazed you have kept it this long." Was it a hint of relief that brightened the dark eyes?

Wyatt felt bright flags of color wave in his face. "Have you ever known me to break a promise?"

"No." Mischief replaced Bern's grave expression. "Would you like to take Shana into the kitchen and speak to her there?"

Wyatt flung back his corn-colored hair. "No, sir. Everyone here has the right to know. Do you want to tell them, or shall I?" He looked from puzzled face to puzzled face. A slight frown creased his mother's forehead. His father's eyes twinkled. Had Bern Clifton been unable to stay silent? No, for Sasha and Shana chorused, "What promise?"

At a nod from Wyatt, Dr. Clifton quietly said, "This young man came to me a good five years ago. He declared his love for Shana and asked permission to marry her when they were both old enough."

Wyatt's ears burned at the words and Shana's gasp, but he manfully took his medicine, never letting his gaze move from the girl's shocked face.

"Wasn't I to have anything to say in the matter?" Icicles tinkled in Shana's voice and a tidal wave of red swept into her tanned skin.

"Of course." Bern blandly went on, although his sparkling eyes showed how much he was enjoying himself. "Wyatt simply felt the right thing to do was to come to me, my dear. He gave his word he would not express his feelings until you were both twenty-one, unless you showed marked interest in another man. From the look on your face, I believe Wyatt has kept his promise. His honor is above reproach." Bern exchanged a meaningful glance with Sasha, who smiled tremulously in return. "Son." He extended a powerful hand. "If you can win my daughter, you have my blessing."

Wyatt tore his gaze free from Shana and knelt by her mother's chair. "Once you placed her in my care," he said huskily. "Should God grant me the gift of Shana's love, do I still have your blessing?"

Sasha looked deep into his eyes. Wyatt had the feeling she saw his very soul. Her lips curved upward. "With all my heart," she told him.

The revelation of Wyatt's love—or his audacity—proved too much for Shana. Hands over her scarlet face, she fled from his triumphant whoop to the safety of her room. She slammed the door, barely missing Kobuk's plumy tail, and threw herself on her bed. The malamute took his usual place on the bearskin rug next to it. "Go away," she ordered when Wyatt knocked.

"You have to come out sometime," he called. An exultant laugh followed. "When you do, I'll be here. I told you not to bet I couldn't catch you!" The sound of racing steps told Shana her scheming suitor had gone back to the main room. Was he even now gloating over the shock of his surprise?

The thought brought anger. How could he? How dared he complicate her life even more, when she already had more than she could handle?

Be fair, a little voice reminded. *He couldn't know you would be called to North Carolina. He did the honorable thing. Once he knew his boy's love for you had become a man's, he went to your father. He abided by your father's edict not to speak unless he saw you were beginning to care for someone else.*

Someone else? Preposterous! Shana's eyes widened. She pressed both hands to her chest, where her traitorous heart beat wildly. "God, am I in love with Wyatt?" she demanded in a whisper. Little things came back to her. His care through the years. His constant presence when she needed him. His comfort when her pet fawn died. His defense against the greedy, clutching hands of the drunken storekeeper. She shivered in revulsion at the memory.

Wait! Had that incident five years ago roused Wyatt to awareness of her as a woman? "God, I don't care for Him that way," she confessed. "At least not yet." A deep blush dyed her oval face. She stirred uneasily and allowed her hand to fall to Kobuk's ruff. She felt the dog's rough pink tongue against her skin. Loneliness filled her.

"Lord, if Wyatt goes, I could take at least that much of Tarnigan with me. Is it fair to him, when I'm not sure how I feel? Oh, dear, just when I think I've made it over one obstacle, here's a new one, although Wyatt wouldn't appreciate being called an obstacle." Diamond drops sparkled in her long, dark lashes. Like the mountain ranges of Alaska, her life had become one peak after another, each higher and harder to climb than the one before!

Chapter 3

The next day brought a northern storm that rattled even closely shuttered windows. Winds straight from the peaks took the girl's breath when she stepped to the porch of Nika Illahee and drove her back inside. Only fools or *cheechaquoes,* what white men would could tenderfeet or newcomers, exposed themselves to such fury unless they were far from home when the devil winds caught them by surprise.

Shana shivered. The previous winter she and Wyatt had been caught by the wind a few miles from Tarnigan. They had taken stock of the situation and decided their best refuge was to hastily construct a snow house. Kobuk snuggled down between them, adding his warmth to their shelter. When gray daylight came late the next morning, the three companions headed home. It took all their strength to reach the outskirts of the village before another arctic blast attacked.

Now Kobuk barked defiantly into the face of the storm and followed Shana inside. The Indians of Tarnigan had felt "the daughter of Clifton" would surely ruin the furry malamute by allowing him the run of her home. She had laughed, then proved how mistaken they were when twice Kobuk and his mistress bested the finest dog teams for miles around. Suspicion of the powerful dog's worth quickly died. Vindicated, Shana had the satisfaction of knowing all Tarnigan recognized Kobuk more than lived up to his ancestors' reputation.

In the living room, Shana slipped from her parka, knelt on the wolf-skin rug in front of the blazing fireplace, and hugged Kobuk. "I'm going to miss you so much." She sighed. "I can't take you with me. You'd never be happy." A shadow crept into her heart. "I wonder if I will be. I know I must go, Lord, but why am I not happier about it? Shouldn't I be glad to serve You, no matter where?" She thought of missionary stories she had read. Of the hardships and struggle, the eventual realization it was all worthwhile. "Be patient with me, please, Lord," she prayed. "Surely once I get there. . ." Her voice trailed off. Long, snowy months stretched between December and a time safe to travel.

"Enough brooding," Shana scolded herself. She jumped up. "Remember, Shoshana Noelle Clifton, the Lord loves a cheerful giver. A cheerful goer, too, I'll bet!" She giggled and felt better.

Heavy thumps sounded at the heavy front door. It burst open, and a snowy figure flung himself inside, accompanied by a gust of frigid air. Wyatt Baldwin's strong shoulder pushed the door shut against the shrieking storm.

"Good grief, what are you doing out on a day like this?" the girl demanded.

"Just because it's stormy, does it mean a man can't call on his lady-love?" Mischief twinkled in Wyatt's blue eyes.

Shana's heart lurched, but she refused to dignify his

jest with an answer. "Get yourself out of those wet boots and parka and to the fire before you catch pneumonia," she ordered. "Here. I'll put them to drip in the bathtub."

"I'll do it, but thanks, ma'am." Wyatt exaggerated his drawl. "Much obliged."

"I hope you don't think that's a southern accent," Shana said crushingly. "Even southern Alaska would scorn it."

"A humble thing, but my own." He fished a pair of worn moccasins from his parka pocket, slid them on, and disappeared in the direction of the bathroom. His curly golden hair shone in the firelight when he returned on silent feet, then hunkered down in front of the fire next to her chair and held his hands to its warmth. "Wonder if the Hollow gets blizzards."

"They get snow, but it probably doesn't last like ours." Shana stared into the leaping flames, wondering how to open a subject they must discuss—now, while Dad was in the kitchen watching Mother make dried-apple pies. "Wyatt?"

"Yes?" His sapphire gaze turned toward her.

She found herself strangely tongue-tied and mentally chastised herself. The young man before her was no stranger. She had shared her innermost thoughts with Wyatt Baldwin since they both learned to talk. Perhaps that was why she felt differently. All the long years she believed he was as open as she, Wyatt had carried the secret of his confession to her father. In some indescribable way, that secret, now that it had been revealed, had built a barrier.

Never one to back away from hard tasks, Shana crashed headlong into the invisible wall. "You mustn't go to North Carolina if it's only to follow me," she said in a low voice. Head bent, fingers laced together, she added, "I may not ever be able to care as—as you do."

Really, an unfamiliar little voice mocked inside. *Then why did your heartbeat quicken when Wyatt called you his lady-love? And why is your face redder than wild strawberries in summer?*

Wyatt's gaze was steady. "I'll take my chances."

Another wave of red shot up from the rolled-back, white collar of Shana's warm woolen gown. Wistfulness crept into her voice. "I wish you wanted to go for the reason I do," she faltered. "Don't you see? If it's just for me, you may find everything horrid and be sorry you ever left Tarnigan." She raised her head until her troubled dark gaze met his. "I will feel it's my fault."

For once, Wyatt's happy-go-lucky personality gave way. He reached up from his position on the rug and lightly touched her fingers before clasping both hands around his knees. He waited a long moment before he spoke. When he did, his face set in the lines of a man.

"Shana, I appreciate your honesty. We've never lied to each other and we won't start now. I wish I could tell you I feel as called to the Hollow as you. I don't. I do have a tremendous curiosity about the place. I always have. God speaks to His children in different ways. Perhaps my belief that I have to go with you, coupled with the desire to see the place my father loved and served, is the Lord's way of nudging me in the right direction."

Again he fell silent. She considered what he had said. *If only—*

Wyatt broke into her musings. "I never want to make

you feel uncomfortable. We're too good friends for that. Now that you know my feelings, we don't need to discuss them further." His gravity slipped and he gave her the lopsided smile that changed him back to the boy she knew far better than the determined man she had just glimpsed. "One thing. If I forget and come out with endearments—such as lady-love, sweetheart, or darling—" He shrugged. "Well, just ignore them. I've been thinking those words for a long time—but that doesn't mean you've given me the right to use them." He broke into a hearty laugh, the last thing she expected.

Shana's hands flew to her flushed cheeks. She scrambled from her chair. "Wyatt Baldwin, you are outrageous!" she gasped.

He bounded to his feet. Strong arms inexorably drew her to him. Too surprised to struggle, Shana stood quietly. Wyatt's head bent. He whispered, "Then just this once, I may as well be totally outrageous." His lips touched hers, lightly, reverently. For the space of a heartbeat, Shana stood stock-still, filled with wonder at the kiss. She felt the hard beat of Wyatt's heart, felt his arms tighten as if he would hold her in a circle of protection forever.

A second, an hour, an eternity later, Bern Clifton's rumbling laugh in the kitchen separated the couple as effectively as a knife slicing bread. Wyatt's arms dropped to his sides. Shana stepped back. "How could you?" Her face burned with shame. After telling him she didn't care the way he wanted her to, how could she have submitted to his kiss? What must he think?

Tears of rage came. Without another word, she turned

and ran—as much from her own traitorous self as from Wyatt.

He caught her at her bedroom door. "Don't run away from me," he said huskily. "I won't do it again. Not until you tell me it's all right."

She found her voice. "What kind of an apology is that?" she cried.

He proudly flung back his head. "I make no apologies, Shana. Saying I am sorry would deny my love. That I will never do." He wiped away a lone tear that escaped her tight control and left a silver streak on the girl's smooth cheek.

The gentle touch almost proved Shana's undoing. Feeling the need to sort out the new emotions rising within her, she opened her bedroom door and stepped inside. Wyatt backed away, but his gaze never left her face. Just before Shana closed the door, she saw a slow smile form on the lips that had kissed her so tenderly.

She flung herself to her bed. How could she face Wyatt again, she wondered in despair. His action had changed everything. No longer were they boy and girl, carelessly playing together in a land both harsh and wonderfully satisfying. Wyatt's inexperienced kiss had roused the sleeping womanhood in Shana as nothing else could have done. She tried to whip up resentment. "How could he, Lord?" Her attempt at fury failed miserably. There had been nothing rude in Wyatt's kiss, only the need to stake his claim, to let the woman he desired for his mate know the depth of his feelings.

What about her own feelings?

Unwilling to answer the pounding question, Shana

hastily rose from the bed, rebraided her hair, tied it with the scarlet ribbons she loved so much, and smoothed her collar. If the dark eyes peering back from her mirror shone more brightly than usual, if color streaked her face, surely Dad and Mother would not notice. Wyatt must not. If he did, it would give far more significance to the little tableaux in the living room a few minutes ago than Shana desired. With a quick prayer for strength, she swept out her door and to the living room.

The room stood empty and quiet, and both relief and disappointment swelled in her heart. She swallowed hard. Too bad if Wyatt had gone, just when she'd been prepared to pretend nothing out of the ordinary had happened. What was a kiss, anyway? Her heart thumped against her ribs. She hated dishonesty, even when it was only herself she lied to. She could not write off as trivial an incident that had affected her so deeply.

She walked to the kitchen on hesitant steps. A cheerful room, it boasted windows on two sides, a colorful tablecloth and chair covers. "Where's Wyatt?"

Sasha looked up from her pie making. "He said he had to get home." She expertly pared extra dough from the plate she held aloft in one hand. "Did you get things settled between you?"

The innocent question set Shana afire. "I—I think so." They had, hadn't they? "He knows I'm making no promises. He also is intensely curious about the Hollow." She seated herself in a chair next to her father, who took his nose from a medical magazine long enough to raise a quizzical eyebrow. "Dad, is it really all right to let him go with me?" A dreadful thought occurred to her. "You don't think the people in the Hollow will feel we are doing something wrong by coming, do you? Together, I mean. After all, we aren't married or related."

"I've given it some thought," Bern admitted. "Your friendship has always been accepted here in Tarnigan. But the Hollow? Dr. Aldrich will know, of course. Since the War and Armistice, conventions have been shaken. I don't know how much it's affected the Hollow. I do know they lost boys and men in the conflict."

"I wouldn't worry about it," Sasha put in, dark eyes confident. "If it's God's will for you and Wyatt to serve Him there, He will work things out." Her busy hands stilled. "I'd think anyone Dr. Aldrich sponsors would be given a fair trial. After that, your and Wyatt's own decorum will determine the way you are treated and whether you are accepted."

"Well spoken." Bern reached out a long arm and pulled his wife to his lap. "I do have a concern, Shana. You're a well-trained nurse and physician's assistant. What does Wyatt think he's going to be able to do in the Hollow?"

He posed the same question later that evening when the Baldwins braved the continuing storm and dropped by. "You can't just tag along after Shana," the doctor bluntly told Wyatt.

"I know. I wish I'd spent less time trapping and hunting and more time learning medicine from you and Dad, like Shana did," Wyatt mourned. "I can't change that, but I can follow you around and study. In short, take a crash course between now and spring. It will give me enough medical knowledge to intelligently follow orders. Right?

Thanks to you all, especially Mother, I also have a good general education." He smiled at pretty Inga, who had carried out a regular program of schooling for him, Shana, and other Tarnigan children. "Maybe the Hollow can use a teacher. If not, I always have these." He flexed his muscular arms. "Shana might need a cabin of her own. So might I, and I'm just the person who can build them."

Wyatt restlessly shifted position and frowned until his silky, golden eyebrows came together. "There's just one thing. Would it be better if we arrived in the Hollow separately? Once we get to Vancouver or Seattle, I could hang around and take a later train." Hot color flooded his face. The apology he had withheld earlier flashed a wordless signal to Shana. "I don't want to do anything to dishonor you."

Shana shrugged the question away, not wanting to face the implication behind his words. But she did not want her witness to God's love to be marred by Wyatt's presence. Her mother gave her a small serene smile, and Shana sighed, remembering what her mother had said earlier. As usual her mother was right: If this was God's will, then He would take care of all the possible problems. There was no point worrying.

Chapter 4

Shana Clifton always remembered the months following her call to a distant place as a time of waiting, bittersweet, filled with both anticipation and regret. Once the fateful letter committing Wyatt and her to their mission sped on its way by *coureur de bois* (woods runner), Shana threw herself into holiday preparations with all her usual fervor. Every passing day brought a pang. She might never again spend Christmas in Tarnigan. Even if she someday completed the work God had for her to do in that faraway land and returned, things would never be the same. Time had a way of altering even the most beloved patterns.

With Wyatt's help, Shana smothered Nika Illahee in fragrant evergreen boughs, hauled in on a sled pulled by the prancing Kobuk. Satin ribbons as scarlet as the girl's cheeks formed bows and loops against the dark greenery. Candles stood waiting in every window, ready to be lighted on Christmas Eve in honor of the Christ Child.

Sasha busied herself with sewing simple gowns of sturdy material, their only beauty in the workmanship of nimble fingers. She whisked the dresses out of sight when Shana raced into the room, saving them for her daughter's Christmas birthday. Costly garments would set the girl apart from the women of the Hollow, so

Sasha laid aside fine laces and contented herself with bits of bright trim on collars and pockets.

Only Shana's heavy silk traveling gown hinted at the riches she and her mother had inherited from Shana's grandfather, Nicolai Anton. Money from the sale of priceless furs Nicolai had taken in fair trade with Indians and trappers had helped provide much-needed medical equipment for Tarnigan. More than enough remained to carry Shana to her destination. She could live as comfortably as surroundings warranted, even supplement Dr. Aldrich's equipment, if necessary. Wyatt had saved most of what he earned by trapping, so he also had no pressing need.

If tears dampened the garments Sasha created with such loving care, only God knew. Along with wealth, the proud conqueror Nicolai had passed down a heritage of fortitude and endurance that silenced inner protest. Even an aching heart must respect the code of the north, the unwritten rule stating men and women must stand or fall according to their own choices.

Neither would Sasha allow Shana to carry away the memory of sighs and tears. She raised her chin and buried the loneliness creeping into her heart like permafrost under the tundra. She stored away each trilling laugh, every sight of girl and dog tussling on the wolfskin rug before the fire, each tender good-night kiss. In the months or years when obedience to God's calling separated mother and daughter by thousands of miles, Sasha would lift her memories from the treasure chest of her soul, and stroke them like nuggets in a chain of gold.

"Wyatt will care for her," Inga whispered to Sasha

on Christmas Eve when the families joined others in the small church first pastored by Bern Clifton's father, who had been buried a few years before, not far from Nicolai Anton.

"I know." Sasha pressed her friend's fingers. Long years of friendship coursed between them—and the strength God gives those who love and trust Him.

Shana saw the look the two mothers exchanged, and her own heart was comforted. The two women would sustain one another in the loss of their children. Shana stared at the candlelit altar, wondering at herself. In the time since she accepted God's calling, a strange thing had begun in her life. Her body remained in the land she loved, acutely aware of all she was leaving. Her parents. Kobuk. The Baldwins. Her Indian friends, especially Strongheart and his lovely wife Naleenah. Yet at times, she felt curiously detached, as if her spirit had already taken flight and gone.

Only Wyatt knew how Shana felt. She would never forget the poignant look in his eyes when she haltingly tried to explain. "I understand, Shoshana. I am the same." He raised his head and stared at the distant Endicotts, eternal watchmen over the valley in which Tarnigan lay. "I believe our hearts and minds are separating from what we hold dear to help make the actual parting less painful."

In a flash, Shana realized the truth of what he said. "Is this God's way of ensuring we will actually go?"

"Perhaps." He turned from the mountains, dropped gentle hands on her shoulders, and looked into her eyes. "Or His way of reminding that when His Spirit lives in us, we need not fear the future."

Shana said through trembling lips, "I am glad you are going with me, Wyatt."

"So am I." His blinding smile sank deep into her troubled heart. The next moment he changed from philosopher to facetious. "About time you admitted I'm a pretty handy guy to have around. Race you home. On your mark. Get set. Go!" This time she had no head start. Wyatt outdistanced her by a few steps.

Now the fragile moment shimmered in the candle-lit church. Shana bowed her head and silently prayed, *God, we can't know what's ahead. Help us take comfort from knowing You do. I still don't know why You're sending me so far away from all I know and love.*

A startling thought broke into her prayer. Was this how Jesus felt when He left His Father to come to earth? How could God stand it when He sent His Son, not to the warm welcome Shana and Wyatt would surely receive, but to a hostile world? What great love God had for His children to send Jesus to die for them! How could anyone refuse to believe in God, after He sacrificed His only Son? How small her own sacrifice, when compared to the giving of Jesus' life!

Joy to the world! The Lord is come;
Let earth receive its King;
Let every heart prepare Him room,
And heaven and nature sing,
And heaven and nature sing,
And heaven, and heaven and nature sing.
Joy to the world; the Savior reigns

Shoshana Noelle, a rose born on Christmas Day, could sing no more. The peace and joy that first dawned in a rude Bethlehem stable flooded her soul. No matter what lay ahead, she could bear it—and bear it joyfully. She looked at Wyatt and thrilled to his deep voice singing the ageless carol. The same exaltation that had come to her shone in his uplifted face. His hair glinted in the candlelight, and his wide shoulders were set straight and strong. No wonder Mother had confidently placed her in his care!

A sense of awe stole through the girl. Tease he might, irritate her he surely would, yet the love of such a man was not to be taken lightly. On this Christmas Eve, more than ever before, Shana accepted the truth. Wyatt Baldwin, not quite twenty-one, was a man, full-grown and master of himself. The fact he had turned that mastery over to the Lord only increased his worth.

As though he sensed her intent regard, his gaze turned toward her. His blue eyes darkened. For a moment, Shana felt he was a stranger, an exciting man she scarcely knew. Her pulse sped, and she hastily looked away. When she glanced back, her childhood companion smiled down at her. Yet the disturbing glimpse of unknown, unexplored depths haunted Shana, and set her heart on tiptoe thinking of what lay ahead.

Christmas Day passed in a flurry of snow and laughter, with tears just below the surface. New Year's Eve came and went, ushering in sub-zero weather that froze the snow-covered valley to a rock-hard surface. One day as Shana ran beside a sled drawn by Kobuk and his mates, her face bright with the joy of exertion, the sharp premonition of homesickness to come struck her heart with such force that she stumbled and fell behind the dogs. Next winter she would be far away in another land. Why, she had only been in Fairbanks a few times, and never as far as Vancouver, British Columbia, but soon she would be thousands of miles from her home.

Jesus left His home too, she reminded herself, recollecting her Christmas Eve experience. Again she felt herself withdrawing from the only life she had ever known, the sense of distance insulating her from pain.

Meanwhile, Wyatt had changed from outdoorsman to student overnight. Most of the time he steadfastly resisted Shana's attempts to lure him for a run behind the dogs. The one time, he did go with her, he kept pace with her easily, shouting medical questions at her between strides.

"How do you splint a broken leg?" he bellowed. As soon as she answered, he fired another question at her. "What's the treatment for pneumonia? Why does moldy bread cure infection? What's the best relief for the pain of an abscessed tooth?"

She answered his questions automatically, while her fascinated eyes watched the way his muscles covered the snowy ground so easily, his mind absorbing the new information. It seemed to her that she was watching him stride forward into manhood. And yet when he suddenly gave her sideways shove, sending her sprawling into a snowbank, she was perversely relieved to see him lapse back into boyishness. Giggling, she struggled to her feet, pelting him with snowballs all the while.

At last the long-awaited letter from Dr. Aldrich arrived. The Baldwins and Cliftons gathered before the fire in the living room at Nika Illahee. Arthur read:

Dear Arthur,

God is so good! I cannot stop thanking Him for the strange paths by which He accomplishes his purposes. Long ago when I first heard your stories of the need in the Hollow, I felt as called as Peter, Andrew, James, and John must have felt when Jesus quietly said, "Come. Follow Me."

My work here has not been easy. Fighting poverty, poor diet, and mountain superstitions means giving everything I have, knowing many times it will not be enough. Each time I lose a patient, a small part of me is buried along with the child, the mother, the bearded mountaineer who has "fotched" my mail. Or whose callused grip of my hand makes me fear for my bones. Or who has bestowed on me a rare smile of unconscious charm.

I often think of the English preacher and poet John Donne's immortal lines from his 1624 Devotions for Emergent Occasions:

"No man is an island, entire of itself; every man is a piece of the continent, a part of the main; any man's death diminishes me, because I am involved in mankind; and therefore never send to know for whom the bell tolls; it tolls for thee."

Think of it, Arthur! Three centuries have come and gone, yet Donne's words are as relevant to life in this secluded Hollow as if the poet had been born and raised here. I know you in Tarnigan must share my feelings, the necessary interdependence of those who live far from so-called civilization.

Forgive an old man's ramblings. They come from an overflowing heart. I also felt the need to let Wyatt and Shoshana know that no matter how hard the tasks here in the Hollow, it is all worth it. My people join me in rejoicing at the coming of your son and your friend's daughter. Don't be concerned about Mrs. Grundy and her raised eyebrows. We're too far back in the hills to slavishly follow her manners and morals. Besides, I have explained to those here the impossibility of Dr. Clifton leaving his work long enough to bring his daughter to the Hollow. These people accept the practicality of his appointing your son to act as her brother and protector. It is as natural as breathing for the older children in families here to look after the "least-'uns." As a sop to conventions, Nurse Shana, as she will be called, will live with a young widow and her small child. Emmeline is a little older than Shoshana and highly respected. I once had hopes of training her as an assistant, but young love, early motherhood, and the loss of her husband interfered.

Is Shoshana knowledgeable enough to pass state nursing exams? What about Wyatt? My people have great respect for my certificate. Mounting others on the wall of the white-washed cabin I use for a clinic would raise esteem.

My lamp is sputtering a warning the oil is nearly gone, and daylight nears. I look forward to spring and the coming of the two courageous young people. Their youth, strength, and dedication may be the salvation of the Hollow.

Below the signature were a few scrawled words, punctuated with a heavy black exclamation mark:

Wyatt and Shoshana won't have to ride muleback into the Hollow, as you and I did, Arthur. A road of sorts now permits automobile travel. Advise day of arrival. I will make sure they are met!

"What a grand person!" Shana exclaimed. A thrill of pure excitement flowed through her. "Dad, do I know enough to get my certificate?"

Bern Clifton considered. "I don't know why not. What do you think, Arthur?"

The mischief in the blond doctor's eyes made him look only a few years older than his son. "She might squeak by."

"Well, I like that!" The corners of Wyatt's mouth

turned down and he leaped to Shana's defense. "Hasn't she helped with every malady known to mankind? Didn't she stitch up the trapper she found mangled by a wolverine when we were miles away from Tarnigan? Wouldn't he have died if she'd run all ladylike and shrieking to get one of you?"

Arthur's eyes almost disappeared in laugh wrinkles. "Seems to me she did." His merriment subsided. He turned to Shana, whose face shone with pleasure at Wyatt's spirited support. "I'm only teasing. You will pass. Easily."

"Thanks to you and Dad, Mother and Inga," Shana murmured gratefully. She smiled at Wyatt. "If you study as hard between now and when we leave Alaska as you have been since Christmas, I won't be the only highly trained assistant."

He flushed beneath her warm approval. "Thanks for the lollipop, pal. What I don't learn here, you can pound into my head on the way to North Carolina."

Chapter 5

Winter reluctantly loosened its grip. Streams and rivers freed from their icy prisons babbled with the ecstasy of being alive and free-flowing once more. At daybreak on a late spring morning, the two missionaries and an Indian guide set out on their long journey. Heads high and unafraid, eyes damp but shining, they faced whatever perils might arise between their points of departure and destination.

"I won't look back," Shana promised herself. "Jesus said in the ninth chapter of Luke that he who puts his hand to the plow and looks back is not fit for the kingdom of God." She bid farewell to family and friends as composed as though she would return by nightfall, then followed Wyatt and Mukee up from the valley floor.

Alas for Shana's good intentions. Kobuk broke free from Bern Clifton's firm hold and caught up with the travelers atop the rise from which Shana had so often observed Tarnigan. She felt herself tremble when the dog flung himself on her with a joyous bark. She fought the urge to bury her face in his fur and never let him go. "Home," she sharply ordered. "Home, sir!"

The malamute trotted a few steps down the slope. He halted, looked back, and whined. His pricked ears and rigid stance showed puzzlement that his mistress did not follow.

"Home," Shana called again. Her voice sounded thin. "Kobuk, go home."

The dog threw back his magnificent head and howled. His desire to stay warred with years of training. Body drooping, he backed away a few steps and dropped to his haunches. His excited barks shattered the stillness.

"Ko–buk." Faint but clear, Dr. Bern Clifton's voice rang in the morning air. *Ko–buk* echoed from the hills.

With a look of reproach Shana knew she would never forget, her canine friend headed back to Tarnigan. Through blurred vision Shana saw Kobuk reach the group of miniature figures in front of Nika Illahee. A final mournful howl floated up to the three on the hill. Shana turned away. Mukee's impassive face softened into kindliness. "Kobuk, he be all right."

Shana said nothing. Could a dog raised and loved as the malamute had been adjust to the absence of the person he loved most on earth? She had heard of animals that sickened and died when separated from their masters. "Please, God, don't let that happen to Kobuk," she whispered. Child of the wild, she saw no incongruity in asking God's protection for her dog. The One who knew when a sparrow fell would surely show compassion on a lonely, abandoned malamute.

Wyatt's face wrinkled in sympathy and he wordlessly held out his hand. Shana laid hers in it and felt strength flow into her. Without another backward glance, they left the crest of the hill and began their arduous journey.

To Shana's relief, the trip itself brought a measure of healing. The wilderness grapevine had long since broadcast the news that son and daughter of the

Tarnigan doctors would soon tread the Alaskan mountains and valleys. The trio found welcome in remote and unexpected places. Vaguely familiar French and Indian faces appeared, their owners grinning and chattering with delight when the nomads of the north arrived at cabin or village. Shana recognized former patients. Wyatt discovered trappers he had met while running his lines. All shared what they had, and the visitors gladly accepted the rude shelter and coarse but strengthening food offered.

Other provision for their care had been made. In spite of knowing the uncanny way those who dwell far from civilization communicate, Shana and Wyatt found it hard to believe just how quickly word could travel. "How could they know?" they marveled when Mukee calmly pulled an overturned canoe from its shelter of bushes by the side of a rushing river.

A rare smile blossomed on Mukee's lined face. He grunted and his obsidianlike eyes shone. "Perhaps the birds of the air tell them daughter of Clifton and son of Baldwin come." He motioned them into the canoe, picked up a paddle, and sent the craft flying over the water. When the stream changed course from the direction they needed to go, Mukee waited until his charges clambered out, then beached the canoe far back from the water's edge.

"There will be other streams and rivers," Shana said. "Shouldn't we carry it?"

The corners of Mukee's mouth twitched. "Other rivers, other canoes," he said. "We use. We leave. Mukee bring back when he come again."

The guide's prophecy proved accurate. Only once did they fail to find a canoe when needed, placed there by unseen hands. That time, two bronzed Indians awaited their coming and safely transported them on their way.

"We be here when you come," they told Mukee.

"How will you know?" Wyatt demanded, fun dancing in his blue eyes. "It will be many days."

Shana covered her mouth to keep from giggling at the Indians' scornful dismissal of Wyatt's ignorance. "We know."

"Will they wait here?" Wyatt asked after the others left.

Mukee shook his head, a mute reminder that people who dwelt in the wilderness had better things to do than stand by the side of a river or stream until he arrived. Time enough to go there when needed.

At last the travelers, whose trek together had firmly cemented their friendship, reached Fairbanks. Mukee immediately replenished his supplies and turned back. Shana silently watched him go. She mentally reviewed the paths his moccasin-clad feet would retrace, each stretch of white water, every lonely mile. Only the excitement of purchasing tickets to Anchorage and boarding the Alaska Railroad could overcome the sadness of parting from their faithful guide.

A new world opened to Shana and Wyatt. Eyes used to far distances and few people widened at the crowds in Fairbanks, and then at Anchorage, where they took passage on a steamer bound for Vancouver and Seattle. At dinner time, Shana slipped into the dark silk traveling dress her mother had made, the dress that had ridden from Tarnigan in pack and canoe. When she shook out the wrinkles, the exquisitely stitched garment had no need to hide in comparison with more glamorous gowns. Shana's lovely face, velvety dark eyes and hair, and strong white throat rose above the dark silk like an exotic white flower growing in rich black earth. More than one man cast wistful glances at the girl. A few attempted to scrape an acquaintance but fell back from Wyatt's black scowl, assuming he must be a relative.

Unconscious of the power of her charm, Shana was more concerned with the unaccustomed sight of glaciers and heaving seas than with her clothing. She and Wyatt spent every daylight moment at the rail of the ship. The Inside Passage especially appealed to them, with its forested islands, fjordlike coast, tumbling waterfalls, and glimpses of wild animals.

Seattle left them both confused and eager to leave. "Like squirrels in a cage," Wyatt disgustedly labeled the inhabitants who hurried to and fro. Neither he nor Shana rested during their one-night stopover. They agreed the scream of fire engines, the rattle and rush of a city that seemed never to sleep outweighed the beauty surrounding Seattle. Even distant Mount Rainier on one side and the snowcapped Olympic Mountains on the peninsula across blue Puget Sound couldn't make up for "too many people in too small a place," as Shana called it.

The cross-country railroad trip brought more wonders. "Who'd have dreamed it would be like this?" Wyatt murmured, nose pressed to the window glass with the curiosity of an unselfconscious child. Shana, who rode facing him, did the same, much to the amusement of fellow passengers. "Alaska has a lot of different kinds of land but precious few cities and fewer villages. Here you can't go more than a few miles without coming to a little town."

"Wait till you get to the desert and the plains," the kindly man across the aisle advised. "You'll travel many a mile 'tween towns and more 'tween mountains."

Shana turned brilliant eyes toward the weather-beaten speaker who said he'd be getting off in Denver. "If I had to live where I couldn't see mountains, I think I'd die," she told him.

The man's keen gaze bored into her. "Just how I feel, ma'am," he said heartily. "That's why I picked Colorado when I went to ranchin'. You say you're from Alaska? Well, I reckon Colorado comes 'bout as close to matchin' your home for mountains as anyplace I know."

Shana and Wyatt fervently agreed when they saw the mighty Rockies.

They told their new friend good-bye in Denver. Before he left them, the rancher said, "The Great Smokies ain't like our Alaska 'n' Colorado mountains, but accordin' to pictures, they're mighty purty. Good luck with your doctorin' and nursin', young'uns. If you ever come back this way, look me up." He smiled until his eyes almost disappeared in crow's-feet, then ambled up the aisle and down the steps. The whistle shrieked a warning. The engine rumbled to life. The train chugged forward, gathering momentum with every turn of the wheels that carried Wyatt and Shana toward their new home.

"I hope the people in the Hollow are as friendly as this man," Shana soberly told Wyatt.

"If they aren't, we can always come back and look him up," Wyatt drawled. "He'd probably give us a job punchin' cows."

"Why would anyone want to punch a cow?" Shana demanded.

Wyatt exploded into mirth, but lowered his voice. "Haven't you ever read western novels? Men who work with cowherds are called cowboys, cowpokes, and cowpunchers."

"Who cares what a cow heard?" Shana grinned at him, but relented when he rolled his eyes. "Of course I've read western novels." A little trill of laughter escaped her. "When I was fourteen I was madly in love with Gene Stewart in Zane Grey's book *The Light of Western Stars.*"

"You were!" Wyatt sat up as though she'd dumped an icicle down his back. "How come I didn't know anything about it?"

"My goodness, Wyatt. Don't tell me you'd pry into the secrets of a fair young maiden's heart."

"You bet I would!" His blue gaze brought an unwilling smile to her face. He grinned, gave a mock sigh, and placed one hand over his own heart in an exaggerated gesture. "Aw, shucks, Shoshana Noelle. If I'd known years ago you had a yen for cowboys, I could have been one. Can't you just hear me yelling *yippy-ki-yi* and herding caribou your way?" Awe crept into his laughing eyes. "All this time and I never knew how to make an impression."

He paused and added irrelevantly, "I never heard of North Carolina having an overabundance of cowboys, did you? Especially in the Hollow."

Shana felt warmth steal up from the collar of her dress. "Don't be silly. I'm not going to the Hollow to catch a cowboy or any other man."

"Indeed, you shouldn't be," he pompously approved. "Not when you already have an outstanding specimen of Alaskan manhood biding his time until you decide to say yes to his offer of hand and heart."

"I certainly am glad for your lack of conceit," she mumbled.

"Faint heart never won fair lady," Wyatt reminded. He closed one eye in a wink. "I just want you to keep in mind that if a pore, lonely cowpoke wanders into the Hollow, I saw you first!" He yawned, stretched, and added, "We can't get to North Carolina any too soon for me. These train seats weren't meant for my legs." He shifted them restlessly, trying to find a place to stretch out their length. Shana giggled at his frustration.

Many a quiet laugh brightened the lengthy miles for Shana and Wyatt. Time after time those around them said things that tickled their funny bones. Such as calling trickles of water that wouldn't make a respectable creek in Alaska "rivers." Or pointing out "mountains" in the distance that rose no higher than the smallest Tarnigan foothills. Only their laughter kept their long journey from deflating their spirits.

At last, after days of travel, they reached Asheville, jumping-off place for the Hollow. Shana's heart pounded. Tarnigan, Kobuk, even her parents seemed part of a different lifetime.

A stocky, silver-haired man with dark eyes stepped forward. He held out a gnarled hand. "Miss Clifton? Mr. Baldwin? I am Dr. Aldrich. Welcome."

Shana's spirit soared. Time, hard work, and worry had bowed the doctor's shoulders. The three robbers had, been unable, however, to dim his unquenchable spirit. More important, Dr. Aldrich's look of gratitude and compassion made the travel-stained, weary girl feel that somehow she had come home.

Chapter 6

"The scenery is like a series of masterpieces painted by the matchless hand of God," Shana breathed to Wyatt. Fascinated by her introduction to her new home, she forgot the jouncing of Dr. Aldrich's old car over what he called "a road of sorts." Loveliness surrounded them, the Great Smokies at their best. Mountain laurel crowded close to the trails, great treelike shrubs wearing glossy dark green leaves and pink or white flowers. Some wore purple markings.

"What are those?" Shana pointed out the uncurtained car window toward clumps of trees, some thirty feet high and more. Waxy white clusters shone brilliant against the gray branches. Her eyes felt enormous from trying to take in everything at once. Her ears rang with the songs of countless unidentified birds.

"Those?" Dr. Aldrich glanced in the direction she pointed. "Dogwood." He tightened his hold on the wheel of the bucking vehicle. "According to legend, Jesus was crucified on a dogwood tree. The tree supposedly felt such terrible pain and shame, Jesus had compassion on it. Until then it had been a mighty tree. Jesus said never again would it grow to such large proportions that it could be put to such a use. It's also said Jesus caused the four bracts—the modified leaves—beneath the small, greenish-white flowers to form in the shape of a cross. Then He put a spot of scarlet in the center to remind the world of His shed blood." The doctor smiled sheepishly. "It's just a legend but I have to admit, I never see a dogwood without thinking about it."

"That's great. Are there other legends?" Wyatt wanted to know. Sun shone on his hair and turned it to molten gold.

Shana saw warm approval in Dr. Aldrich's face before he replied, "Oh, yes. See those redbuds? The ones with reddish-brown bark and heart-shaped leaves? They're called Judas trees. Legends say after Judas betrayed Christ, he hanged himself on a redbud tree."

Shana looked at the tall trees with the black-veined design on their trunks and shivered. "Don't they bloom?"

"Earlier in the spring, before the leaves appear. They're a sight to behold." He smiled at his enthralled passengers. "Of course, before then you'll see an autumn to remember. It's one of my favorite times of year." The winding, upward road grew steeper. Dr. Aldrich shifted to a lower gear. "We're almost to the top of the hogback. Close your eyes and don't open them until I tell you."

Wyatt winked mischievously before obeying, then shut both eyes. Shana did the same. "You don't need to tell us what we're going to see," Wyatt boasted. "Dad said the valley lies tucked in the folds of the hills like a cornhusk doll folded into a bit of leftover calico."

Dr. Aldrich chuckled. "He did, did he? Sounds just like him." The car slowed, chugged, and came to a stop where the road flattened. "I'm going to open the door and help you out. Keep your eyes closed," he warned. The doctor suited action to his words and cleared his throat. "All right. Take a gander for yourselves."

Shana opened her eyes. Blue haze that gave the Great Smokies their name shimmered in the distance. Thick forests composed of more than two hundred species of trees spread over the highest and most rugged portion of the Appalachian mountain chain. They stretched from where the watchers stood to farther than the keenest eye could see.

Long moments passed before she tore her gaze free from the horizon and reluctantly let it drift downward. A small feeling of dismay unnerved her for a moment. In spite of Arthur's warning, she simply hadn't been prepared. She and Wyatt had secretly decided passing years would surely have brought change, improvement. They had not. The westering sun, eager to retire for the night, ruthlessly exposed both the picturesqueness and shortcomings of the Alaskans' new home. So had it done more than two decades ago when Wyatt's father first stood on the hogback and looked into the Hollow.

Patches of corn and other vegetables snuggled up to log cabins in small cleared areas that feebly held back the looming, encroaching forests. Hounds bayed, their deep-throated cries clear in the still air. The laughter of children mingled high and sweet with the ring of pick and shovel on rock where men wrestled out stumps and cleared more land.

Shana involuntarily reached for Wyatt's hand. Thank God he had come with her, no matter what his motives! His fingers tightened on hers and swept away some of the forlorn feeling in her heart. She firmed her lips and lifted her head to stare again at the mountains. Why mourn that the valley itself held poverty, hard work, apathy, when she had those glorious, ever-present ridges above her?

" 'I will lift up mine eyes unto the hills, from whence cometh my help,' " she softly said.

Wyatt continued the quotation from Psalm 121. " 'My help cometh from the Lord, which made heaven and earth.' "

"My motto, as well," Dr. Aldrich told them. "Are you ready to go on? Go down, I should say." He chuckled again.

Shana and Wyatt silently climbed into the car. Waves of weariness dulled the new nurse's senses. They jumbled her impressions until only Wyatt and that mountain-top moment remained clearly in her mind. Down, down, down, the old car crawled. Here and there, figures in denim and calico raised curious faces. Men raised their hats. Women bobbed their heads. Children stared.

Dr. Aldrich waved to all. So did his passengers, but their host and sponsor didn't stop the car. "Time enough later for you to meet the folk," he told them. "Right now, you two look pretty done in."

Wyatt yawned mightily. He grinned at Shana when she couldn't help following suit with a yawn of her own. "Lead me to a bed. Any bed. Or a hunk of ground under a tree. It really doesn't matter."

"We can do a bit better than that," Dr. Aldrich said dryly. "You'll stay with me, at least for the present." He motioned to a small whitewashed cabin at the near end of a large, cleared area. A short dogtrot, or covered passage, connected it to a similar, but larger cabin. "Our clinic," he explained proudly.

Our clinic. Two small words that unequivocally welcomed and accepted Wyatt and Shana as partners against sickness. Wyatt straightened. A spark kindled in his blue eyes. Shana felt some of the fatigue drain from her body.

Dr. Aldrich didn't stop but drove slowly over the dusty road that led past a few discouraged-looking buildings. Shana felt her lips twitch when she noticed a freshly painted sign over the door of the largest. *Mercantile* rather than *General Store* seemed a bit pretentious for such an aged building. On closer examination, she revised her first impression. Old and sleepy-looking it might be, but a neatly mended screen door kept out flies, and the windows on either side of the door shone brighter than sun after a lazy glacier.

"Is the store always this way—or is the shininess in our honor?" Wyatt mischievously asked. His eyes sparkled and Shana's lips twitched in sympathy with his rising spirits.

"A little of both. The windows are always clean, in spite of the dusty road," Dr. Aldrich told them. "The newly painted sign is definitely in your honor." He grinned. "Actually, so is the sign itself. There's never been one before. When the storekeeper put it up, it sure made a stir." He laughed reminiscently. "Some folks 'lowed it was purely pretty. Others said 'twas all foolishness; there weren't nary a body for miles around but who knew where the store was!" The doctor's reproduction of his beloved mountaineer's speech held no malice and his passengers laughed along with them.

They reached the far end of the clearing. Dr. Aldrich halted the car before a double cabin attached by the same covered dogtrot as his own cabin and the Hollow Clinic. Rough and unpainted, time had laid a kindly hand and mellowed the boards to weathered gray. Wild roses clambered up the supports of the communal porch, whose worn floor boards showed evidence of a recent scrubbing. Starched white curtains fluttered at the window of the cabins. Their coarse material fit their humble surroundings, yet bore mute witness to someone's loving care. Twin water buckets rested on each end of the porch railings.

"Your new home, Nurse Shana," Dr. Aldrich quietly told her. "The left-hand cabin. Emmeline Clark and her son Gideon share the one on the right. Good. She's coming out now."

Wyatt's low, "What a beauty!" turned Shana's fascinated gaze from the unexplored mysteries of her new dwelling-place to the young woman slowly coming down the steps. She mentally echoed Wyatt's admiring appraisal. Emmeline's coronet of pale-gold hair framed a pure oval face, shy blue eyes, and a hesitant smile that silently pleaded *please like me.* Her full-skirted, blue-sprigged calico dress failed to hide high-arched, shapely bare feet but stole not one whit from her natural dignity, as she gracefully walked toward Dr. Aldrich and the newcomers.

A small, male replica peered from the shelter of his

mother's arms. Shana judged him to be about two. She glanced at Wyatt, who hadn't taken his gaze from Emmeline since she first appeared. Something sharp and hurtful thrust into Shana's heart. Never had she seen Wyatt show interest in any girl except herself. Now he looked thunderstruck. *As well he might,* jealousy taunted. *This mountain girl is as lovely as the wild rose blooming over the doorway.*

Dr. Aldrich beamed and said, "Emmeline, this is Nurse Shana. I know you'll be friends."

"I'd admire to," Emmeline replied in a low, musical voice. "Folks are all so glad you came. Gideon hardly ever cries. With the dogtrot between, we won't be a bother to you." She held out a slim, workworn hand.

Shana marveled. No wonder the doctor had coveted this girl's services. Her smile alone could bring as much healing as all the medicine in his black bag! She pressed Emmeline's hand and spoke more to the wistfulness in the other girl's eyes than to what she had said. "I am so glad we'll be living together." She glanced at the dogtrot and laughed. "I mean, be neighbors. Did you make the curtains and plant the rose?"

Emmeline's face lighted up as if a hundred candles flamed behind her eyes. Her laugh reminded Shana of a waterfall in spring. "The rose has been there as long as the cabins. I fixed up inside for you. Folks gave what they could. Would you like to see?"

Shana respected her the more for making no apologies. "Very much."

Wyatt found his tongue. "Not before I meet this young lady," he objected. "I'm Wyatt Baldwin. I'm not a doctor or a nurse, but I'm learning."

Emmeline turned her smile on him. The sword in Shana's heart thrust deeper at the delight in Wyatt's face when the girl said, "Many a man and woman here remember your doctor pappy and what he did for their kinfolk. I welcome you." She curtseyed quaintly, then turned back to the other girl, eyes eager. "Come and see, Nurse." Still holding Gideon, she mounted the steps, her slender back straight as a soldier at attention.

Shana crooned with pleasure when she stepped inside the cabin. Plain, white-washed walls gave a feeling of restfulness. The wood stove had been polished to within an inch of its life. A rag rug covered most of the scrubbed floorboards. Packing boxes nailed to the wall served as cupboards and hid behind plain white curtains that matched those at the window. An unmatched collection of freshly washed dishes sparkled on the shelves. A bright afghan mercifully hid the sagging sofa's defects.

Shana peeked into a small, curtained alcove, and exclaimed in delight. It contained a narrow bed covered with the most beautiful red and white patchwork quilt Shana had ever seen. Another braided rug lay beside the cot. A small table held a shiny kerosene lamp, well-filled and artistically shaded by a rose red paper shade. A coarse linen runner covered the top of an old chest of drawers on which stood a plain white pitcher and bowl.

Shana thought how little those in the Hollow had, how they could ill afford to give. She blinked to keep back a rush of emotion. She turned to Emmeline. "It's beautiful. I can never thank you enough."

The mountain girl's eyes widened. One hand absently patted her son's shining blond hair. After a moment she softly said, "There's no need to be thankin' us. It's we who are beholden."

Shana valiantly blinked back tears at the response. Barefoot and simple, Emmeline Clark, child of the woods, might be, yet Shana realized the girl's heart was as pure as mountain snow.

Chapter 7

Strange as it might seem, growing up in Tarnigan gave Shana Clifton and Wyatt Baldwin a boost in adjusting to life in the Hollow. Thousands of miles and customs separated the two places, yet they shared a common need: Residents had to be both self-reliant and dependent on neighbors in order to survive. Any doubt or suspicion on the part of those who lived in and around "the Holler" soon vanished like fog on a brilliant day.

Shana's first day in the Hollow began with a rooster blasting the morning air with his cock-a-doodle-doo. His arrogant stance and loud crowing clearly implied the bird's belief the sun got up every morning just to hear him.

Shana stirred, pulled her covers higher against the cool air coming in the wide-open, screened window. Dr. Aldrich had told her folks in the Hollow never locked doors or windows. His eyes twinkled when he said, "It's considered downright unneighborly, insulting, even."

"You don't have crime?"

"A few moonshiners in the hills. A mild feud or two that breaks out mostly in shouting matches or rivalry at rifle contests. Nothing that will touch you. Just stay on the main trails if you have to visit patients without me.

Folks can be a mite touchy about strangers wandering around where there might be a still."

The rooster crowed again, louder and more insistent this time.

"All right. I'm getting up." Shana threw a warm flannel robe over her nightgown, thrust her feet into deerskin moccasins that brought back memories of home, and pattered from alcove to sitting room. She touched a match to the already-laid fire and watched the sweet-smelling wood shavings burst into flames, then hopped back in bed until the cabin warmed.

A smile of pleasure curled her lips, remembering how Emmeline suggested Shana lay her morning fire the night before. "That way it won't take near as long to warm up your cabin," she explained. " 'Course in winter, you'll put in a backlog and keep a fire all night. It gets cold here."

Shana laughed outright. "Not as cold as in Tarnigan. I've run with my sled dog Kobuk in weather that's far below zero."

Emmeline's blue eyes opened wide. They reminded Shana of the deep blue shadows found in the massive Alaskan glaciers. Or cloudless summer skies. "How excitin' that must be! I've never been anywhere much except the Hollow and to Asheville a few times." Her face shadowed. She started to speak, then broke off.

Shana saw hunger in the other girl's face. "What is it, Emmeline?"

"I want to be somebody, somethin' more than what I am."

The eternal cry. The germ of an idea popped into Shana's

mind. "If given a choice, what would you like to do?"

Emmeline didn't hesitate. "Be a nurse. Like you. If I hadn't married so young, I'd have learned what I needed to know from Doc Aldrich. I still want to, but how can I?" She hugged Gideon so fiercely he looked up at her in surprise and wiggled to get free. "It takes all my strength just to raise enough crops to keep body and soul together and care for my boy."

"Do you regret marrying young?"

A poignant light came to Emmeline's sensitive face. "No. I loved Gideon's pa always. 'Twas natural for us to marry soon as we got old enough. We were happy. When my man died, I had our son." She stroked Gideon's pale gold curls. "Nurse Shana, I want better for him. I want him to have more than a mule and a patch of worn-out land. I'd do anythin' to get it for him."

For the first time, Shana felt the power having more than enough can bring. "Is there a woman here who would look after Gideon so you could work with Dr. Aldrich and Wyatt and me?"

Clear red stained Emmeline's cheeks. "I reckon, but I'd be too proud to ask unless I could offer them a sum. Doc Aldrich don't know that, though."

Shana touched the other girl's hand. "I inherited money. More than I need. I've already spoken to Dr. Aldrich about sending for medical equipment the clinic doesn't have. Emmeline, will you let me pay for Gideon's care while you learn nursing?" She held her breath. In the time she had been in the Hollow, Shana had learned the mountain people found it far easier to give than to take, or be "beholden" to others.

Before Emmeline could answer, Shana quickly added, "You know God called me to North Carolina. It may be for the rest of my life." Her lips quivered at the thought of permanent separation from Tarnigan. "On the other hand, it may be only for a time. Don't you see? Dr. Aldrich can't live forever. Should God call me away, the people here will have no medical help, unless someone is trained. You could also earn money to help with your dreams for Gideon."

Generations of ancestors who possessed little more than pride warred with the truth of what Shana had said. The struggle showed in Emmeline's face. At last she let her son slide to the floor, and rose in quiet dignity. "There's a granny-woman among my kinfolk who'll be glad to keep my boy. She said so long ago, but I couldn't bring myself to let her unless I could pay his way." The flush receded from her face. Her eyes shone with anticipation. "If you're sure you want to do this, I'm beholden."

"I do, with all my heart."

Emmeline gave a little cry and pressed Shana's hand to her cheek. "You won't be sorry. I'll make you proud." She caught Gideon up and ran out, happy tears streaming from her glittering eyes.

News that the Widow Clark was aimin' to study medicine with Doc Aldrich and his fotched-on helpers hit the Hollow like a bomb. As usual, the inhabitants reacted in different ways. Some thought it a good idea. Others, notably the unmarried men, found it a pure shame. Such a pretty widow could get any man she wanted with the snap of her fingers. Hadn't some of them already said so to her face and offered to be pa to her boy?

At Shana's insistence, Granny King kept mum about the fact she would receive a small sum for keeping Gideon. "I don't mind buttonin' my lip," she told the new nurse. "Some folks might think it was right down onneighborly to take money for watchin' a young'un." She sighed. "Truth is, hit's an answer to prayer. Gettin' old in the Hollow ain't easy and I never been one to take charity."

"This certainly isn't charity," Shana reassured. She'd fallen in love with the little old lady the first time she met her. "You're allowing Emmeline to gain knowledge that can help the whole Hollow, maybe even save lives."

Black eyes twinkled in the walnut-shell face. "Nurse, you kin talk the birds outta the trees." She cocked her head to one side and grinned. "No wonder that feller of yours wouldn't let you outta his sight. I'll dance at your weddin', if you don't wait too long to get hitched."

Shana laughed and felt color rise from the neck of her cotton gown. She patted the wrinkled hand, promised to drop by again when she could, and escaped.

Now a familiar ache replaced Shana's smile. Every day she saw less of Wyatt. He had taken to his lessons like an otter takes to the sea. He whooped with delight when he learned Emmeline would be studying along with him. After the first week he confessed, "I never saw the like of our new student nurse. She gobbles up Dr. Aldrich's medical books so fast it's all I can do to keep ahead of her, in spite of studying last winter and this spring."

His frank approval sent Shana's heart to her toes, but

she had to be fair. "When Emmeline works with me, I seldom have to show her anything twice."

"I'd like to see her spend some time in a training hospital after you and Dr. Aldrich teach her what you can here," Wyatt commented. "The Hollow offers almost everything she will need to know, but not all. We haven't faced them all yet, but according to Dr. Aldrich, the Hollow never lacks for variety when it comes to ailments." He ticked off on his fingers. "Influenza. Broken bones. Measles, mumps, chickenpox, consumption, rheumatism, croup, scarlet fever. Gunshot wounds, some accidental, some questionable—" He sighed. "It's really not that much different from Alaska. I remember a few wounded trappers and Indians being packed into Tarnigan under mysterious circumstances."

Shana nodded, then watched Wyatt's blue eyes darken as he changed the subject. "About Emmeline. Think she'd go?"

"I don't know. Why don't we wait and see?" Shana's treacherous heart beat fast with hope. In the short time since she reached the Hollow, she had learned to love Emmeline as the sister she never had. Yet sharing Wyatt's time and attention with the other girl made the prospect of Emmeline's absence loom promising and attractive.

Dog in the manger, she scolded herself. *You turned Wyatt down. You told him to count on nothing. Now when he shows interest in Emmeline, you want to snatch him back. You're jealous of one of the sweetest, most Christlike girls you've ever known.*

"I am not!" she protested aloud. Wyatt raised his

brows at her in surprise, and Shana flushed and turned away. *It's just that I never thought Wyatt would turn out to be so fickle,* she told herself. *A few weeks ago he was swearing undying love for me. Now. . .* She couldn't finish the thought. What if Wyatt gave up on a girl who had taken his friendship, even his love, for granted? What if the protective nature she knew so well reached out to the mountain girl who fiercely longed to be someone and was willing to do whatever necessary to make it happen?

"I don't think I could stand it," she whispered to herself later that night when she was alone in her room. With a lightning flash of illumination she realized the truth. She loved Wyatt. Not with the childish adoration carried through the years into girlhood. She loved him with every beat of her heart, with the love she had so often seen in her mother's and Inga's eyes when they looked at their husbands.

The realization kept her tossing and turning all night long. At last, as morning's light brightened the windows, she sat up in bed and put her hands to her aching head. "God, why did it take me so long to know?" she cried into the stillness of her cabin. "Why did I have to come half a world away from Tarnigan to realize I can never marry anyone but Wyatt? I want to be his wife, to bear his children. Have I put him off too many times? Is it too late?"

Self loathing brought Shana out of bed. In all the novels she had read, she had despised heroines who awakened to the preciousness of a fine man's love only when another woman came onto the scene. Shallow, she had called them. Now she understood. Her blind eyes had remained closed until a catastrophic shock shook her very foundations. She quickly dressed, scorned breakfast, and braided her hair into two fat braids. Honest to the core, she knew she must tell Wyatt of her stupendous discovery.

A merry laugh outside her cabin sent her to the door. She flung it wide and stepped outside. At the other end of the dogtrot, Wyatt stood smiling down at Emmeline. Gideon leaned against Wyatt's leg, arms wrapped around it. Shana bit her lip, undecided whether to call a greeting or go back inside.

Shana shifted her weight. A board creaked under her foot. Wyatt looked up. "Morning. Ready to go to the clinic? We'll drop this young man off on the way." He picked up Gideon, set the child on his sturdy shoulder, and said, "Ow! Stop that, you rascal," when Gideon buried his chubby hands in Wyatt's golden curls and hung on for dear life.

The completeness of man, woman, and child shut Shana out and drove a splinter of pain into her heart. She mustered her poise and smiled at Emmeline, dewy fresh in her simple cotton dress with its white collar and cuffs. "I'll be along in a little while. I haven't had breakfast."

"All right. Coming, Emmeline?" They went off together like three children happy just to be together.

The day's beauty turned clouded and gray. Shana waited the length of time it would normally take to eat breakfast, then slowly walked the dusty road leading to the clinic at the other end of the clearing. She passed the mercantile, too dispirited to smile at its incongruous sign. Now that her childhood playmate obviously admired Emmeline so much, how could Shana tell him her feelings had changed? It wouldn't be fair to hold him to a promise that his heart could no longer keep.

Pounding footsteps raced toward her and broke into her misery. Her heart lurched. In all their years of acquaintance, she had never seen Wyatt so distraught. The gray-faced man reached her, grabbed her arm, and gasped, "Hurry. It's Emmeline." He dragged Shana toward the clinic at full run.

Shana couldn't speak, only feel. What had happened to bring agony to Wyatt's eyes, agony that sounded a death knell to the love Shana had not recognized until it was too late?

Chapter 8

Shana and Wyatt burst into the Hollow Clinic. Emmeline lay on the examining table, white-faced and silent. Blood stained her left hand and the white forearm where Dr. Aldrich pressed a heavy pad, obviously torn from a petticoat. He ignored his nurse's frantic, "What happened?" and barked, "Get the suture tray. She may need stitching."

His tone of command freed Shana from her daze. She ran for the tray of sterilized instruments and supplies always kept ready for emergencies. Sewing up gashes in patients was a common need in a community that worked with ax and saw, plow and hoe, guns and knives.

Wyatt stood to one side. Shana wondered why he looked so ill. His short term of study with the Tarnigan doctors had exposed him to far worse sights than a wounded arm. A moment later, Dr. Aldrich uncovered the wound and Shana understood Wyatt's concern. No jagged gash marred the rounded arm, but deep punctures. Tooth marks. Shocked, Shana asked again, "What happened?"

Wyatt passed an unsteady hand over his face. "We left Gideon at Granny King's. I suggested taking a shortcut through the woods to the clinic. Halfway here, the bushes rustled. A wild dog sprang toward me from the side of the trail." He swallowed and huskily added, "Emmeline leaped in front of me. When she lifted her arm to ward off the attack, the dog sank his teeth into her."

Emmeline's eyes looked enormous, but she whispered, "Wyatt grabbed a downed tree branch and killed the dog. If he hadn't been there. . ." Her whole body shook as with a chill.

"If I hadn't been there, you would never have taken the shortcut," Wyatt fiercely flailed himself.

"No use crying over spilt milk," Dr. Aldrich told them. His heavy eyebrows knit into a shaggy line across his furrowed forehead and he warned Emmeline, "This is going to hurt." He drowned the wounds with antiseptic, let them bleed freely, and poured more antiseptic over them. He finished off with a generous dose of evil-smelling carbolic acid and a mixture of herbs Shana didn't recognize. "Local medicine." He grunted. "Draws the poison out."

Shana barely heard him. Fear brushed its wings against her, then clutched with both claws. What if the wild dog were rabid? If not, why would he attack? Her fear increased. She thought of the Indian who had staggered into Tarnigan after being bitten by a rabid wolf, and the horrible death that followed. *Dear God, please don't let that happen to Emmeline,* she silently screamed. *Save her. She loves You and longs to serve. Please, God.*

Shana looked at Wyatt's bowed head and knew he was praying for the girl who had risked her life to save his. She felt comforted. Had not Jesus promised in Matthew

18:20 that where two or three gathered in His name, He would be in the midst of them? Surely God would spare one so pure and willing to serve as Emmeline! *Thank You for hearing and answering our prayers,* Shana's heart cried.

God did hear and answer their prayers.

"The dog wasn't rabid," Dr. Aldrich told Shana and Wyatt the next day. "I examined him, and I couldn't see any signs of sickness. One of the men recognized the animal. Says the dog was a mean stray that had been beaten until he hated every human he encountered."

Shana breathed a sigh of relief and tried not to notice the look of joy on Wyatt's face. When Emmeline had faced death for Wyatt, how could Shana begrudge her his love? She blinked away tears of gratitude and pain.

Emmeline's wound didn't even infect, thanks to the quick medical attention. As the torn flesh healed, Shana tried to open her wounded heart to God's healing grace. Eventually only small scars remained on Emmeline's arm, and she was able to resume her studies and training. But Shana's heart still felt as torn as ever.

One sunny afternoon when business was mercifully slow, Dr. Aldrich called a meeting of his "staff," as he designated his nurse and two helpers. His thick white hair waved wildly above his keen black eyes. He didn't shilly-shally but went straight to the point. "Wyatt, Emmeline, how would you like to spend next six months in Charlotte, working harder than you ever have or ever will?"

Shana felt her heart leap to her throat. Wyatt cocked his head to one side. An eyebrow lifted and a wary look came to his face.

Emmeline finally said, "Charlotte?" The mountain girl's eyes turned round as the silver moon that sailed above the Hollow. "That's better than a hundred miles from here, and it's got more folks than grass blades in a meadow!"

"I know. It also has a topnotch hospital run by one of the finest surgeons I know." Dr. Aldrich fitted the tips of his fingers together. "I'd like to put you two under his tutelage until Christmas."

Emmeline twisted her fingers until they shone white. "I—I thought you'd be teachin' us everythin' we needed in order to help folks."

"You'll learn a heap more during your six months in Charlotte than I can show you here in years," Dr. Aldrich told her. "When you come back, you'll be far more valuable to me and to our people."

Shana felt the blood drain from her face. A lifetime ago, she had wanted Emmeline to get training away from the Hollow. After the other girl's courageous act, Shana bitterly regretted her selfishness. Now with a quirk of fate, not only Emmeline but Wyatt would be gone for six endless months.

"What about Shana?" the young man demanded.

Surprise filled Dr. Aldrich's face. "She will stay here and help me, of course. I've already arranged for her to take exams in Asheville and get her nursing certificate." He considered for a moment. "Emmeline, do you think Granny King would mind moving into your cabin while you're gone? Gideon's used to it."

"I'm to leave my baby?" Emmeline paled and put her hands in front of her.

"Only for six months. Child, you once told me you would do anything in the world to get a better life for him than what most of our mountain folk have." The doctor's face wrinkled in sympathy. "Perhaps it's too much to ask, but if you will go, stick it out, and learn, it will be the finest sacrifice you ever make."

Shana thought Emmeline aged ten years in the next ten seconds. She bowed her head. When she raised it again, she quietly said, "I'll go. For him." Without another word, she rose and started for the door. Dr. Aldrich's voice stopped her with one hand raised to open the screen.

"Wyatt? How about you?"

He stared at the doctor. He looked at Emmeline. Last of all, he turned to Shana in wordless appeal. An eternity later, he asked, "Well?"

Could a heart ache this much and not shatter into tiny pieces? Shana wondered. Desolation rose within her. Long, lonely months stretched ahead should he choose Charlotte. Yet how could she protest? Ever since the accident, Wyatt had treated Emmeline more tenderly than ever, as if she were a delicate piece of porcelain that suddenly showed previously unsuspected depths of strength. Longing to beg him to stay, Shana said in a colorless voice, "You have to do what you feel is right."

He stared at her for a long moment, and the eyes she knew so well were unreadable. "If Dr. Aldrich believes we can learn faster, I have no choice." Now that the die had been cast, Wyatt reverted to his usual, laughing self.

"Emmeline, we can keep each other company in our banishment to Charlotte. Right?" He grinned.

Shana barely heard the murmured reply. Pride inherited from both her father and mother sustained her. If Emmeline could forsake her child for six long months in order to ensure a better future for him, then Shana Clifton must ignore her aching heart and give her best to those in the Hollow.

That pride carried her through the parting with Emmeline and Wyatt. She took care not to be alone with him and tossed her head when he looked deep into her eyes. Yet his questioning gaze remained in her mind long after the *chug-chug* of Dr. Aldrich's old car faded on the other side of the hogback.

The same pride also sharpened Shana's mind when she took the tests for her certificate. She did well on both written and oral exams and thrilled when she received a letter of commendation from the board of examiners.

Summer passed, the hard work broken only by brief letters from Charlotte and longer ones from Tarnigan. Sickness ravaged the community until Shana had little time to think beyond its forested borders. She traveled into the mountains on foot and on muleback, tending the sick, fighting the belief fever patients should be bundled and made to sweat in a room devoid of the slightest bit of fresh air. Nights found her too tired to do more than tumble into bed until roused to a new day, new worries over the people she had come to love.

Autumn lived up to Dr. Aldrich's predictions. Shana reveled in the gold and red, the orange and russet tones of leaves that drifted onto forest trails and paths. The mornings grew colder. Frost sparkled on twig and branch. Granny King said her "rheumatiz" told her they'd have a hard winter. "Bet you can't wait for Em'line and your feller to come back," she teased.

Shana didn't reply. Time enough at their return for folks in the Hollow to learn Wyatt no longer cared. Emmeline's last letter had been straight from the heart.

Did Wyatt tell you what's happened? she wrote. *I never thought I'd love another man, and I'll be beholden to God for the rest of my life. It's so wonderful. He wants to be a good pa to Gideon too. Don't tell Dr. Aldrich (we want to surprise him) but we plan to spend the rest of our lives in the Hollow. Nurse Shana, none of this would have happened if God hadn't led you to North Carolina. We aim to wait and get married in the Hollow. Will you stand up with us?*

Even though Shana had feared such a thing, the reality rocked her senses. Her first thought was to flee, to return to Tarnigan and forget North Carolina, the Hollow, and the false-hearted Wyatt Baldwin. She shook her head. No. God had called her here. Until He directed otherwise, here she must stay—even though it meant watching Wyatt and Emmeline's happiness at the expense of her own. Would they live in the cabin at the other end of the dogtrot? The thought was unbearable.

Chastened by prayer and the determination never to let anyone but God know the extent of her wounds, Shana relied more heavily on her heavenly Father than ever before. The last leaves of autumn lay buried under winter's first snow. A skiff of ice in her water bucket reminded her that Christmas and the return of the happy couple lurked just ahead. Shana threw herself into caring for the sick, studying her Bible and making certain passages her own. The Psalms came alive to her as never before. She relied heavily on those that promised a shield, protection, strength, memorizing them and repeating them whenever she thought of the future. From disbelief and anger, through acceptance, Shana worked her way to a fragile peace.

Now the days raced along. A week before Christmas. Six days. Five. Four. Three. Wyatt and Emmeline were due on the twenty-third. Fortunately, nothing beyond the usual drip of colds and hack of sore throats plagued the community. Dr. Aldrich went to Asheville, leaving Shana in charge of the clinic. A few hours later, snow began to fall. When darkness came, Shana wearily trudged home. Snow crunched beneath her feet. Never had she felt so defeated. Even telling herself Christmas was for celebrating Christ's birth, not wondering how she could live through the holidays without betraying her feelings, didn't help.

Dr. Aldrich, Emmeline, and Wyatt didn't come that night. Granny King looked wise. "Don't fret yourself, child. They'll be here for Christmas, no matter what. What Doc says, Doc does."

Christmas Eve dawned clear and bright. Inches of white laid their gentle hand over the Hollow, softening its rough edges, beautifying the unlovely buildings. Wreaths made of wire covered with cedar boughs and red calico bows hung on her door and Shana's. A large package from Alaska rested beneath a tiny tree the girl had forced herself to decorate with carefully strung popcorn and cranberries.

Gideon raced down the dogtrot on chubby legs. "Momma come today?"

"I hope so." The sooner she faced meeting Wyatt and Emmeline, the sooner she could begin to fade into the background. She hugged the child, sent him back to Granny, and nerved herself for the ordeal.

They came just before dusk, honking the horn and hollering like banshees. Shana peered from her window when the car came to a halt in front of the double cabin. The last rays of daylight shone on Emmeline's laughing face, on bulky Dr. Aldrich, on a tall stranger. Shana's fingers curled into tight buds. Emmeline and Wyatt must have brought a minister. She turned from his pleasant countenance and gazed at the man she loved. Why must he look so handsome, so happy, so unattainable? Hot tears she had dammed threatened to spill. She turned from the window and whispered, "God, I can't do this alone."

The door burst open. Wyatt bounded inside and across the small space between them. "Shana?" His strong arms circled her. "I know I promised to wait until you said I might, but hang it all, it's Christmas!" His lips, cold from the clean outdoors, found hers.

For the space of a heartbeat, she returned his kiss, forgetting everything except her love for the man who held her. Then she tore free, eyes blazing. "How dare you?" A sob of pure fury escaped her.

"Sorry." He didn't look at all repentant. "As I said, it's Christmas."

"What would Emmeline think if she knew you were in here making love to another woman?" Shana raged.

A twinkle appeared in his eyes. "She'd tell me faint heart never won fair lady. That's what she's been telling me ever since we went to Charlotte. So has John."

Shana's head reeled. "John? What on earth are you talking about, Wyatt Baldwin?"

"Dr. John Wilson. He fell in love with Emmeline the first time he saw her. It didn't take her much longer, a day or two, perhaps." Wyatt's teasing gave way to startled recognition. "Shoshana Noelle, you didn't think—you couldn't have thought—" He caught her by the shoulders and his mouth set in a grim line. "Thanks for trusting me," he said sarcastically.

The dam broke. "How could I know? Emmeline's letter never mentioned John's name, just yours."

"And you cared this much?" Wyatt put a finger beneath her chin and tilted it up. "Why, Shana!" Wonder and gladness rang in his voice.

The final barrier between them crashed. "Ever since we came here. I was going to tell you, but you were always with Emmeline, and she's a wonderful person, and—"

Wyatt stopped her pitiful explanation the only way he knew how. With a kiss. This time Shana responded with all the love she had secretly hoarded, the way mountain squirrels stored up nuts for winter. At last she broke free, flushed and happier than she had been since leaving Tarnigan. "Wyatt, please, don't ever frighten me so again."

"Only if you promise not to get foolish notions. Haven't I proved you're the only girl in the world for me?"

Made daring by her newly declared love, Shana couldn't help saying, "You have to admit. Emmeline is lovely."

"Of course. So is a columbine, or a wildflower. I just happen to like black-haired, black-eyed girls with lots of sass." Wyatt cocked an eyebrow in the endearing mannerism she had missed so much. "Going to be a good girl and marry me tomorrow? A preacher's coming, and I can't wait any longer for you to be my wife." He looked at her with eyes she felt examined her very soul. "People in the Hollow will have to be our family, Shana. It's too far for our folks to come, even if it weren't the dead of winter."

Shana thought of Nika Illahee, her dear homeland. Those she loved more than life itself would be getting ready to celebrate Christmas. Dad, Mother, Arthur, Inga. Strongheart and his Naleenah. A pang of homesickness went through her. If only she could be married in Tarnigan, in the church where Benjamin Clifton had proclaimed the Word of God until his death. Yet as Wyatt said, it was just too far.

But wait! Didn't the best of Tarnigan stand before her, strong and tall? The same dear boy, now a man, who had stood beside her all the years of her life? The love in Wyatt's eyes came from a heart that beat true and always would. It shone brighter than the aurora borealis in all its splendor. She nodded, and rested in the circle of his arms. As long as Wyatt Baldwin loved her, she was home.

The next morning, Shoshana Noelle Clifton donned the simple white gown and veil she had found in her Christmas package from Tarnigan. Emmeline's delight over a matching gown and veil completed Shana's happiness. Through a sheen of tears, she wondered, *How did Mother know?*

"I've been keeping the mail service between North Carolina and Alaska busy." Wyatt grinned. "We decided your twenty-second birthday would be about right for a wedding. After all, Shoshana Noelle, when else could a Christmas rose be wed?"

Epilogue

Tattered banners of crimson, green, and violet fluttered in the sky over the tiny village of Tarnigan. Fantastic patterns painted the white hills and valleys in the shadows of the Endicott Range. The yellow glow from Nika Illahee's lighted windows paled by comparison.

High atop a snow-covered slope, a parka-clad girl and man stood gazing at the beauty. Months and years had fled since Wyatt Baldwin and Shana Clifton left Alaska to answer the call of God. After Dr. John Wilson had arrived to help Dr. Aldrich and Emmeline in the Hollow, Wyatt had been accepted in medical school. Shana continued nursing. The same day Wyatt received his license to practice, he and Shana left for home. Alaska was growing. She needed her sons and daughters.

The Baldwins raced to Tarnigan a few steps ahead of a winter storm. How good it felt to be clad in the clothing they wore when they left so long ago! To paddle a canoe, tramp for miles without seeing anyone, then be welcomed in isolated places as though they had left only days before. Although they knew they should have waited until spring, their goal was to reach Tarnigan by Christmas. Tonight, Christmas Eve, they had at last reached their goal.

"Look, Wyatt," she said. "Someone opened the front door of Nika Illahee." She laughed. "The wilderness grapevine must still be working." Her grip tightened. "Someone's coming out."

He laughed, the same joyous laugh she'd loved since childhood. "Not someone, darling. Something." Wyatt cupped gloved hands around his mouth and called, "Hallooo." *Hallooo* came back from the hills.

A frenzy of barking echoed and reechoed. Shana felt her heart leap. "Is it. . .do you think he—?" Heedless of the steep slope, she began to run. Down, down, down. Halfway there, a furry avalanche hit her head-on. Girl and dog fell together and rolled in the snow. "Kobuk. Oh, Kobuk, you remembered!" Shana buried her face in his fur and wept.

The malamute gave a single howl, then quieted beneath her touch. Wise in the ways of the north, Shana heard in his cry the story of waiting, watching, hoping: the eternal hope that never dies in the hearts of those who love deeply. It rang in her heart like a paean of praise. God willing, she and Wyatt would never leave Alaska again. From now on their Christmases would bloom here, in their one true home.

Colleen L. Reece

An accomplished author with 116 books to her credit, Colleen loves to travel and, at the same time, do research for her inspirational historical romances. Twice voted "Favorite Author" in the annual Heartsong Presents readers' poll, she has an army of fans that continues to grow. Colleen is currently writing a compelling mystery series for girls ages 9–15 entitled "Juli Scott Super Sleuth." She is also a teacher and lecturer while working full-time on her writing in her home state of Washington.

A Letter to Our Readers

Dear Readers:

In order that we might better contribute to your reading enjoyment, we would appreciate your taking a few minutes to respond to the following questions. When completed, please return to the following: Fiction Editor, Barbour Publishing, Inc., P.O. Box 719, Uhrichsville, OH 44683.

1. Did you enjoy reading *An Old-Fashioned Christmas*?
   ❑ Very much—I would like to see more books like this.
   ❑ Moderately—I would have enjoyed it more if ____________________

____

____

2. What influenced your decision to purchase this book? (Check those that apply.)
   ❑ Cover ❑ Back cover copy ❑ Title ❑ Price
   ❑ Friends ❑ Publicity ❑ Other

3. Which story was your favorite?
   ❑ *For the Love of a Child* ❑ *God Jul*
   ❑ *Miracle on Kismet Hill* ❑ *Christmas Flower*

4. Please check your age range:
   ❑ Under 18 ❑ 18–24 ❑ *25–34*
   ❑ 35–45 ❑ 46–55 ❑ Over 55

5. How many hours per week do you read?____________________

Name ____

Occupation ______________________________________

Address ____

City ____________________ State ____________ Zip ____________

E-mail ____

If you enjoyed

An Old Fashioned Christmas

then read:

PATCHWORK HOLIDAY

One Heirloom Quilt Comforts
Four Couples in Search of True Love

Twice Loved by Wanda E. Brunstetter
Everlasting Song by DiAnn Mills
Remnants of Faith by Renee DeMarco
Silver Lining by Colleen L. Reece

If you enjoyed

An Old Fashioned Christmas

then read:

TWO HUMOROUS MOTHERS, TWO LONELY WIDOWS,
FOUR STORIES OF REGAINING CHRISTMAS PEACE

All Done with the Dashing by Pamela Dowd
No Holly, No Ivy by Wanda Luttrell
O Little Town of Progress by Wanda Luttrell
My True Love Gave to Me. . . by Christine Lynxwiler